Re-Evaluating Women's Page Journalism in the Post-World War II Era

Kimberly Wilmot Voss

Re-Evaluating Women's Page Journalism in the Post-World War II Era

Celebrating Soft News

palgrave
macmillan

Kimberly Wilmot Voss
Nicholson School of Communication and Media
University of Central Florida
Orlando, FL, USA

ISBN 978-3-319-96213-9 ISBN 978-3-319-96214-6 (eBook)
https://doi.org/10.1007/978-3-319-96214-6

Library of Congress Control Number: 2018952286

Cover credit: maystra/iStock/Getty Images Plus
Cover design by Fatima Jamadar

This Palgrave Macmillan imprint is published by the registered company Springer Nature Switzerland AG
The registered company address is: Gewerbestrasse 11, 6330 Cham, Switzerland

This book is dedicated to all the women's page journalists who served their communities, practiced quality journalism, and changed the definition of women's news.

Preface

The women's pages of newspapers were a consistent place for women to work in journalism from the 1880s through the 1970s. (There were some opportunities for female reporters for sob sisters, stunt girls, and Eleanor Roosevelt's press conferences, but they were fleeting.) Newspapers across the country had women's sections—of varying qualities in the early decades. Much of the content focused on what was considered traditional female issues—clothes, homemaking, and child rearing. In the post-World War II years, the sections came into their own. Women's page editors oversaw increasingly large sections and mixed the traditional with the progressive. Yet, the perception that the sections were fluff continued for years.

This book focuses on the stories of the women's pages and the journalists who created them in the post-World War II years through the end of the sections in the early 1970s. It focuses on what women's page editor-turned publisher Marjorie Paxson called the "Golden Era" of the women's pages in the 1950s and 1960s. This examination of the women's pages documents women's news and writes women's page journalists into history. Material is drawn from the sections themselves, along with oral histories, personal interviews, and archival materials.

When the Washington Press Club Foundation (WPCF) created its Women in Journalism oral history project, it included four women's page editors. They each described significant, important journalism in their sections. It was far from the previously described fluff portrayed in journalism history—if the sections and their editors were included at all. (Journalism historian Marion Marzolf explained the role of newspaper women in 1977 as being part of the footnote.) A review of another dozen women's page editors revealed that the experiences of those included in the WPCF were not unique. In other words, women's page journalism was more significant than previously described. This was likely because these sections were never actually examined.

The women's page editors educated their readers about women's roles as times changed. Some sections included detailed series about divorce laws and women's status. For example, the articles in the women's sections in Milwaukee and Honolulu about no-fault divorce were so significant that they were reprinted in stand-alone sections for readers. The sections also included news about the state and local Commissions on the Status of Women, which addressed new employment opportunities for women. In addition, many of the women's pages included profiles of women in the workforce who could serve as role models for readers.

It's also important to remember that the traditional topics still held value, especially for fashion and food. In the 1950s, clothing styles were less democratic than they are today. The local women's pages often dictated what was acceptable and what was not. While it's difficult to imagine today, many women still made their own clothes—sometimes based on patterns found in the women's pages. This was news that women read in the newspaper every day.

There still has not been enough examination of the content of the women's pages and thus this book will explore the complexity of the sections. It was the place where a majority of women journalists worked for decades. While they were marginalized, they made the most of the space they were in. Women's page editors are a lost part of journalism history and women's labor history. The reasons for the oversight include the embarrassment of newspapers about how women were treated, the closing of newspapers, and mass retirements.

The women's pages were ingrained in the communities they covered. Working with local women's clubs, the women's sections helped build their communities, including establishing libraries, creating social service programs, and promoting historical preservation. They celebrated engagements, weddings, and birthing of their readers. They also shared grief—including the death of their own children. The editors helped establish social mores in the advice columns that ran in the sections—both local and national. These columnists addressed segregating neighborhoods, mothers working outside the home, and the role of unmarried women.

If the front page of the newspaper was guided by conflict and prominence, the women's pages could be anything the journalists wanted the sections to be. Typically, the sections became the hearts of the newspaper—connecting people. The women's pages not just found community problems but also helped to find solutions through women's clubs. They created a foundation for women who were entering the public sphere. Like other women who toiled between the "waves" of women's liberation, women's page journalists were innovators who redefined women's news, shining a light on the challenges of infertility and exposing the impact of child abuse. They gave a voice to the voiceless. They made society news more inclusive and made sure that high society's charitable causes were worth it.

The goal of this scholarship is to uncover the content of the women's pages and to document the careers of the women who contributed to the sections. This research allows the stories of women who worked in newspapers for decades to be told. It provides context for the challenges and victories that women faced in journalism for decades.

Orlando, FL Kimberly Wilmot Voss

Acknowledgments

I was first introduced to women's page editors nearly two decades ago. I was born as the sections were being eliminated and never knew of barriers to what I wanted to cover as a journalist. I never knew about the great women's page editors who were the trailblazers before me. They were not part of common journalism history. It was my mentor Dr. Maurine Beasley, my dissertation advisor at the University of Maryland, who told me about these amazing but not-researched women. I cannot thank her enough for her guidance. I also want to thank my editor, Glenn Ramirez, for his encouragement and guidance.

As I got to know the first few women, I realized that there was so much more to uncover. I appreciate the archivists at the University of Wyoming, the University of Nevada-Reno, and the University of Nevada, Las Vegas, for their help. Most of all, I want to thank the archivists at the National Women and Media Collection and Marjorie Paxson for recognizing the need to document the lives and careers of female journalists. They hosted me for numerous visits in Missouri and invited me to speak at the 20th anniversary of the Collection. They have continued to make copies for me and update me on their new papers. Their dedication to women and journalism is amazing.

I want to acknowledge the people who helped me understand the work of the women's page editors including the families of Carol Sutton, Ruthe Deskin, and Roberta Applegate. I also appreciate the many people who shared their memories of the women's pages at the *Miami Herald, Milwaukee Journal*, and the *Seattle Post-Intelligencer.*

My thanks to my husband and research partner Lance Speere who knows so much about these women. He and I visited lauded Dallas women's page editor Vivian Castleberry in Dallas. Our son is named after Vivian's husband, Curtis Castleberry. Our younger son is named after the longtime director of the Penney-Missouri Awards, Paul Myhre. Our family is connected to the women's page editor community.

Contents

1

Introducing Post-World War II Women's Pages

Women and Newspapering

When it comes to journalism history, women were nearly non-existent for decades. In 1977, journalism historian Marion Marzolf wrote the book *Up From the Footnote*.[1] As the title indicated, when the few women were included in the stories of newspapers, they were typically found in the footnotes. Even when it comes to newspapers' own histories, women also get short shrift. The 2003 book *Orange Journalism* highlighted several significant Florida women but not women's page journalists other than a brief reference to Anne Rowe at the *St. Petersburg Times*.[2] Like many stories of women in journalism history during this time period, it was usually the woman who reached a management position or became an investigative journalist that caused her to have historical significance. Rarely do women who wrote for women's pages get historical acclaim. Yet, in the post-World War II era, women's page journalists were worthy of study. They were winning national awards and creating a new direction for content being copied across the country.

The positions of women's page editors, in terms of stature, at their newspapers varied. Some women were more respected—usually if a male editor understood. Examples of these men include James Bellows, Lee

K. W. Voss, *Re-Evaluating Women's Page Journalism in the Post-World War II Era*,
https://doi.org/10.1007/978-3-319-96214-6_1

Hills, and J. Edward Murray. Yet, there were many more men who did not understand or, at least, were not enlightened. Decades later, when asked if the well-respected and typically progressive Florida newspaper *St. Petersburg Times* (now the *Tampa Bay Times*) was ahead of its time in treatment of or regard for women in the 1960s, newspaper executive David Lawrence responded:

> Well, I would say yes, but not so far ahead of that time that it was a world-beater. There were people there who were women who had substantive responsibilities, but for many years their responsibilities were very much connected, most of them, to women's news, softer kinds of things. A very smart woman named Anne Rowe, later Anne Rowe-Goldman, was in charge of the women's and feature sections. She clearly could have been editor of the paper. The whole business was sort of shabby on the subject. Women made distinctly less, had lesser jobs, and did not have much of a path to get more responsibility and more money.[3]

Women are most likely to be included in journalism history if they make it to the front pages of newspapers, cover sports, or become wartime correspondents—when they dare to take on men's turf.[4] When specialized reporting is studied, it is usually a matter of politics, business, or sports. For decades, the women's pages of newspapers were largely ignored. Until the 1970s, most women journalists were restricted to women's sections other than those who briefly served as stunt girls, who raced around the world, and sob sisters, who covered heart-wrenching trials.[5] A few women covered First Lady Eleanor Roosevelt's women-only press conferences beginning in the 1930s. Other than during wartime did a token few women leave the women's section. They were rarely part of newsrooms at most metropolitan newspapers. Yet, in the years between World War II and the beginnings of the women's liberation movement in the late 1960s, many women's page journalists were also redefining women's roles. While men dominated the news and sports positions, the soft news beats were a place for women to find their niche.

For much of the scholarship on journalism history, the story of women's pages has been consistently defined with a broad stroke, described as the four Fs of family, fashion, food, and furnishings. The women's pages were also the place to find high society news, advice columns, and wedding information. More often, the term fluff was applied to women's page material. Yet, the sections were rarely examined to see if there was more to it. Recent scholarship has begun to shine a light on the women who covered soft news.[6] The truth is more complicated as many women's pages had long been refining roles for women.[7]

Reporter Susan Paynter said that her work in Seattle demonstrated how women's page news was evolving by the 1960s. "The women's pages became, really, the center of social-issues reporting," she said. "The news side wasn't doing it at all." She said that by the time the news side realized they had been scooped by the women's pages, "It was too late, because the ball was in our court and we were running with it."[8] The Seattle newspaper was not alone in these changes. By the late 1960s, the women's pages of the *Charlotte Observer* were covering the social stigma of syphilis and life inside a women's prison. The *Detroit Free Press* covered prostitution in the city—including ranking those who just wanted a free meal to those who exchanged services for drugs. The women's pages of the New York newspaper *Newsday* included 13 ways to avoid a child molester.[9]

It is easy to simplify the content of the women's pages rather than examine the complexity of the material. In looking at the women's sections, there was some fluff and undoubtedly some of the material reinforced women's role in the private sphere. Yet, there were also stories of career women and community development by clubwomen. Just as Joanne Meyerowitz re-examined the original source material used to support Betty Friedan's thesis in *The Feminine Mystique* and came to a different conclusion,[10] women's pages should be looked at with fresh eyes. It has been shown that there were progressive women's sections throughout the 1960s, as various newspapers won Penney-Missouri Awards, the preeminent annual national award competition for women's page journalists sponsored by the University of Missouri. The content of these sections was a mix of the traditional as well as progressive news.

Primary-source material and growing scholarship have demonstrated that there was likely more value to the women's pages of the 1950s and 1960s than previously thought. It most visibly began with the Washington Press Club Foundation's oral history project "Women in Journalism."[11] The four women's page editors interviewed for the project told stories about including progressive articles in their sections prior to the Women's Liberation Movement in the 1960s. The interviews also showed that there was a women's page community with similar approaches to progressive content. Retirement stories and obituaries showed that many women's page editors had rejected the traditional model and explored the changing roles for women. Later studies revealed that several women's page journalists were working to update their sections in post-World War II years before the sections were eliminated in the 1970s.[12]

Impact of World War II

In fact, it was likely World War II that led to the changes that were obvious more than two decades later. During this time, women were taking on man's work, most visibly represented by Rosie the Riveter. In one 1943 *Tampa Tribune* cartoon, a woman is shown sitting on a bed looking at her husband, who was in front of a mirror and wearing a welding-mask. The caption read, "Stop admiring yourself and take it off, Otis; I have to get ready for work."[13] Across the country, women were taking on new roles, holding positions previously denied to them based on their gender.

The lack of men meant that women journalists had new opportunities. For example, Roberta Applegate covered hard news for a wire service during the war and was then the first woman to cover the Michigan capitol for the Associated Press. In another example, Betty Ewing had the chance to interview with the wire service United Press. The United Press employed 100 women during wartime, or 20 percent of its staff.[14] The man doing the hiring was a Texan and, with their native connection, Ewing began covering Atlanta. While there, Ewing became the first woman to invade the male sanctuary of the Georgia Tech sports box. She had not anticipated the outcry that it caused; she was simply friends with the football coach's daughter.[15] Just as she was getting to know Atlanta, she was told that she had been promoted to bureau chief in Richmond, Virginia—a part of the country that she knew nothing about. She, and a female assistant, would be in charge of covering the entire state. The office was across from the statehouse and the two women spent their days running back and forth. Among the stories she wrote included covering a plane crash that killed 27 people, the Maryland versus Virginia oyster wars, and a Virginia power strike.[16]

Marjorie Paxson graduated from journalism school when the nation was at war, recalling: "Our involvement started in December. The classes at the University of Missouri were still full of men. And within six weeks, suddenly all the guys were gone. I think the enrollment at J School was cut about in half."[17] The new job opportunities allowed her to cover hard news for a wire service, the United Press in Nebraska—something almost unheard of during peacetime. In fact, the only topics she could not cover were football games and executions.

Dorothy Jurney also got to be part of hard news at a Washington, DC, newspaper because of the war. A former Northwestern female classmate wrote of Jurney's new position, "That must be a dream, too bold to be expressed even yet, of every dame who ever got mixed up in newspapering."[18] The editor later wrote he hired Jurney reluctantly as he had "an antipathy toward women in news shops."[19] Jurney soon was promoted to assistant city editor and eventually she became acting city editor. According to her boss, Jurney had become "one of the greatest finds ever to enter our doors. She was an excellent copy reader, a good writer, an editor of rare judgment, an exceptional executive—and one of the hardest workers it ever has been my privilege to know."[20]

Then, the war ended and Jurney—despite her experience—was demoted, like most of the women journalists who had taken men's jobs during the war.[21] In peacetime, a top editor called Jurney and said there was a young man who was a cub reporter in the sports department who management wanted to make the city editor. The managing editor instructed her to teach him his job. He told her that she was not a candidate for city editor because she was a woman.[22]

Jurney was typical of the many women journalists who lost their jobs. Ewing, as another example, lost her position in Atlanta and instead returned to Texas and for a job at the *Houston Press* covering society news. When Paxson took her job with the United Press, she had to sign a waiver that guaranteed that she would give up her job for a man who returned from the service. She left the position after the war ended and would spend most of the rest of her journalism career in the women's pages until she went into newspaper management.

Milwaukee and Chicago women's page editor Colleen "Koky" Dishon attended the University of Kentucky and worked as a non-union printer's apprentice before she joined the *Zanesville News* when male reporters left to serve in World War II. She continued her on-the-job journalism education. She was only 20 years old when she was assigned to cover the 1944 Republican convention in Chicago to get the "women's angle." Gossip columnist Hedda Hopper, she later recalled, walked up to her and said "Honey, don't you think you're too young to be here?"

Dishon next joined the Associated Press in Baltimore, Maryland, when the wire services, too, were hiring women to take the place of men at war. She became the chief AP reporter covering the launchings of warships often named for the communities that had raised the funds to help build them. She also wrote stories about sick babies brought from across the country to Johns Hopkins Hospital's well-known infants' ward. And she covered the April 12, 1945, death of President Franklin Delano Roosevelt. Then, like most of the women who were working at the wire services, Dishon lost her position as the war ended and the soldiers returned.

Milwaukee Journal women's page editor Aileen Ryan noted the women's exodus when peace returned: "When the war was over neither democracy for all nor a place in the newspaper sun for women was won. Men took their jobs back."[23] So, when the war ended, most women returned to the women's pages—but they took their news experience with them. Many of these women approached their work in a new way and found new purpose. It did not mean they transformed all of the traditional content. It would not have made business sense as advertising reflecting the traditional roles of women and men paid the newspaper's bills. And, in a time when suburban communities were flourishing, department stores were ready to help consumers fill their homes with appliances. The newspapers—especially the women's section—were often growing bigger and bigger with the increase in advertising dollars.

After the war, when many women lost their jobs, they also lost their government-sponsored child care. By 1947, more than three million women had been laid off from their wartime employment and not all were happy to go back home.[24] There were picket lines with signs such as

"How Come No Work for Women" and "Stop Discrimination Because of Sex."[25] Of course, this does not include the many women who were employed in the working class, often time taking care of the children or homes of other employed women. Miami women's page journalist Marie Anderson recalled the war in a 1960 speech to other women's page editors: "The child-care problem is desperate. We had child-care programs during the war. Why not now? Young girls are being encouraged only to get a husband or teach. Why can't she be a mathematician and have a husband, too?"[26]

Post-World War II Journalism

Eleanor W. Stanton, a former women's page editor at the *New York Sun*, delivered a lecture in 1943 for the Newspaper Institute of America in which she admitted that she used to look with "scorn" at women's pages of the past. She had changed her mind after seeing the changes that women's editors were making, which she described as "revolutionary." She said, "The day of the old-fashioned women's page with its senseless drivel, and mushy advice to the lovelorn is passed."[27] She noted that current women's pages were aimed at both homemakers and professional women. While there were still beauty columns, recipes, and fashion news, there were also stories about politics and current issues. She explained that sections had the potential to be significant—even if she is not in the newsroom: "She may miss some of the thrills of straight reporting, but one who has tried both soon learns that the so-called thrills of the city room are few and far between. And the editor has the daily thrill of building something that is her own."[28]

An examination of women's page content reveals a snapshot of a changing time for gender roles in the 1950s and 1960s. For example, consider the newspaper story "Women Are Root of Trouble." That was the message from British psychiatrist Joshua Bierer, who was on an American lecture tour in 1966. He said the United States was becoming "a matriarchy and this is an unhealthy thing." His views were debated by numerous women, including feminist author Betty Friedan and columnist Marya Mannes, who called into question his statements. The article, which ran in newspapers across the country, was clearly pro-women, but it was a sign there was a worry about women's roles in society.[29]

As social history grows, more study has been done of how events have shaped the world. This is often done by looking at the media coverage of the time as the keeper of the communities' and nation's historical record. This, however, can be too simple. For example, the 1950s has been romanticized as the development of the suburbs, with women raising children at home. But women were going to work in record numbers. Between 1940 and 1960, the number of working wives quadrupled.[30] In the 1950s, the employment of wives from middle-class families rose from 5 to 25 percent.[31] Many women's page editors recognized this fact and created content for women who were working inside and outside the home—and a combination that often also included paid and volunteer work. After all, the growing consumer culture meant more newspaper advertising which, in turn, led to more pages in the women's section.

According to Associated Press women's page journalist Dorothy Roe, in the late 1950s, many women's page editors put out newspaper sections from 4 to 6 pages daily, as well as an additional 12 to 18 pages on Thursdays and Sundays. Many of the big newspapers had more than 30 women on the staff. Most women's page editors "say it's practically impossible to get trained girl reporters to work on the women's pages. They all want to be city desk reporters. This is despite the fact that the girls have far more latitude in writing, a greater variety of assignments and often more recognition when they choose the women's field."[32]

By the 1950s, many of the women's sections in newspapers had already started making substantial changes. A roundup of the *Omaha World-Herald* content from 1958 included wedding and engagements news, Mary Lane's advice column, social stories, and food features.[33] Florence Burge started in the women's pages of her Reno, Nevada, newspaper in 1959 when she cut out club coverage that was not news and shortened wedding stories. "Burge saw the changes as both a 'natural evolution" and "fairly drastic." She viewed the changes in the section as related to the growth of the city.[34]

Women's Pages in the 1960s

In the 1960s, Marie Anderson, the daughter of a local judge and with her roots in the Miami Junior League, helped to nurture the relationship between women's pages and women's clubs. She encouraged organizations to take on important causes and then honored them when they did. They created libraries and kindergartens, helped the needy, and later encouraged women to run for office. In a speech to women's page journalists, Anderson said, "Be a motivating source in your community. If your town doesn't do something, call attention to it."[35] The combination of women's clubs and women's pages allowed for a natural growth beyond traditional content.

For some women's page journalists, their lives did not represent a traditional woman's path anyway. Several of the women journalists, such as Anderson, Applegate, and Paxson, did not marry nor have children. Others had to work to support their children after divorce. In other words, they had to work for their own security. While there was a view women simply worked for "pin money," according to a 1970 study of Florida women's page editors, seventy-one journalists wrote that they were the "sole support of herself."[36] Several married but never had children, but many others also juggled roles of mothers, wives, and journalists.

The challenges that women's page editors often faced and tried to mediate were between tradition and progress that would pit women against each other. Many women's page editors found ways to represent women's issues without resorting to the "catfight" treatment that is too often featured in news stories about women. Take, for example, Paxson's advice to women's page editors on stories about women who were rising through the ranks:

> Let's stop downgrading women executives. How many times have you heard and printed the comments, 'I hate to work for a woman boss'? No specifics, just that. I have worked for some men who weren't so great as bosses, but nobody will sit still for a generalization about male bosses. As women, let's give other women a chance.[37]

She also defended professional women who wanted to take time off to have children—pointing out that these women often returned to the workforce later. She said, "Let's stop criticizing women for giving up jobs to have children."[38] She also asked if the women had looked into the lack of day care facilities and the increasing number of job discrimination complaints in their communities. These employment topics would not make it to the front pages for many years.

These kinds of stories were mixed in with the traditional fare about fashion, family, food, and furnishings. Rather than finding these messages contradictory, these women found them as co-existing. They found women were interested in a mix of recipes and political issues—the kind of content long embraced by women's magazines. By creating a mix of hard news and soft news, they created a new kind of "quilted" content that will be explored in this book. It was a reflection of their lives in which they enjoyed gardening and entertaining—yet were also concerned about pay inequities and other injustices.

The women editors had limited management experience. They did not have the power to hire or fire their reporters, nor have authority over budgetary matters. Yet, they did have the power to control the content in the sections and the appreciation of their readership. In some ways, it was obvious they were assigning progressive content, at other times it was a more subtle way of presenting news. After all, the presentation of news can lead to a different understanding of issues. Take the example of a 1962 Associated Press wire story, written by Jean Sprain Wilson, about *Miami News* award-winning women's page editor Billie O'Day. The profile focused on her work as a journalist and a musician, as well as her interest in football. Three of the newspapers that ran the story featured the following headlines: "Reporter by Day, Conductor at Night,"[39] "Woman Scribe is Conductor of Symphony,"[40] and "Football and the Classics Keep Her too Busy for Love."[41] The third headline is especially interesting as the question of dating was not even mentioned until the end of the lengthy story. The differing presentations of a new story can lead to different understanding of a news issues.

In the 1960s, more women's pages were also addressing racial issues—to varying degrees. Women's page editor Edee Greene was known for including the photos of black brides in her section at the *Fort Lauderdale*

News—something not done at most newspapers. The *Miami Herald's* women section included a series profiling African-American residents in Miami in 1962, well before the front pages of newspaper addressed societal inequities. Roberta Applegate, who wrote the series, recalled that she was "frankly amazed that the reaction has been so one-sided: favorable."[42]

Then, just as society was beginning to pay serious heed to the changing role of women, the women's pages were eliminated. Some of the women journalists were able to move into other sections, while others were demoted or lost their jobs. Paxson said one of her lowest career points came when she was meeting with a group of professional women and she described her firing and demotions due to the end of women's pages. Paxson recalled, "One of the participants heard me out and then told me, 'Marj, you have to accept the fact that you're a casualty of the women's movement.'"[43] Paxson said she agreed with that assessment.

Changing Women's Page Content

Mixed in with the advertisements in the 1950s and 1960s, there were several newspapers that included stories in these sections that were part of the women's movement's platform—stories about domestic violence, the Equal Rights Amendment (ERA), and abortion reform.[44] It was also the part of the newspaper that first featured stories about the federal and state Commissions on the Status of Women. These stories reached large audiences and impacted the work of other women's page editors and women leaders.[45] The circulations of the papers were high so the work of the women editors reached large segments of their own communities and sometimes beyond them. This was because leading women's page editors read each other's publications to find content ideas.[46]

The women's sections also included large doses of soft news such as stories about food and fashion. These topics are often overlooked by historians but valued by readers. These beats allowed the female reporters numerous opportunities to travel as they covered fashion shows and judged cooking contests. Recipe columns connected newspapers and their readers. Newspapers have a direct connection to the community that a national magazine does not. Food editors in the women's pages largely wrote about local stores, local restaurants, and local cooks. For example, the *Akron Beacon Journal* food editor Polly Paffilas wrote:

> The newspaper food editor is the homemakers' best friend, mother confessor and mentor. Mrs. Jones calls us when she can't understand a recipe in a national magazine or when Graham Kerr talks about clarified butter. Mrs. Jones doesn't call the magazine or the TV station. She calls me.[47]

Although the women's pages played important roles in their communities, it was clear that they would soon be under attack as society was changing. A *Glamour* magazine editorial asked its readers in 1971, "What has your women's page editor done for you lately?" The columnist attacked the content of the newspaper sections for speaking down to women and reducing women to traditional roles in the home.[48] While that may have been true in some places, the answer to this question at many American newspapers was "a lot." While some content reinforced a women's place in the home, other stories challenged stereotypical gender roles and validated professional women. Women's page editors had spent more than two decades after World War II laying the groundwork for women's changing roles in society that would help support the Women's Liberation Movement.

In an example of how strange some of these ideas of women's liberation were to American readers, consider a 1972 article in the *Saturday Review*. The author found herself introducing the term "Ms" to readers. She explained that it was "a new term to indicate female as Mr. indicates male; it is pronounced miz or miss."[49] On the other hand, many women had been using the term "Ms" for years. Florida Representative Elaine Gordon recalled her first day in the House in 1972 when she used black tape to cover the "r" in order to clarify that she was "Ms Gordon" rather than "Mrs. Gordon."[50] A 1971 story in the *Milwaukee Journal* women's pages featured the views of US Rep. Bella Abzug and her introduction of a bill that would eliminate the use of "Mrs." and "Miss" on government forms.[51] In another story that year, a Michigan man who took his wife's last name after marriage was featured in the women's pages.[52] At the *Milwaukee Journal*, the tradition was to only use last names for men on second reference but to use a title for women. The use of "Ms" was added in 1974 and finally the practice was stopped altogether in 1980.[53]

Women's Pages in Black Newspapers

There is not much scholarship about the women's pages in black newspapers. Just as is common in the newspaper histories of white newspapers, there are few—if any—mentions of the women's pages in books about specific newspapers. Biographical sketches of black women journalists have largely focused on big names in journalism such as Ida B. Wells-Barnett, Charlotta Bass, and Ethel Payne.[54]

Journalist Rebecca Stiles Taylor covered women's news at the *Chicago Defender* from 1939 to 1945; it was one of the largest black newspapers at the time. She was a journalist and an active club woman. Her column "Mostly About Women" covered women's club news and commentary.[55] She was hired by publisher Robert Abbott to develop the women's pages and to increase women readers. In order to take the job, she required a full page for coverage of the women's club the National Association of Colored Women. This was significant as the organization had stopped publishing its newsletter, and the newspaper column allowed news to reach members. She wrote about education, political issues, and international events. She also sought to connect women: "Negro women must find some way to reach thinking white women."[56]

African-American journalist Mattie Smith Colin is best known for her civil rights coverage of Emmett Till's body as it arrived in Chicago and later at the child's funeral when his mother insisted on an open casket. She was raised in Chicago and studied journalism at Roosevelt and Northwestern universities. She was hired by the black newspaper the *Chicago Defender* in 1950. After covering Till, she went on to cover food and fashion for the newspaper—for a section then called "World of Women." She wrote about runway shows and fashion designers.[57] At times, she was also covered by the newspaper—such as a 1957 talk she gave and a gathering for women she hosted in 1969.[58] She was an invited guest at the presidential inauguration of Lyndon B. Johnson. John H. Sengstacke, a later publisher of the *Defender*, said Colin was a stellar reporter and was as highly regarded as Ethel Payne—known as the "First Lady of the Black Press."[59]

Women's journalism organizations were concerned about how to include news from black communities in their sections. Women's journalism organization Theta Sigma Phi's publication *Matrix* addressed the issue in 1968 by inviting *Ebony* magazine editor Ponchitta Pierce to pen a piece called "Negro News—Why Isn't More on Women's News." She wrote, "It seems to me that women's editors are in a strategic position to correct the imbalance in racial news that now characterizes much of our national and local news." She also encouraged the women's page journalists to cover all the people of their communities. "You must go directly into the non-white world and bring your white readers," she noted. "In addition women editors and writers will have to give a much broader meaning to the term 'society,' making sure that it is inclusive rather than exclusive."[60]

Women's History and Women's Pages

Women have long been left out of the written version of history other than the stories of First Ladies, industry firsts, or women in other high-profile roles. In recent years, historians have made valiant efforts to write them back into history. In journalism history, this has largely meant telling the stories of women who broke out of the women's pages. These stories are important and allow for an understanding of progress. What is often not examined is the woman who was in the more traditional role. When this occurs, a simplified version of "tradition" is created. Yet, it was these women's page editors who found a way to balance the traditional and progressive.

The content of the women's pages has long been defined in journalism history as that which reinforced a woman's role as wife and mother. As one reporter wrote: "It never occurred to me that anything meaningful could come out of the editorial department whose beat, after all, includes food, clothing and shelter. The women's page was for frivolous, boring, puffy, irrelevant, 86-ways-to-make-tuna casserole news."[61] When looking at these sections through today's more liberated eyes, it is easy to pass judgment. Yet, a closer examination shows change was being made in these sections. Amid the bridal news, fashion photos, and recipes, which were significant for readers, there were also questions about women's roles in the post-World War II era as significant gender change was beginning.

One group that regularly supported the women's page journalists was the local women's clubs. These clubs were active across the country. In large cities like Miami, there were more than 100 women's organizations. As has been noted, "The story of how women's civic associations changed in the 1950s is part of a larger narrative about American political development and the forces that shape political change."[62] These clubs took political and social stands, as well as raised money for social causes. According to historian Anne Firor Scott, "While the social shibboleth was that 'woman's place' was in the home, the fact was that for a certain kind of woman (typically of the middle class) 'woman's place' was clearly in the voluntary association."[63]

These women were taking on a new, more serious public role. As researcher A. Lanethea Mathews-Gardner has noted, "Leaders from each association walked a fine line between adopting new and more overtly political modes of organization at the national level and, at the same time, convincing local members that their fundamental purposes as civic groups were not in jeopardy."[64] Women's page editors, too, walked that line between tradition and progress. As journalism scholar Pamela Creedon wrote, to remain in any field "women must conform in some ways to the norms."[65] While often these women did conform, they made a difference and before long were willing to take on a more public role.

Years later, as the women's liberation movement got underway, Paxson recognized a growing awareness of women in the newsroom. She wrote an article for the *Iowa Publisher* newsletter in October 1967 about the progress women were making in journalism, although she also recognized that sexism still existed. "The walls of resistance to women in the newsroom are yielding, a complete turnaround from 1945," she wrote.[66] But due to gender-based stereotypes, women were coming into the newsroom at a disadvantage. She wrote, "Most city editors are men, and there is an inborn prejudice against sending a woman on certain kinds of stories."[67] She concluded the article by telling young women they did not have to make a choice between a personal life and a professional life: "A woman needn't worry either about having to make the old choice between marriage or a career. More than half the women who work in this country are married. A smart girl has her cake and eats it, too."[68]

While much of the women's page content was focused on the upper class, there was a new focus to make society news more inclusive. As an example, women's page editor Kathryn Robinette of the *Palm Beach Post* was inclusive in her reporting—reaching beyond the high society of her city. One of the commonalities Robinette had in common with the other women's page journalists was her ability to reach out to those in all social classes. After her death, Michael Brown, general manager of The Brazilian Court hotel, said of Robinette, "She had a way of making the plain feel equal to royalty. She printed the real-world side to the story versus just a Palm Beach side."[69] She was a native of Chicago, Illinois, and earned a master's degree in English from Northwestern University. In 1966, she left a Savannah newspaper to become women's editor of the *Palm Beach Post-Times*. She was known for working from 7 a.m. until 1 a.m. during much of the week and attending several parties a night. According to restaurateur and longtime friend Jerry Beebe: "High social status was not a prerequisite to coverage. If your cause was legitimate, she'd scoop you up and off you went."[70]

Importance of the Women's Pages

Women's page content supports a revision in the history of women's pages. While traditional women's pages, often filled with society, home, and wedding news, appeared in many newspapers, this was not the full story. There were many sections that were progressive in their content and writing style. Obituaries of numerous women's page editors noted that they were the ones who changed or updated their sections.[71] Not recognizing the differences among sections at various newspapers leads to the invisibility of women in journalism history[72] and overlooks the important roles played by women journalists in pressing for change in their individual communities.

In journalism history, the women's pages are often described as a "ghetto" for female journalists—sometimes called "pink ghettos."[73] If the women's pages are dismissed as "fluff sections" and a "ghetto" for women, the work of women journalists, who fought in their own ways for change, is devalued. These female journalists were pioneers, which makes their stories valuable. As Jennifer Inge Bortolus wrote of another significant woman journalist, Peggy M. Peterman, "while many of the pioneering women of the nineteenth century individually do not appear to be symbols of greatness, it was their collective effort that brought about many social changes."[74] They made their marginalized spaces their own.

One of those who encouraged that collective effort was Paul Myhre, director of the Penney-Missouri Awards. He often applauded the work of the women in the mid-1960s. He was a supporter of adding significant content to women's sections, and his letters to the editors included several references to "we" and "our" mission in making changes. He wrote in a 1966 letter to Greene:

> It's wonderful to hear what the Florida contingent is doing for this laborious cause. You and Marj Paxson thundering from Olympus in your territory and Gloria Biggs and Marie Anderson rocking the managing editors back on their heels in New York.[75]

Myhre wasn't the only man who understood the power of women's pages. Often changes for the sections were based on a few men in management who wanted better women's pages and better roles for women journalists. For example, *Miami Herald* women's page editor Dorothy Jurney worked with Arizona newspaper editor J. Edward Murray in the New Direction for News project, which documented news coverage of women's issues. In their correspondence, Murray mentioned the difficulty that he and other male editors faced during the early years of women's liberation: "Some editors, like me, who have tried their best for a long time to learn how to be fair concerning the news of women now find themselves too often accused of never having thought about the problem at all."[76]

Three men who helped improve women's page journalism in the 1950s and 1960s were James Bellows at the *Miami News*, *New York Herald*

Tribune, and *Los Angeles Times*, among other papers; Al Neuharth at the *Miami Herald* and as founder of *USA Today*; and Lee Hills at the *Miami Herald* and *Detroit Free Press*. Documentation of what they did and what may have driven them can be found in their own writings. Bellows wrote his memoir, *The Last Editor*, and Neuharth wrote a memoir, *Confessions of an S.O.B.* Both men had friends and family contribute sections to their books. While Hills did not write a memoir, Bellows and Neuharth mentioned Hills in their books; Neuharth even referred to Hills as a mentor. Much of the information about Hills, however, comes from an oral history conducted with Jurney who worked with Hills for many years.

Bellows was an early advocate for women journalists and was one of the few men to champion many to positions of authority in his newsrooms prior to the women's movement. In 1959, when women typically covered only soft news, Bellows sent Rollene Saal, a woman's section feature writer to cover the World Heavyweight Championship fight in Miami.[77] The journalists of the women's pages gave him a plaque reading the "Grand Boss Award." Saal, who went on to be editor-in-chief of Bantam Books, wrote: "Back then we were Jim Bellow's gals. Jim was tall, handsome in that loose-limbed Gregory Peck way. Every one of us in the Women's Department was a little in love with him."[78] He hired a collection of talented women including food editor Bertha Hahn and society writer Myrna Odell. Saal noted, "Jim hired these women, was able to give us space to stretch in, and admired and encouraged our work."

Bellows said that his small stature when he was young had formulated his view of what it was like as an underdog. He said that was probably why he identified more with the women and their "second-place citizenship in the newspaper fraternity."[79] As he wrote in his book: "Early in my newspaper days I noticed that the few women in the newsroom were much more eager to accept unusual assignments and work hours than men. Of course, in retrospect, I realize they had nothing to lose, because they were going nowhere to begin with."[80]

By the 1980s, Bellows would go on to mentor Mary Anne Dolan, who would become one of the first female managing editors at a newspaper. In his memoir, Bellow wrote:

> Feminism was a great movement, and it did wonders for newspaperwomen. Maybe I was unduly influenced by the fascinating time I spent with Germaine Greer and Maya Angelou, among others. Certainly, (second wife Maggie Savoy) Maggie helped my education. But I also think of my appreciation for my mother and respect for her strength under pressure.[81]

In the 1950s, while the managing editor of the *Miami Herald*, Hills called Jurney and asked her a question: "Could you take on the women's editorship so that we could get something in the paper that is worth reading?"[82] Hills agreed the coverage of clubs and brides was too narrow a focus for the women's section and wanted stronger content.[83] She was up for the challenge and was hired by the *Herald*, where she stretched the definition of women's news for a decade.[84] She soon hired her friend Marie Anderson as her assistant. They were later joined by Michigan journalist Roberta Applegate who had covered hard news during the war.

Neuharth was one of the first men in newspaper management to speak about the need for more women in management positions at his newspapers. In 1968, he spoke to the winners of the Penney-Missouri Awards and encouraged women to be ambitious: "Go after some of those jobs that have always had 'For Men Only' signs hanging on them. Women can have the top jobs in the newspaper profession if they want them."[85] The promotion of Gloria Biggs as the first female publisher of a Gannett newspaper was intended as a change for his company but did not produce the results he hoped for. "Even after I broke the ice with Biggs as our first woman publisher, there were no Gannett females lining up at my office door seeking promotions," Neuharth wrote in his memoir. "That disappointed me. But I pushed on."[86]

Biggs began her journalism career in 1953 as the "number two woman in a two-woman women's department"[87] at the *Evening Independent* in St. Petersburg, Florida, before being named the women's page editor in 1957 at the competing *St. Petersburg Times*. In 1966, she became women's page editor of *Today*, the Gannett-owned start-up based in Cocoa, Florida. (It later became *Florida Today*.) She also became the head of all women's sections for the Gannett newspaper company in Florida. Neuharth, who in 1966 was president of Gannett Florida, justified Biggs' promotion in a letter to her stating, "Having someone of your proven ability and high caliber run the women's show simply adds to the insurance policy for success."[88]

For all of his good intentions, however, Neuharth did not explain how Biggs and other early female executives would receive the mentoring they needed to be successful. The problem became apparent after his subsequent 1974 promotion of Christy Bulkeley to publisher of *The Saratogian* in Saratoga Springs, New York. He wrote in his memoir that Bulkeley, the second women to be named a Gannett chief executive, was initially shocked because she did not believe she was suitably prepared. He responded: "You think you're not ready. Well. You're right. You're not. But you're as ready as I've ever been for any of my promotions and you'll grow into it."[89]

The Need for Women's Page Research

This book is the story of women's page journalists who made changes in their communities and found their own ways to help women. At times, this was because of forward-thinking male editors and at other times, it was a matter of being crafty. For example, Edee Greene would often find her own way to take a new approach in violation of the newspaper's policies. When asked, she would deny knowing the rules. To other women's page editors, she advised various approaches including ignoring old policies until they disappear: "But of course the best weapon is the sneak attack. Improve one area at a time—but don't let the top guns know what you're doing."[90]

According to an academic study: "Early twentieth-century woman's pages also featured innovative new genres covering a changing roster of topics. Dismissed by contemporaries and scholars as homogenous 'drivel,' the woman's section has long been misunderstood because no one has conducted an in-depth, multi-decade analysis of content and evolution."[91] The gendered assumptions of women's interest led to its content being overlooked. Another academic study of the women's pages noted: "Reflecting on the low status of women's genres in mainstream research, scholars have largely ignored news for women. The scant attention paid to women's pages to date, despite the significant insights offered by a few journalists and researchers," results in not much understanding of the sections.[92] According to a study of the women's section of the *Washington Post* in the 1950s and 1960s, most critics have focused largely on the transition into lifestyle sections, "shedding little light on the rich history of the genre." Further the scholarship noted that "most of the existing research on women's pages embraced masculine values as the norm. Reinforcing the stereotype of women's pages as frivolous and dull, this line of critique obscured the significance of women's pages as a feminine genre."[93]

The goal of this examination of the women's pages is not to refute the assertion that the sections contained material that at times was limited—including tips about applying cosmetics, how to get stains out of clothing, and household tips. Rather, this exploration demonstrates that the sections included more progressive content than previously explained—and that even the traditional content had more complex meaning than simply reinforcing a woman's place in the home. It is safe to say that most women journalists were limited to working in the women's pages at most metropolitan newspapers prior to the women's liberation movement. Yet, this does not mean that the women journalists gave in to the limits placed upon them. Instead, they saw the potential in the section that management did not and explored a variety of stories. Their sections often gave space to topics that may not have been covered otherwise.

These women were smart, feisty, and ahead of their times. They left a great legacy for today's women journalists. In addition, they were the ones who spread the message of the women's movement in a way that allowed women in their communities to feel empowered. They also changed the course of women's page journalism. In some cases, it was about promoting women and overtly changing content. In other cases, the changes were more subtle in nature. Regardless, forward-thinking women's page editors were making improvements both shocking and sophisticated as they transformed their sections in ways that also transformed their readership. They also helped change the newspaper industry.

Notes

1. Marion Marzolf, *Up From the Footnote: A History of Women Journalists* (New York: Hasting House, 1977).
2. Julian M. Pleasants, *Orange Journalism: Voices from Florida Newspapers* (Gainesville, Florida: University Press of Florida, 2003).
3. Pleasants, *Orange Journalism*, 50.
4. Kathleen A Cairnes, *Front Page Women Journalists, 1920–1950* (Lincoln: University of Nebraska Press, 2003); *War Torn: Stories of the Women Journalists Who Covered the Vietnam War* (New York: Random House, 2002).
5. Maurine H. Beasley and Shelia J. Gibbons, eds, *Taking Their Place: A Documentary History of Women and Journalism* (State College, Pennsylvania: Strata Publishing, Inc., 2003); Kay Mills, *A Place in the News: From the Women's Pages to the Front Pages* (New York: Columbia University Press, 1990); Marion Marzlof, *Up From the Footnote: A History of Women Journalists* (New York: Hasting House, 1977); Jan Whitt, *Women in American Journalism* (Urbana, Ill.: University of Illinois Press, 2008).
6. Eileen Wirth, *From Society Page to Front Page* (Lincoln, Nebraska: University of Nebraska Press, 2013).
7. Kimberly Wilmot Voss, "Anne Rowe Goldman: Refashioning Women's News in St. Petersburg, Florida," *FCH Annals: Journal of the Florida Conference of Historians*, March 2011: 104–111.
8. Susan Paynter oral history with Maria McLeod, "ERA Oral History Interview," Washington State Historical Society, transcript, May 22, 2008, 5, http://www.washingtonhistory.org/files/library/Paynter.pdf.
9. "Pages for Women," *Time*, May 19, 1967.
10. Joanne Meyerowitz, ed., *Not June Cleaver: Women and Gender in Postwar America, 1945–1960* (Philadelphia: Temple University Press, 1994).
11. "Women in Journalism Oral History Project," Washington Press Club Foundation, http://wpcf.org/women-in-journalism/.
12. Kimberly Wilmot Voss, "Forgotten Feminist: Women's Page Editor Maggie Savoy and the Growth of Women's Liberation Awareness in Los Angeles," *California History*, Spring 2009: 48–64; Kimberly Wilmot Voss, "Florence Burge: Representing Reno's Women in a Changing Time," *Nevada Historical Quarterly*, Winter 2006: 294–307; "Colleen 'Koky' Dishon: A Journalism Legend," *Timeline*, Summer 2010.

13. Doris Weatherford, *A History of Women in Tampa* (Tampa, Florida: Athena Society, 1991), 145.
14. David Davies, *The Postwar Decline of American Newspapers, 1945–1965* (Westport, Conn.: Praeger Publishers, 2006), 4.
15. Betty Ewing interview with Dawn Letson, August 4, 1991. Available in Betty Ewing Papers, Woman's Collection, Texas Woman's University.
16. Betty Ewing, "27 Persons Killed in Airline Crash, United Press," *The Port Authority News*, May 16, 1946; Betty Ewing, "Virginia, Maryland Oyster War Revived," United Press, *Middlebury* (Kentucky) *Daily News*, February 5, 1947; Betty Ewing, "Virginia Power Strike Called Off," United Press, *Middlebury* (Kentucky) *Daily News*, November 1, 1946.
17. Marjorie Paxson, "Women in Journalism Oral History Project," Washington Press Club Foundation, Session 6, 144.
18. Mary Welsh Hemingway letter to Jurney, September 11, 1958, Papers of Dorothy Jurney, National Women and Media Collection, State Historical Society of Missouri.
19. Charles Stevenson letter of recommendation, February 28, 1949, Papers of Dorothy Jurney, National Women and Media Collection, State Historical Society of Missouri.
20. Stevenson, letter of recommendation.
21. Marjorie Paxson described this in her introduction to the National Women and Media Collection, State Historical Society of Missouri.
22. Dorothy Jurney, "Women in Journalism Oral History Project," Washington Press Club Foundation, Session 4, 126.
23. Aileen Ryan, "Woman's World: 'No So,' Writes Aroused Editor," *Once a Year*, 1961, Milwaukee Press Club Papers, Box 10, folder 21.
24. Stephanie Coontz, *A Strange Stirring: The Feminine Mystique and American Women at the Dawn of the 1960s* (New York: Basic Books, 2011), 50.
25. Ibid.
26. Rodger Streitmatter, "Transforming the Women's Pages," *Journalism History* 24, no. 2 (1998): 72–81.
27. Eleanor W. Stanton, "Editing a Woman's Page" Newspaper Institute of America. Special Collections, Southern Illinois University Library.
28. Eleanor W. Stanton, "Editing a Woman's Page" Newspaper Institute of America. Special Collections, Southern Illinois University Library.
29. Joy Miller, Associated Press, "Women Are Root of Trouble," April 23, 1966.

30. Mary Ryan, *Womanhood in America: From Colonel Times to the Present* (New York: Franklin Watts, 1983), 279.
31. William Henry Chafe, *The American Woman: Her Changing Social, Economical, and Political Roles, 1920–1970* (New York: Oxford University Press, 1972), 218.
32. Dorothy Roe, "Associated Press Newsfeature support," February 20, 1959.
33. Wirth, *From Society Page*, 114–115.
34. Elizabeth McCormick Malmgren, "An Analysis of Changes in the Reno Evening Gazette Women's Pages" (master's thesis, University of Nevada, 1978), 62.
35. Nancy Beth Jackson, *The Junior League: 100 Years of Volunteer Service* (New York: Association of Junior League International, Inc., 2001), 119.
36. Jean Jarvis Sneed, "The Florida Newspaper Woman of 1970" (master's thesis, University of Florida, 1970), 25.
37. Talk by Marjorie Paxson, Penney-Missouri Awards Banquet, March 31, 1966, 2, Penney-Missouri Awards Papers, State Historical Society of Missouri.
38. Ibid.
39. Jean Sprain Wilson, "Reporter by Day, Conductor at Night," *Cedar Rapids Gazette*, September 23, 1962.
40. Jean Sprain Wilson, "Woman Scribe is Conductor of Symphony," *The Gettysburg Times*, February 9, 1963.
41. Jean Sprain Wilson, "Football and the Classics Keep Her Too Busy for Love," *Greeley Tribune*, September 12, 1962.
42. Memo from Roberta Applegate to George Beebe. February 16, 1962, Papers of Roberta Applegate, State Historical Society of Missouri.
43. Marjorie Paxson, *New Guardians of the Press: Selected Profiles of America's Women Newspaper Editors* (Indianapolis, Indiana: R.J. Berg and Co., 1983), 126.
44. Marzolf, *Up From the Footnote*, 20.
45. Rodger Streitmatter, "Transforming the Women's Pages: Strategies That Worked," *Journalism History* (1998).
46. This fact was mentioned by Vivian Castleberry and Dorothy Jurney in "Washington in Journalism Oral History Project," Washington Press Club Foundation, http://wpcf.org/women-in-journalism/. Castleberry also mentioned that women's page editors Maggie Savoy and Gloria Biggs often interacted.

47. Polly Paffilas, "Comments from the Food Section," *Matrix* (Winter 1971–1972): 15.
48. "What Has Your Women's Page Editor Done For You Lately?" *Glamour*, September 1971, 92.
49. Pamela Howard, "Ms." *Saturday Review*, January 8, 1972, 43.
50. Laura Brock, "Religion, Sex, and Politics: The Story of the Equal Rights Amendment in Florida" (PhD diss, Florida State University, 2013), 61–62.
51. "Mrs. Or Miss? Abzug Bill Says Irrelevant," *Milwaukee Journal*, July 27, 1971.
52. "Man Takes Wife – and Her Last Name," *Milwaukee Journal*, October 5, 1971.
53. Robert Wells, *The Milwaukee Journal: An Informal Chronicle of Its First 100 Years* (Milwaukee, Wisconsin: Milwaukee Journal, 1981), 451.
54. Rodger Streitmatter, *Raising Her Voice: African-American Women Journalists Who Changed History* (Lexington, Kentucky: University Press of Kentucky, 1994).
55. Bill V. Mullen, *Popular Fronts: Chicago and African-American Cultural Politics, 1935–46* (Urbana, Illinois: University of Illinois Press, 1999), 52.
56. Caryl Cooper, "Selling Negro Women to Negro Women and to the World," *Journalism History*, Winter 2014, 241–249.
57. Mattie Smith Colin, "The Guild: On the Runway," *Chicago Defender*, August 20, 1975; Mattie Smith Colin, "Imported Fashions Featured," *Chicago Defender*, October 29, 1975.
58. "Mattie Colin to Give Talk," *Chicago Defender*, June 26, 1957; Doris E. Sanders, "'Femme Faire' Mattie Colin's New Year Entry," *Chicago Defender*, January 7, 1969.
59. Joan Giangrasse, "Mattie Smith Colin, *Chicago Defender* reporter who covered Emmett Till story, dies at 98," *Chicago Tribune*, December 30, 2016.
60. Ponchitta Pierce, "Negro News – Why Isn't More on Women's News," *Matrix*, June 1968, 4–5.
61. Lindsay Van Gelder, "Women's Pages: You Can't Make News Out of a Silk Purse," *Ms Magazine*, 112.
62. Lanethea Mathews-Gardner, "The 1950s, Women, Civic Engagement, and Political Change," American Political Science Association Conference, Chicago, Illinois, September 2, 2004, 4.

63. Anne Firor Scott, *Making the Invisible Woman Visible* (Urbana, Illinois: University of Illinois Press, 1984), 282.
64. Noted in A. Lanethea Mathews-Gardner, "The 1950s, Women, Civic Engagement, and Political Change," American Political Science Association Conference, Chicago, Ill. September 2004, 35.
65. Pamela Creedon, "Framing Feminism: A Feminist Primer for the Mass Media," *Media Studies Journal*, 1993: 71.
66. Marjorie Paxson, "Where the Girls Are Going," *The Iowa Publisher*, October 1967, 13.
67. Paxson, "Where the Girls Are Going," 13.
68. Paxson, "Where the Girls Are Going," 14.
69. "Society Editor Remembered for Her Common Touch," *Palm Beach Post*, July 30, 1997.
70. Ibid.
71. For example: Dave Person, "Former Kalamazoo Gazette Editor was energetic, charming," *Kalamazoo Gazette*, September 10, 2010; Judi Hunt, "Newswoman Sally Raleigh Dies," *Seattle Post-Intelligencer*, March 29, 1993; "Home Décor Editor Excelled at The Blade," *Toledo Blade*, April 19, 2009.
72. Joan Wallach Scott, "The Problem of Invisibility," in *Retrieving Women's History*, ed. S. Jay Kleinberg (New York: Berg Publishers Limited, 1998), 5.
73. Barbara Bratman, "A Century and a Half of Women – and 'Women's News,'" *Chicago Tribune*, June 8, 1997; Sarah Jaffe, "From Women's Page to Style Section," *Columbia Journalism Review*, February 19, 2013; Jan Whitt, *Women in American Journalism: A New History* (University of Illinois Press, 2008), 47.
74. Jennifer Inge Bortolus, "Fighting for Others: Peggy M. Peterman's 31 years at the *St. Petersburg Times*" (master's thesis, University of South Florida, 2000), 2.
75. Paul L. Myhre to Edee Greene, November 10, 1966, Penney-Missouri Award Papers, State Historical Society of Missouri.
76. J. Edward Murray, publisher of the *Daily Camera* (Boulder, Colorado), letter to Dorothy Jurney, February 11, 1981, Papers of New Directions for Newspapers, National Women and Media Collection, Missouri State Historical Society.

77. Jim Bellows, *The Last Editor: How I Saved the New York Times, the Washington Post, and the Los Angeles Times from Dullness and Complacency* (Kansas City, Missouri: Andrews McMeel, 2002), 79.
78. Bellows, *The Last Editor*, 78.
79. Bellows, *The Last Editor*, 217
80. Bellows, *The Last Editor*, 217.
81. Bellows, *The Last Editor*, 217.
82. Marie Anderson, "Women in Journalism Oral History Project," Washington Press Club Foundation, transcript, Session 1, 24.
83. Marzolf, *Up From the Footnote*, 209.
84. Dorothy Jurney, "Women In Journalism," *The Bulletin*, January 1, 1956, 5.
85. "Sex Gap in Communications," Penney-Missouri Awards program, 29, Papers of the Penney-Missouri Awards, National Women and Media Collection, State Historical Society of Missouri.
86. Al Neuharth, *Confessions of an S.O.B.* (New York, NY: Signet, 1992), 242.
87. "Biography of Gloria N. Biggs," June 1977, Gloria Biggs Papers, National Women and Media Collection, State Historical Society of Missouri.
88. Al Neuharth to Gloria Biggs, February 4, 1966. Gloria Biggs Papers, National Women and Media Collection, State Historical Society of Missouri.
89. Neuharth, *Confessions*, 242.
90. Edee Greene, "Penney-Missouri Workshop Talk," March 22, 1965, 9, Papers of Florence Burge, University of Nevada, Reno, 82-36/II/1.
91. Julie A. Golia, "Courting Women, Courting Advertisers: The Woman's Page and the Transformation of the American Newspaper, 1895–1935," *Journal of American History*, December 2016: 608.
92. Mei-ling Yang, "Women's Pages or People's Pages: The Production of News for Women in the Washington Post in the 1950s," *Journalism and Mass Communication Quarterly*, Summer 1996: 364.
93. Ibid.

2

The Growth of the Women's Page Community

For decades, every metropolitan newspaper had a women's page that employed numerous women journalists. Their backgrounds varied, of course, but some generalizations can be made. Many were college graduates, which was not necessarily true for other journalists. There has long been a debate if a college journalism degree was needed or a newsroom apprenticeship was a better path.[1] The answer for many journalism education programs was to produce student publications and internships. Women were long part of these programs. According to a study from the 1939–1940 school year, there were more than ten colleges that offered women and journalism or home economics journalism classes. Other programs also offered classes focused on women's page content.[2] Home economics journalism was officially recognized by the study *The New Majority*, funded by the Gannett Foundation and conducted at the University of Maryland.[3] The major was cited as a way for women graduates to gain employment. It was noted, "Journalism school training was a must for the female who wanted to go into newspaper work, although males can go to work without experience."[4]

Women earning journalism degrees were using them to gain entry into the workforce in advertising, publicity, and journalism jobs. An article in a 1932 issue of *Matrix* recommended that women could get jobs in

K. W. Voss, *Re-Evaluating Women's Page Journalism in the Post-World War II Era*,
https://doi.org/10.1007/978-3-319-96214-6_2

numerous communication fields. The writer noted, "The school of journalism should teach its women students the art of collecting news and the accepted manner of writing it."[5] A study of women journalism graduates from a dozen schools in the 1941 graduating class showed that they had achieved success. Most were married and still stayed in the workforce. The study also found that these graduates were doing better financially than professional women in general. The scholar wrote, "In her personal life, the graduates found that an education was an excellent education for life."[6] There were many significant home economics journalism programs including those at the land-grant schools of Iowa State University, Kansas State University, and the University of Wisconsin. These programs taught women to cover news for the women's pages.

Other women's page editors had traditional journalism degrees. For example, Carol Sutton was one of several women in the news editorial sequence at the University of Missouri during her undergraduate years. She said no one discouraged her from going into journalism, particularly the news sequence. This was not common for the time as many journalism schools offered courses that encouraged women to remain in the traditional women's sections.[7] But, the University of Missouri was known for admitting women into its program many years before other journalism schools and treating them as equals.[8]

In Dallas, Vivian Castleberry entered college as a journalism major at Southern Methodist University and she quickly started writing for the school's weekly newspaper, the *Campus*. By the time she was a junior, she was working as many hours at the newspaper as she could. She had worked her way up from features editor to assistant editor when she decided to run for editor, an elective office. Her opponent, who lost to Castleberry, was another female student—this was because male students were largely off at war. It was a significant election as there had never been a female newspaper editor in the university's history.

Women's page editor Maggie Savoy attended the University of Southern California in the late 1930s. She wrote that as a depression-era child, she "tramp-scholared" her way to a Phi Beta Kappa, working ten-hour days to everyone else's eight hours.[9] Savoy graduated from USC in 1940 with a bachelor's degree in journalism and honors.

Dorothy Jurney attended Western College for Women for two years. She then completed her junior and senior years at Northwestern University with a major in journalism and an emphasis in economics. After graduation, Jurney had every intention of pursuing a professional career, like many of her female classmates. She said: "My friends were career minded, there was that impetus that we should all be working—we should be working women and have careers. But nobody ever pointed out, or we were not smart enough to realize, that the horizons were not very high."[10] Jurney was frustrated later by women who were not using their educations outside of the home. She later said, "I was very disappointed when I found that the women who were in college around the time of World War II were not career-minded."[11]

Choosing the Women's Pages

Most journalism histories indicate women sought to escape the women's pages; they preferred to work in other sections of the newspaper. While there were likely women who did seek to work elsewhere at the newspaper, others saw the promise the sections held. For example, after World War II Colleen "Koky" Dishon returned to her Ohio newspaper and covered religion. She later recalled sitting at her newsroom desk, reading the weak content in the women's section and asking herself, "Why don't I fix this?" Dishon requested she be appointed editor of the women's section. She described the current stories as nonsense, citing headlines "dressing for him" and "how to get stains out of clothing." Her editor, George Smallsreed, tried to talk her out of the decision to head the women's pages. "You're too good for that," he said. She prevailed and began trying new concepts. She eliminated much of the household-hint stories and began writing feature stories with a news peg. Her goal was to "take the yardstick we used for news and move it over to the features section."

Dishon found a kindred spirit in Ohio native Charlotte Curtis, then the women's page editor at the cross-town rival the *Columbus Citizen*. "We competed for stories during the day," Dishon wrote of their relationship, "and then met to discuss how we could save newspaper sections from ailing dullness and wafer-thin substance." The women agreed that women's sections could be improved with stronger writing and more news. It was Curtis's unique writing style that later led to her position as an editor at the *New York Times*.

Carol Sutton vowed she would not join the women's pages after graduation from college. From 1955 to 1960, Sutton was a general assignment reporter at the *Louisville Courier-Journal*. In 1963, Sutton became the women's editor. Sutton also seemed to be of this frame of mind as she worked to stretch the women's pages—applying her news background and feature writing specialty to the section. Sutton was so excited about the opportunity of leading the section that she could not sleep. She felt it was a very creative part of the newspaper, and she wanted to bring the section "into modern times."[12] Prior to her editing the section, it rarely included controversial topics. That changed under Sutton's direction. She said the previous content "didn't suit the women of the early 1960s."[13] The section began to cover reproductive issues including birth control and abortion. She remembered: "It was a lot of responsibility, very challenging. The whole social atmosphere was changing."[14]

In 1957, Edee Greene joined the *Fort Lauderdale News*. Bothered by the typically traditional content, Greene hoped to avoid the women's section. She later said, "I ran my legs off to keep from having to work in the women's department."[15] She eventually left the city room to head the women's department in 1958 after being promised by executive editor Fred Pettijohn the opportunity to change the entire outlook of the section.[16] Her groundbreaking approach was rewarded with a full-page article in the industry magazine *Editor & Publisher*. When Pettijohn was asked about hiring women, he responded that when he was in a position of authority in the newsroom, he hired women.[17]

Women's Page Community

A wide women's page community in the 1950s and 1960s met socially and professionally—and they also reached out to women's page editors beyond their state's borders. Often, these women had spotty support for progress at their own newspaper so they found support systems elsewhere. They kept in contact through letters and regular meetings, encouraging each other and cheering each other on. Sutton helped spread the news of Gloria Biggs's promotion from women's page editor to publisher in the Gannett chain in 1973. In Sutton's words, "That's one for our side!"[18] Marjorie Paxson wrote to Biggs after reading of the promotion to *Editor & Publisher*: "I'm so proud of you I could pop. Nice going. Very nice going."[19] Biggs's promotion was considered a victory for all of the women journalists. Paxson, who would later become a publisher herself, went on to joke "Will you still speak to lowly women's editors like me now that you're up there in the front office?"[20]

When Marie Anderson announced her retirement from her university position, Biggs heard the news from Florida women's page journalist Nancy Taylor.[21] Biggs wrote to Anderson: "This letter will tell you how glad/sorry I am about your retirement. I say 'glad' because I know it was your idea to take that step. I say 'sorry' because it's absolutely ridiculous for all that talent of yours not to be exercised in ways that are meaningful to you."[22] They stuck together as their sections—and often their jobs—were eliminated. In their later retirements, they continued to visit each other, as letters showed.

It is clear from the meetings they attended and the letters sent between them that there was an extremely close community of women's page editors. And for many of these women, it was a lifelong relationship. Anderson and Jurney traveled the world together, and one photo shows them both riding an elephant. In the 1980s, Miami women's page journalist and library advocate Helen Muir achieved an ambition by walking across the Brooklyn Bridge—she was accompanied by her 1950s women's page colleagues Anderson and Jurney.[23] While a women's page editor in Dallas, Castleberry visited Miami to shadow Jurney and Anderson at the *Miami Herald* to learn how to improve her section. Several of the women's page editors also gathered together at the American Press Institute-sponsored conferences at Columbia University in the 1950s.

Penney-Missouri Award Workshops

The Penney-Missouri Awards were the ultimate recognition for women's page reporting, which began in 1960. Sponsored by the J.C. Penney Company and run by the Missouri School of Journalism, the competition rewarded progressive content that went beyond the traditional women's page content. The awards competition was created to recognize progressive women's pages. The national awards were considered the Pulitzer Prize of women's sections.[24] These awards included workshops that allowed the women to network and impact change on a national level. Winners presented their approaches at the workshops.

Florida newspapers were the place to be for women's pages in the 1960s, and their editors dominated the four circulation categories of the Penney-Missouri competition. For example, during Kathryn Robinette's career at the *Palm Beach Post*, she earned three Penney-Missouri Awards—in 1966, 1968, and 1972. Winners received the good news in telegrams that arrived on Christmas morning, and Robinette was clearly thrilled. She responded to the first telegram by writing, "That shout you heard wasn't the south rising again—it was me. The news that I had won second place in the J.C. Penney-Missouri Journalism competition was just too great to be taken in a calm, sedate manner."[25] Marie Anderson won so many of the awards for her work at the *Miami Herald* that she was retired from the competition.

Women's page journalists from across the country came together on a regular basis to the Penney-Missouri Awards workshops hosted annually in Columbia, Missouri. These meetings allowed the kind of networking that the male editors often had access to over the years. For example, the Society of Professional Journalists did not accept women until 1969. While at these meetings, not only were friendships established, but a mission to improve the sections was encouraged. Penney-Missouri Award Director Paul Myhre encouraged change and developed his own friendships with the women's page editors. Letters from Edee Greene were signed "Love and kisses."[26] Myhre's mother-in-law lived in South Florida, and he occasionally visited with the women when in the state. Greene also regularly met with Myhre's mother-in-law.[27]

George Pica, who was later hired to run the Penney-Missouri program, witnessed the growth and impact of the program. James Cash Penney, the founder of the J.C. Penney Company, chose the University of Missouri School of Journalism to conduct the program because he was born in Missouri. Penney, Pica said, believed the school had the prestige necessary to reshape women's sections into effective vehicles for his company's advertising. According to Pica:

> I suspect that in many ways the program he helped create succeeded beyond his expectations and helped that area of journalism evolve in a direction he never envisioned. I don't think J.C. Penney wanted the women's sections so much to change as to become better at what they did—telling women what they ought to be spending the family's income on. Instead, the program spawned a generation of aggressive, innovative lifestyle journalists whose work was as likely to win a Pulitzer as it was to win a Penney-Missouri Award.[28]

Multiple Penney-Missouri Award winner Marjorie Paxson said the recognition was valuable to her career:

> It was a big help. If nothing else, it lets you know that you're not alone, you're not the only one out there who has these ideas about getting more hard news and substantive news into your pages. You're bored with writing the trivial club notices and lengthy descriptions of weddings and engagements—and if you're bored the readers are probably bored, too. But you're not alone. Other people are fighting the same fight and you get all sorts of ideas from them.[29]

Photos of the workshops show the women socializing in addition to attending the workshops—and often meeting at Myhre's house. There were numerous thank you letters that cited the great parties at his residence. These letters show the women also knew Myhre's wife, Mary, quite well as they were often addressed to "Paul and Mary."

The Missouri connection continued through the years, as many of the female students from the University of Missouri were recruited to work in women's pages. One example was Mary Mills, who joined the *Miami Herald* women's section in 1967. She took the place of Nancy Taylor, who moved over to the *Miami News* to work as an assistant to Billie O'Day.[30] Another example was Sandra Lantz, who in 1961 joined the women's section of the *Sun-Sentinel*. Myhre wrote of Lantz, "Sandra has the instincts, the initiative, and the will to be a good newspaper woman and writer."[31] She was welcomed with open arms by the women in the section. According to Morales, the older, married women were happy to live vicariously through the young woman who had found an apartment on the beach. Morales wrote of a colleague, "One of the girls said she'd be willing to put her family on the auction block and take the apartment next door."[32]

Later Morales left the newspaper and Edee Greene, women's page editor in Ft. Lauderdale, Florida, made sure to look in on Lantz. After speaking at a company event, Greene brought Lantz to her home and made her a dinner of grilled cheeses sandwiches. Greene wrote, "We talked long, long as I wanted her to known that she was not ALONE down here—and that if she needed a mother's shoulder to cry on—mine was broad."[33] Greene continued to be someone who looked out for younger female reporters—and that wasn't always easy. Many women's page editors described having to convince new female college journalism graduates that their sections were worth working for. Greene said in a 1963 talk, "I sell her on the thought that we're no pink tea operation."[34] In 1965, Greene and Paxson were at a workshop to encourage high school and junior college students to go into journalism.[35] Greene explained that her staff was made up of a variety of women, including a "French warbride," a "beatnic who drives a sports car," and a "mother of two adopted children."[36]

Journalism Organization Theta Sigma Phi

Throughout the early part of the century, male and female journalists were often members of separate professional organizations. For example, the Society of Professional Journalists did not allow female members until 1973. Women journalists often belonged to the sorority Theta Sigma Phi, which had statewide chapters. The organization is now known as the Association for Women in Communications. Many of the women's page editors were leaders in the state chapter, but it was Paxson who made a national name for herself. Anderson wrote of Paxson, "She certainly has done an excellent job of putting Theta Sig on a more professional and businesslike basis."[37]

Paxson was the national president of the Association for Women in Communications during its transformation from a sorority to a professional organization. Paxson was elected the national president of the 4500-member professional journalism organization. She held that office from 1963 to 1967. When she took office, the organization—which was founded in 1908 as a sorority for journalism students—was more of a social group. According to Paxson: "I turned the organization from a narrow, journalistic social sorority concept to a professional approach. I motivated volunteers who paid dues for the privilege of working in the organization … to change direction."[38] Paxson's campaign for a more professional approach to issues concerning women in journalism was not always well received. The race for the presidency was bitter. Many members resisted Paxson's emphasis on professional training. She was at a local Theta Sigma Phi meeting when she learned she had won. She got a telegram from Anderson: "Congratulations, I guess."[39]

According to Chicago journalist Mary Jane Snyder, it was an important time for the organization. She said:

> Those were decisive years when a philosophy of change was at stake. We needed a woman with strong leadership qualities, a real professional. Marj was the right person at the right time. She hits the ground running. She's a woman with high expectations who has the talent to mesh divergent people together, yet do it in a non-threatening manner so everybody feels comfortable.[40]

Paxson's goals included establishing a national headquarters. At the time, the group's files were housed in a member's garage. She spent much of her free time traveling and speaking to local chapters across the country. While president, she visited 40 chapters and traveled more than 75,000 miles. She also wrote to regional groups—corresponding with more than 4,000 members for an average of 25 a week. In her final address as president, Paxson called for the organization to change its name from the Greek symbols and move toward a more professional title, Women in Communications, Inc. Ultimately, it took several years for this to take place. She later said: "I always had a high regard for the organization. It did spread across the country and there were a lot of prominent women in it. I felt like it could be a force to help women as things changed in the sixties."[41]

In the years following Paxson's presidency, the women journalists she had recruited stayed involved and pushed for professionalism. In 2003, she was inducted into the organization's national Hall of Fame. Her honor proclaimed: "Her career is truly a documentary of women in journalism. She has lived the evolution of change from society section to lifestyle section … society editor to managing editor and publisher."[42] She was able to take her women's page experience and use it as a foundation for women in newspaper management.

Other Press Organizations

Likely, the first American press club was the Chicago Press Club, established in 1880 to develop contacts between journalists and local leaders.[43] By 1919, press clubs existed in most major American cities serving professional and social roles. These clubs often excluded women and thus women-only press clubs were established, as explored by historians Maurine Beasley[44] and Elizabeth Burt.[45] Over the years, women journalists had made attempts to become part of several men's clubs but were unsuccessful.[46] In Milwaukee for example, women journalists fought throughout the years to become members of the Milwaukee Press Club—considered the oldest, continuously running press club in the country. Aileen Ryan, a three-time Penney-Missouri Award winner at the *Milwaukee Journal*, wrote this exclusion often came as a shock to young women journalists beginning at newspapers that they viewed as tools to change social injustice. She paraphrased the views naïve female employees might ask, "Aren't newspapermen the foes of prejudice, champions of tolerance, fighters on the side of justice, searchers after truth, exposers of inequalities, fair-minded exponents of human rights?" Ryan said her response would be, "We can only point out that newspaperwomen are not even permitted to become members of the Press Club."[47] The female journalists protested, but it was not until a threatened American Civil Liberties Union lawsuit that they became members in 1971.[48]

This is not to imply that all press clubs excluded women—organizations such as the Nevada Press Club had already elected its second female president by 1966.[49] But, it was clearly common to exclude women as was the case in many cities where women created their own gender-exclusive clubs.[50] In Florida, Florence DeVore started the Florida Women's Press Club in 1951 to address inequities that women journalists faced.

Greene was president of the Florida Woman's Press club from 1965 to 1967. She was also president of the Broward Chapter of the Theta Sigma Phi from 1966 to 1967. When Paxson's national presidency of Theta Sigma Phi was over, she immediately became treasurer of the Florida Women's Press Club.[51] Rowe was also an active member in the state press club, as well as in Theta Sigma Phi. One member recalled "a number of instances when prospects and progress of women in the newsroom dominated informal conversation at press club meetings."[52] These meetings were opportunities to begin questioning women's roles at their newspapers—and society.

The Florida Women's Press Club also served as a reunion for the women with Jurney, who had moved to Detroit by 1960. In 1966, Jurney came to Palm Beach for the organization's annual meeting and met with Greene, Rowe, and Biggs. She then spent a week with Anderson in Miami.[53] These women also served as judges for the awards of women's press club. In 1967, the Florida women judged the work of the Ohio women's page editors. Anderson noted that those newspapers were not covering as much of the hard news compared to the Florida women's sections. She wrote, "Most of these were just reports of someone's talk to a woman's club but at least the clubs were getting speakers on the subject and the papers were covering them."[54]

Like most press clubs, the Florida club featured newsworthy speakers. One example was *Miami Herald* editor Don Shoemaker's speech in Daytona Beach on September 13, 1958. He identified himself as a supporter of women's rights using a term not common at the time: "May I say at once that I am a confirmed feminist."[55] At the press club meeting, Shoemaker went on to say:

> I have an unauthenticated hunch that there are far more successful newspaperwomen than there are lady lawyers, doctors, merchants, and chefs. If I remember my history, Nellie Bly got around the world well before Stanley went to Africa to say 'I presume' to Dr. Livingston. From Alicia Patterson and her triumphant *Newsday* to some of the smart copy girls on the *Herald*, there is proof positive that whatever men can do, women can do better—er, let us say, as well.[56]

His talk addressed race segregation in the south. It was an issue that Shoemaker knew well. He oversaw a journalistic project about segregation that resulted in the 1957 book *With All Deliberate Speed: Segregation-Desegregation in Southern Schools*. The title was a reference to the Supreme Court ruling in *Brown vs Board of Education*. The justices wrote that schools needed to be desegregated "with all deliberate speed." Shoemaker described the book as "a journalistic summation of three turbulent years since the Supreme Court decision against segregation in the public schools."[57] Segregation was a hot button issue throughout the south, especially true when it came to busing children—a topic that would be debated for years. Women's page editors faced segregation in their own sections when it came to brides. This was a concept that was supported by the women's page community—not necessarily their management.

Pay Equity

Numerous studies during the 1960s and 1970s found that women's page journalists were often underpaid. It was a topic that Anderson addressed at a national conference in 1963.[58] A study of the *Orlando Sentinel Star* noted, "Salaries during Andersen's control of the paper were low, especially for women."[59] According to a 1970s study of women's page editors, one person responded, "Positions of authority are not as easily reached; pay is definitely unequal." Another person responded: "Very simple—men are given bigger and better salary increases on a more regular basis."[60]

At her own newspaper, Anderson appeared to also have fought for raises for her reporters. An undated letter from Helen Wells thanked Anderson for her raise: "My morale has gone up 100 percent to know that you appreciate my struggles and I've never had a raise that I appreciated more."[61] Anderson also fought for a raise for *Miami Herald* Club Editor Roberta Applegate. In a note telling Applegate of her raise, Anderson wrote: "You continue to be someone I can turn to when I need help, whether it is in production, story gathering or training new people and advising on community problems."[62]

A 1964 *Miami Herald* story addressed the new federal equal-pay-for-women law and the limited effect it would have for Miami women. The reporter outlined the problem: "In 1961, the average earnings of women were 60 percent lower than those of men. An analysis of 1900 companies showed that every third company had dual pay scales." The reporter then noted that the law required equal pay only for the equal work performed in the same place and gave the examples of companies that gave women and men different job titles.[63]

In 1964, Applegate was the only woman on a panel interviewing President Richard Nixon when he was in Miami. Her questions focused on women and, at times, she interrupted him when his answers got off track.[64] Her story began:

> Richard M. Nixon doesn't believe in offering women top governmental posts or in a place on a ticket as "a sop to win their vote." He doesn't think it will work because "the average woman voter isn't a feminist, and she's not motivated by offers of prominent positions."[65]

This conversation is especially interesting in that it previews Vera Glaser's famous questioning at a 1969 press conference of President Nixon over the few appointments of women in his Cabinet. She had become aware of the lack of women in positions of power and was aware that men were not asking why more was not being done. According to the "A Few Good Women" project, "Taken by surprise, he immediately responded he would change this and so began the first systematic program to recruit women in executive positions in the federal government."[66] It led to significant attention to the lack of women in high-level government positions.

Entertaining Women

When the women were not working for change, they were a very social group. Letters describe elaborate gatherings and lunches. Greene wrote of her lunches with Morales and her dinners with Paxson. Of a particular 1965 meal with Paxson, she wrote: "I showed her the new light fixtures I've bought for the dining room and kitchen and she showed me the speech she's written for the TSP convention. It was a mutual admiration society."[67]

The lives of these women, like the sections they oversaw, were a mix of the traditional, like the furnishings Greene was proud of, and the evolution that was on its way, reflected in Paxson's speeches. Numerous photos of parties at Anderson's home also reflected her socializing.

Of the well-known annual bashes in Miami were the regular teas for women writers, hosted by Helen Muir, who had worked for the women's pages of the *Miami Herald* and the *Miami News*. In later years, *Miami Herald* veterans Jurney and Jeanne Voltz were honored guests, making the trip from Detroit and New York for the events. Muir was also a close friend of Florida environmentalist Marjorie Stoneman Douglas. A regularly told tale was of afternoon visits between the friends in their later years. Stoneman Douglas would walk to Muir's house down the street, where the women would have a nip of sherry. Then Stoneman Douglas would walk Muir back to her house, and they would have a drink of sherry, then Muir would walk Stoneman Douglas back and the pattern would continue.

Complexity at the *St. Petersburg Times*

Overall, the women's page journalists remained friends despite the occasional competition between newspapers. Likely the biggest challenge to the Florida women's page community revolved around the changes in direction and management at the *St. Petersburg Times* from 1965 through 1970. Those years saw the firings of both Biggs and Paxson, while Anne Rowe was promoted. It also included the introduction of the DAY section, which replaced the traditional women's section.

Penney-Missouri Award winner Biggs was forced out of the *St. Petersburg Times* after Don Baldwin came to the newspaper. In a history of the newspaper, the exodus of older workers after Baldwin's arrival is detailed. At one meeting, Baldwin was quoted as saying, "You're all my guys. You're in your job because I put you there." Biggs, then described as the family editor, replied, "Not including me, Don." He replied, "Yes, that's right, Gloria." She was gone within a few months.[68] Her force-out was also revealed in the letters that Biggs and other Florida editors wrote to Myhre. She wrote a short note to Myhre that she had left the newspaper and was staying with family in New York. She had won a Penney-Missouri Award a few months before, and Myhre reassured her that she would still receive the award despite no longer being with the newspaper. In another letter, Baldwin wrote that there were no hard feelings and he approved of Biggs receiving the award.

In 1966, Anne Rowe Goldman became the *St. Petersburg Times* newsfeatures editor. In this role, she became the first woman in the newspaper's history to lead a department that included as many men as women employees. Three years later, the features section underwent what was described as a "dramatic change" in format. She oversaw a staff of 22 editors and writers, plus copy desks and specialists in religion, fashion, food, music, drama, and art.[69]

For Paxson, her demotion was ironic. In the weeks after the elimination of the women's section at the *St. Petersburg Times*, she learned she had won a 1969 Penney-Missouri award for editing the best women's section. She said, "That award was a tremendous achievement. It was proof that your section was relevant."[70] After accepting the award, Paxson returned to her newspaper that no longer had a women's section and knew she had to leave. She said, "I had been given the literal two-step, there was no sense in staying."[71] When editors at the *St. Petersburg Times* learned she was looking for a new job, she was fired. She wrote at the time, "The *Times* fired me on the grounds that I would be leaving in a year or sooner and so it might as well be sooner."[72] Greene's opinion was that Paxson was let go due to Paxson's Penney-Missouri Award win. She wrote, "I think the fact that she won a Penney-Missouri made for a lot of jealousy in a lot of places—which comes under the heading 'How stupid can YOU get?'"[73] Many were surprised by the firing.[74] It was a difficult time for Paxson. Anderson and Greene both spent time comforting Paxson before she rebounded with a newspaper job in Philadelphia.[75]

Godmother of the Women's Pages

Likely, the most influential of all women's page editors was Dorothy Jurney, who worked for several newspapers. Her oral history with the National Press Club Foundation described her as the "godmother of women's pages" due to her progressive approach. Throughout her career, she worked to help build a community of women journalists. In part, this was due to her being denied opportunities based on her gender.

For example, while at the *Miami Herald*, Jurney was considered for a promotion, but she said she already had had her ambitions squashed because of her *Daily News* demotion after World War II. She unknowingly turned down her opportunity when asked by Cle Althouse, the head of human resources at the *Miami Herald*, if she was interested in becoming city editor or managing editor. She replied: "Cle, why should I try? I would be butting my head up against a wall and I'm not going to do that for my own peace of mind."[76] She found out later she was being considered for city editor. (Years later at the *Detroit Free Press*, she learned that Lee Hills said to another editor of Jurney: "There's the person who would make a better managing editor than the one we have."[77])

Despite not moving up the career ladder, Jurney did make an impact. During her tenure at the *Herald*, several women's editors from other newspapers visited to observe her progressive techniques. At one point, she oversaw the revamping of the *Charlotte Observer*'s women's section. She spoke at the American Press Institute in 1956, causing Director J. Montgomery Curtis to remark that Jurney "did the best work on women's interests and women's pages ever done" at the Institute.[78]

In 1959, Jurney separated from her husband and, looking for a new challenge, left the *Herald* for the *Detroit Free Press* at the suggestion of Hills. By 1954, Hills had moved on to the *Detroit Free Press*. As part of his effort to improve the Detroit newspaper, he brought along Jurney, who had gained a national reputation for creating a strong women's section at this time.[79] Under Hills, the Detroit newspaper became known for being "aggressive," especially for focusing on "questionable government practices."[80] Its women's section "ran stories on lifestyles, recognizing their importance at a time when few newspapers ran such stories."[81] Jurney said Hills was a good editor who supported what she wanted to do. In fact, she said, due to Hills's understanding of her work in the women's section, she was invited to Knight (and then Knight Ridder after a company merger) executive meetings around the country.[82] It is not surprising that when the Journalism and Women Symposium began its first newsletter that Jurney contributed an article.[83] It was an organization that supported a community of women journalists, which is what she had devoted her career to building.

Notes

1. Joseph P. McKerns, "Journalism Education," *History of Mass Media in the United States: An Encyclopedia*, 2013, 289–290; Brad Asher "The Professional Vision: Conflicts Over Journalism Education," *American Journalism* 11, no. 4 (Fall 1994): 304–320; Joseph A. Mirando, "Training and Education of Journalists," in *American Journalism: History, Principles, Practices*, ed. W. David Sloan and Lisa Mullikin Parcell (Jefferson, North Carolina: McFarland, 2009), 76–86.
2. Josephine Caldwell Meyer, "A B C for Jobs," *Matrix*, August 1940, 10–11.
3. Maurine Beasley and Kathryn Theus, *The New Majority* (Lanham, Maryland: University Press of America, 1988), 14.
4. Marion Marzolf, *Up From the Footnote: A History of Women Journalists* (New York: Hasting House Publishers, 1977), 249.
5. Jean James, "Women in Schools of Journalism," *Matrix*, June 1932, 13–14.
6. Adelaide H. Jones, "Women Graduates In the 1941–1951 Decade," *Journalism Quarterly*, 1953: 49–54.
7. Beasley and Theus, *The New Majority*, 22–23.
8. As early as 1939, the school boasted that women journalism graduates were working at newspapers across the country. Earl English, *Journalism Education at the University of Missouri-Columbia* (Marceline, Missouri: Walsworth Publishing, 1988), 66.
9. Maggie Savoy, "Untitled" in *Anyone Who Enters Here Must Celebrate Maggie*, ed. Jim Bellows (Los Angeles: Ward Ritchie Press, 1972), 91.
10. Dorothy Jurney, "Women in Journalism Oral History Project," Washington Press Club Foundation, transcript, Session 2, 55.
11. Ibid.
12. University of Louisville. Oral History Project, July 21, 1982 Interview with Carol Sutton, CD #1, Part 1.
13. University of Louisville. Oral History Project, July 21, 1982 Interview with Carol Sutton, CD #1, Part 1.

14. University of Louisville. Oral History Project, July 21, 1982 Interview with Carol Sutton, CD #1, Part 1.
15. Julia Bristol, "Women's Editor: Edee Greene Created a Section Even She Can Read with Relish," *Editor & Publisher*, February 23, 1963.
16. Ibid.
17. Julian M. Pleasants, *Orange Journalism: Voices from Florida Newspapers* (Gainesville, Florida: University of Florida Press, 2003), 72.
18. John Somerville letter Gloria Biggs, March 9, 1973, Papers of Gloria Biggs, State Historical Society of Missouri.
19. Marjorie Paxson letter to Gloria Biggs, March 8, 1973, Papers of Gloria Biggs, State Historical Society of Missouri.
20. Ibid.
21. Gloria Biggs to Marie Anderson, January 31, 1978, Papers of Marie Anderson, State Historical Society of Missouri.
22. Ibid.
23. Helen Muir, *Baby Grace Sees the Cow: A Memoir*, ed. by Alison Owen (Florida: The Prologue Society, 2004), 11.
24. Dorothy Roe, "Women's Features Get Recognition," *Editor & Publisher*, December 17, 1960. 55.
25. Kathryn Robinette letter to Paul Myhre, December 27, 1966, Papers of the Penney-Missouri Awards, State Historical Society of Missouri.
26. Edee Greene letter to Paul Myhre, October 5, 1961, Penney-Missouri Awards papers, State Historical Society of Missouri.
27. Paul Myhre letter to Edee Greene, January 11, 1963, Penney-Missouri Awards papers, State Historical Society of Missouri.
28. George Pica, former Penney-Missouri Awards director, email interview, March 20, 2003.
29. Marjorie Paxson, "Women in Journalism Oral History Project," Washington Press Club Foundation, transcript, Session 3, 63.
30. Marie Anderson letter to Paul L. Myhre, September 4, 1967, Penney-Missouri Awards Papers, State Historical Society of Missouri.
31. Paul L. Myhre letter to Beverley Morales, June 21, 1961, Penney-Missouri Awards Papers, State Historical Society of Missouri.
32. Beverley Morals letter to Paul Myhre, June 15, 1961, Penney-Missouri Awards Papers, State Historical Society of Missouri.
33. Edee Greene letter to Paul Myhre, October 5, 1961, Penney-Missouri Awards Papers, State Historical Society of Missouri.
34. Edee Greene speech, "How to Hurdle Your Girdle or Sex in the City Room," Theta Sigma Phi Seminar, Cleveland, Ohio, August 24, 1963, Penney-Missouri Award Papers, State Historical Society of Missouri.

35. Edee Greene letter to Paul Myhre, April 5, 1965, Penney-Missouri Award Papers, State Historical Society of Missouri.
36. Greene, "How to Hurdle."
37. Marie Anderson letter to Paul L. Myhre, September 4, 1967, Penney-Missouri Awards Papers, State Historical Society of Missouri.
38. Marjorie Paxson, *New Guardians of the Press: Selected Profiles of America's Women Newspaper Editors* (Indianapolis, Indiana: R.J. Berg and Co., 1983), 124.
39. Paxson, "Women in Journalism," Session 3, 66.
40. Diane K. Gentry, "Women in Journalism Oral History Project," Washington Press Club Foundation, 1991, Introduction, 1.
41. Paxson, "Women in Journalism," Session 3, 71.
42. The Association for Women in Communications website, Hall of Fame page, accessed October 1, 2007, http://www.womcom.org/about_us/Hall_of_fame.asp.
43. Katherine Lanpher, "The Boys at the Club: An Examination of Press Clubs as an Aspect of the Occupational Culture of the Late 19th Century Journalist," presented at the Association for Education in Journalism, History Division, Athens, Ohio, July 1982, 5.
44. Maurine Beasley, "The Women's National Press Club: Case Study of Professional Aspirations," *Journalism History* 15, no. 4 (Winter 1988): 112–121.
45. Elizabeth Burt, "A Bid for Legitimacy: The Woman's Press Club Movement, 1881–1900," *Journalism History* 23, no. 2 (Summer 1997): 72–84.
46. Helen M. Staunton, "Mary Hornaday Protests Bars to Newswomen," *Editor & Publisher*, July 15, 1944.
47. Ibid.
48. Kimberly Wilmot Voss and Lance Speere, "Way Past Deadline: The Women's Fight to Integrate the Milwaukee Press Club," *Wisconsin Magazine of History* 92, no. 1 (Autumn 2008).
49. Ruthe Deskin of the *Las Vegas Sun* was the second woman elected to the Nevada Press Club in 1966. Her papers are in the Special Collections of the University of Nevada, Las Vegas. Kimberly Wilmot Voss and Lance Speere, "Where She Stands: Ruthe Deskin and Her Place in the City of Bright Lights and Bigger Personalities After 50 years at the Las Vegas Sun," Nevada Historical Society Quarterly, Fall 2012.
50. Maurine H. Beasley and Sheila J. Gibbons, eds., *Taking Their Place: A Documentary History of Women and Journalism* (Washington, D.C.: American University Press, 1993), 10.

51. Marie Anderson letter to Paul L. Myhre, September 4, 1967, Penney-Missouri Awards Papers, State Historical Society of Missouri.
52. Jean Jarvis Sneed, "The Florida Newspaper Woman of 1970" (master's thesis, University of Florida, 1970), 4.
53. Marie Anderson letter to Paul Myhre, September 12, 1966, Penney-Missouri Award Papers, State Historical Society of Missouri.
54. Marie Anderson letter to Paul Myhre, September 4, 1967, Penney-Missouri Award Papers, State Historical Society of Missouri.
55. Don Shoemaker Remarks to Florida Women's Press Club, Daytona Beach, September 13, 1958, 5, Don Shoemaker Papers, University of North Carolina University Library.
56. Ibid.
57. Don Shoemaker, *With All Deliberate Speed: Segregation-Desegregation in Southern Schools* (New York: Harper & Brothers, 1957), forward.
58. Marie Anderson and Maggie Savoy, "What Does Your Women's Editor Think of You?" *Associated Press Managing Editors Red Book*, 1963, Marie Anderson's papers, Box 3, National Women and Media Collection, State Historical Society of Missouri. Also, Chang conducted a national survey and found that women editors made less than men editors did for overseeing the same sections. Won Chang, "Characteristics and Self-Perceptions of Women's Page Editors." *Journalism Quarterly*, 1975: 61–65.
59. John Rogers Malloy, "A History of the *Sentinel Star*" (master's thesis, University of Florida, 1977), 53.
60. Sneed, "Florida Newspaper Woman," 37.
61. Helen Wells to Marie Anderson, Undated, Marie Anderson's papers, Box 3, National Women and Media Collection, State Historical Society of Missouri.
62. Note from Anderson to Applegate, August 22, unknown year, Roberta Applegate's papers, National Women and Media Collection, State Historical Society of Missouri.
63. Beth Resler, "Not Much Equal Pay For Miami," *Miami Herald*, June 18, 1964.
64. Roberta Applegate letter to G. Milton Kelly, April 24, 1964, Papers of Roberta Applegate, National Women and Media Collection, State Historical Society of Missouri.
65. Roberta Applegate, "Women More Conservative," *Miami Herald*, n.d.
66. A Few Good Women Oral History Project, Penn State University, http://afgw.libraries.psu.edu/background.html.

67. Edee Greene letter to Paul and Mary Myhre, August 5, 1965, Penney-Missouri Award Papers, State Historical Society of Missouri.
68. Robert Pierce, *A Sacred Trust: Nelson Poynter and the St. Petersburg Times* (Gainesville, Florida: University Press of Florida, 1993), 212.
69. Craig Basse, Anne Goldman, former Times features editor, *St. Petersburg Times*, February 6, 2003.
70. Marjorie Paxson, telephone interview with author, June 2003.
71. Paxson, "Women in Journalism," Session 3, 79.
72. Marjorie Paxson letter to Paul Myhre, June 25, 1970, Penney-Missouri Award Papers, National Women and Media Collection, State Historical Society of Missouri.
73. Edee Greene letter to Paul Myhre, June 9, 1970, Penney-Missouri Award Papers, National Women and Media Collection, State Historical Society of Missouri.
74. Paul Myhre letter to Marjorie Paxson, June 30, 1970, Penney-Missouri Award Papers, National Women and Media Collection, State Historical Society of Missouri.
75. Edee Greene letter to Paul Myhre, July 13, 1970, Penney-Missouri Award Papers, National Women and Media Collection, State Historical Society of Missouri.
76. Jurney, "Women in Journalism," Session 1, 49.
77. Jurney, "Women in Journalism," Session 1, 50.
78. Montgomery Curtis letter to Dorothy Jurney, March 26, 1959, Papers of Dorothy Jurney, National Women and Media Collection, State Historical Society of Missouri.
79. Nixon Smiley, *Knights of the Fourth Estate: The Story of the Miami Herald* (Miami, Florida: Banyan Books, 1984), 267.
80. Frank Angelo, *On Guard: A History of the Detroit Free Press* (Detroit: Detroit Free Press, 1981), 207.
81. Ibid.
82. Jurney, "Women in Journalism," Session 2, 59.
83. Kay Mills, "Her Story: 'HerStory' of JAWS," Journalism and Women Symposium, updated March 11 2010, https://www.jaws.org/about-jaws/herstory-of-jaws/her-story/.

3

Powerful Partnerships of Women's Page Editors and Club Women

Associated Press women's editor Dorothy Roe wrote in 1961 that, "No group of women in history has provided such a hilarious target for cartoonists, humorists and professional woman-baiters as the thirty million clubwomen of American."[1] The mocking of women's club members began almost as soon as women attempted to gather outside the home. A May 15, 1869, cartoon in *Harper's Weekly* gauged the reaction to a meeting to one of the earliest women's clubs, Sorosis. The cartoonist featured nervous husbands forced to care for their babies on the stairs.[2] The idea was that women who left the house, even for meetings, would lead to the breakdown of the family.

Yet, these women got things done. They changed their communities and developed their political and business skills along the way. Anne Firor Scott has noted that historians have largely overlooked these women and their voluntary organizations that had been around for decades. She wrote:

> The most obvious way in which voluntary associations had brought about social change was by creating a public role for women who, deprived by custom and law of access to the formal, male-dominated institutions had slowly worked their way to social power by organizing and operating their own groups. Forming societies came as naturally to

K. W. Voss, *Re-Evaluating Women's Page Journalism in the Post-World War II Era*,
https://doi.org/10.1007/978-3-319-96214-6_3

enterprising nineteenth-century women as creating business firms or organizing railroads did to ambitious men.[3]

Most women's page journalists would have agreed with Scott's assessment. As Roe noted: "Today's typical clubwoman is likely to know a lot about any subject she tackles, and if doesn't know at the start, she finds out in short order."[4] Indeed, the clubs often featured expert speakers. In fact, one of the primary sources for women's news was women's clubs.

In South Florida, Roberta Applegate worked to elevate the image of club women in the pages of *Miami Herald*. At times, those stories were picked up by wire services, and her stories ran in newspapers throughout the state and country. Applegate was also a speaker at club meetings. In one such speech, Applegate said:

> For many years, women's clubs have been the butt of jokes—their hats, their pink teas and their gossip. I object to that interpretation of clubwork. Sure, sometimes we wear odd hats, we enjoy teas, and I'm afraid we gossip. But look at men's ties, their get-togethers—and did you ever hear a bunch of men talking? Women have no monopoly on gossip. And women do so much that is fine and outstanding, both in their own right and as a prod to the men.[5]

Much of the work of women's clubs has been left out of historical stories. Yet, these women did important things in their community—especially when they partnered with women's page journalists. The reporters and editors helped to encourage women's involvement in the public sphere—bridging the time between the first and second waves of the women's movement. Early women's clubs worked for suffrage, and later women's club members fought for the ERA. In between, these women worked for numerous community causes.

History of Women's Clubs

Women's clubs have a long history in the United States. Women's page columnist "Jennie June," or Jane Cunningham Croly, herself a women's club member, wrote an 1898 history of these organizations. These clubs not only focused on culture as was common in the earliest days—there was also an element of community development: "Reform-minded women turned the concept of women's sphere, with its concern for family well-being, into a justification for moving from the home into the public arena to confront situations that had an adverse impact on their families."[6] As early as 1922, researchers noted that, "the one powerful agency through which a woman has been able to express her individuality is though the woman's club movement."[7] For example, in 1933, women's clubs were credited with initiating 75 percent of public libraries in the country. James H. Canfield, a librarian at Columbia University and whose wife was a club founder, said, "I know of no one power, no one influence, which has accomplished more for education in this country than the organization known as women's clubs."[8]

These organizations took on bigger roles supporting the troops on the home front during World War II. Marie Anderson was one of the women who did volunteer work at the Servicemen's Pier in South Florida. In April 1941, US Army soldiers transformed Miami Beach into a training camp. The local Junior League asked for women to volunteer at the Filter Center, also known as the Air Raid Information Center. By October 1942, the Junior League was a "commanding presence" at the Servicemen's Center, helping the more than 100,000 Air Force officers being trained in Miami.[9] Anderson said: "It still didn't occur to me to get a job because I thought you worked only if you needed the money. So I became the Available Woman. I was available to every cause that came along."[10]

It was while Anderson was doing this work that she met Kay Pancoast, who oversaw the volunteers.[11] Anderson and Pancoast would continue to stay in touch over the next few years, and it was Pancoast who would eventually bring Anderson to the *Miami News* for a brief stay before her *Miami Herald* tenure began. Many of these women continued to do important work after the war was over. As Roe noted, "The public began to find out that if a community needs a new school community center, or somebody to tame its teen-agers, the local women's clubs could usually get the job done, often succeeding where generations of politicians and aimless 'do-gooders' had failed."[12] According to a study of women's clubs, as early as the 1950s the clubs' policies included supporting "a broad set of issues ranging from federally funded day care to education to environmental preservation to equal pay."[13]

Part of the reason for the success of women's club campaigns was the publicity that women's page journalists gave them. At times, it was for the fundraising activities and other times it was a matter of writing about issues that gave credence to the cause. During Progressive Reform, Dallas women's page writer Pauline Periwinkle followed that model. She said, "printer's ink judicially applied to the club idea is a great lubricator and will make it run further and smoother than anything I know."[14]

In the years after World War II, many middle-class women who had been in the workplace during the war returned to their homes. Many women, however, stayed active in the public arena through women's clubs. For some, these clubs were social activities. Yet, many of these clubs also worked on improving social services, raising money for libraries and civic buildings, and raising awareness for crimes such as domestic violence and child abuse.

As Scott has noted, these women "sometimes function as a kind of early warning system, recognizing emergent problems before they were identified by the male-dominated political process."[15] As communities developed, it was clear that women's organizations helped to pave the way for change. In fact, the president of the General Federation of Women's Club said in 1948: "The day of the sewing circle is past. The time has come when we should discard the outmoded idea that we are a non-political organization."[16]

As recent historians have noted, women's organizations in the 1950s were making a change from civic engagements to political groups: "If the 1950s began as a decade of homemakers and housewives, it opened to a decade for feminists and women's liberation, bringing with it new forms and strategies of political action."[17] They worked on helping disabled or troubled children, sponsored voting drives, and held family planning workshops in partnership with Planned Parenthood.[18]

This is not to imply that all the clubs were well organized nor programming significant activities. A history of the Florida Federation of Women's Club noted that there were numerous odd actions. According to the author, "All too often women in convention failed to study resolutions" that they voted on.[19] First Lady Eleanor Roosevelt, who was a club woman herself, noted that some organizations were short on action. She said, "If all you do is talk and pass resolutions, that has very little value, but if you go into your communities with a real education program, that has great value."[20]

Part of the reason for the clubs' inefficiency was likely the number of women's clubs that existed in many communities. Women often belonged to several clubs at the same time. The concept of being overwhelmed by club work was addressed in a 1963 article in the *Miami News*. The writer described all her work in the Parent Teacher Association (PTA), civic groups, and Girl Scouts. For her this meant a constant course of baking. The article began, "I ain't gonna bake no pies no more, no ma'am, and no cakes and cookies, neither."[21]

At the *Denver Post*, the women's pages featured a "Spotlight on Clubs" in the 1960s. One story focused on the need for more female engineers. Women's page editor Lois Cress began her 1963 story about the Society of Women Engineers with this declaration: "Social pressures for women to use their brainpower are greater during wartime than in peace, a prominent woman engineer charges."[22] In another story, she wrote about the Business and Women's Club of Denver. The group had honored a teacher for her contributions to science.[23]

There were strong women's clubs in Dallas that were making a difference behind the scenes. Vivian Castleberry of the *Dallas Times Herald* worked regularly with these women. For example, the Dallas division of the National Council of Jewish Women took on poverty projects. Members went to the grocery stores in poor neighborhoods and reported on the inequities. They also worked with the Dallas City Council Hospital to document how mothers and their children were being treated. They then issued research reports on their findings that Castleberry's staff could report on. When it came to politics, Castleberry relied on future Texas Governor Ann Richards, who at that time was president of the Dallas League of Women Voters. They were helping create cooperatives for neighborhoods in need. Castleberry said: "As the social issues have reared their ugly heads, there have been women's groups who have been there to do it. And every issue that comes along, women are there first to answer the needs. And those things were not being reported."[24]

Garden clubs may have appeared unassuming, but they often took on issues ahead of their time. For example, in 1970, the garden club was tackling littering and pollution in Dallas. Club President Betty Svoboda said, "Everybody's ready to do something now, not just talk about it." They had created postcards and bumper stickers to remind residents of their cause. She also noted that she was encouraging the 1,000 members of her organization to take down the license plate numbers of those who littered. She said, "I believe in woman power. And with this many women in the council, we're bound to get something done."[25]

Training Women's Club Members

According to a 1946 *Time* magazine article about the clubwomen:

> They had been invited to hear an expert tell them how bad their stuff was. Six hundred showed up. They were all women and all amateur correspondents—presidents and press chairmen of Los Angeles clubs. Like clubwomen everywhere, they habitually send their local papers the kind of disheveled copy that prematurely ages the editors of women's pages. Last week, for the sixth time in six years, *Los Angeles Times* Club Editor Bess Wilson crisply told them to mend their ways.[26]

Her suggestions focused on addressing news values and correct spellings. The women's clubs were ready for the advice. In a December 1950 article in the General Federation of Women's Clubs newsletter, club members were advised to hone their public relations skills. According to the author, one of the club's assets was the club's support of suffrage.[27]

Before she came to Miami, Dorothy Jurney worked hard to help women in her community become news makers in Indiana. She learned the lesson from her father, who likely recognized the value of women's organizations from his suffragette wife. Jurney based her workshop on what she had done at her father's newspaper while women's page editor there. The goals were twofold: to increase readership and to improve the content.

The women's page journalists often helped to raise the status and activities of women's clubs. They did this by educating the women about how to create events and projects that would be worthy of newspaper coverage. A 1953 invitation to women's club leaders from the *Miami Herald* to women's section workshops encouraged women to tackle significant issues.[28] Jurney said, "we upgraded the quality of the work of many of these organizations."[29] It is likely that these clubs were made up of white women as there were only a few typically black women's clubs, and they were generally excluded from club coverage, although Anderson and Jurney were aware of issues in the black community.

The annual Miami workshops began small and grew large enough to draw more than 750 club women at a hotel ballroom. The featured guest speakers were columnists whose work appeared in women's pages: Ann Landers and Dorothy Ricker. An additional speaker was managing editor Lee Hills, further demonstrating his commitment to the women's section. The goal of the workshops was to retain connection to the clubwomen as sources for the women's pages and to explain the publicity chairman's role in producing the type of club news the newspaper can use.[30]

To demonstrate the kind of news the journalists were looking to run, the *Miami Herald* held a contest for the best projects. This encouraged women's clubs to work on significant issues in the community. According to a president of the Dade County Federation of Women's Clubs, which consisted of 60 clubs, "Projects entered in the contest are an inspiration to other clubs."[31]

In the mid-1960s, the *St. Petersburg Times* and the *Evening Independent* also created a training guide for new club publicity designees to help them work with making news out of media coverage. The women were encouraged to adhere to news values: "Some stories concern or are of interest to everyone in the community—others to a handful of people."[32] This kind of training encouraged women's clubs to upgrade their programs to earn a place in the women's page.

The workshops also included a short session on journalism education. This included the importance of spelling names correctly, meeting deadlines, and using photography guidelines. The journalists also stressed the importance of meeting news values: "Not news that Mrs. Thompson will preside—that's what a president does; it is news if she refuses to preside."[33]

The journalists made their point about the amount of unusable press releases by taping them together and lining them across the entire floor of the ballroom.[34]

Edee Greene was also holding these workshops in Fort Lauderdale in the late 1950s and early 1960s. The invitation, in the women's section, noted, "Clubs make news and news make clubs."[35] Speakers at the event, where awards were also given out, included Executive Editor Fred Pettijohn and Managing Editor Milt Kelly. The invitation also noted that some club members may be excused for reasons of "employment or lack of a babysitter."[36] Greene lectured other women's page editors at the national Penney-Missouri Award workshops about her approach to club coverage. She focused on educating publicity women about what was news.[37] She also sat in on a panel with fellow editors Anne Rowe and Dorothy Jurney.[38] Her approach to women's organizations was to coax the members into taking action in the community. According to the industry publication *Editor & Publisher*:

> Often instead of making headlines out of some uncovered short-coming of the community, she investigates, then lays the facts before some organization that will set to work to correct the condition. Her staff, then, reports on the work of the organization, letting its members take the credit.[39]

Photos from the *Miami Herald's* workshops do not show many faces of color, but it would become an issue for women's page editors across the country. The Penney-Missouri Workshops would address the lack of diversity in the sections by the early 1970s. Women in Communications, Inc. noted a 1970 program to help the leaders of black women's clubs work with local newspapers just as they had for white women's groups. The workshops led to regular press releases from black women's organizations in Cincinnati. According to the summer 1970 issue of the *Matrix*, the organization's national magazine, "Their news is getting into print and the citizens of Cincinnati now can know what's happening in all parts of their community."[40]

Clubwomen Coverage Case Study: Roberta Applegate

In her early career, Applegate covered Detroit club activities that she emphasized were about more than high society news—the reputation that many women's sections held. She said at that time, "It's actually straight reporting and presenting trends in women's club activities."[41] They were doing important work, although Applegate did admit that she had tired of eating chicken ala king at the luncheons the clubs regularly held.

Prior to Applegate's transition from covering club women in Detroit and Miami, she served as press secretary for Michigan Governor Kim Sigler, from 1947 to 1949, the first woman to hold that post in the state and most likely the first in the country. In that position, she oversaw twice-a-day press conferences, wrote most of Sigler's weekly radio speeches, and worked with editors of the state's newspapers. The speeches she wrote ranged from proposed state constitutional changes to budgetary issues to policy changes. Most of the governor's speeches were entirely written by Applegate. She later said in a speech of her own, "You are looking at a very healthy ghost whose admissions are off the record."[42]

An examination of Sigler's speeches revealed Applegate's influence. At a time when women were not part of public life, Sigler's words, scripted by Applegate, displayed a unique note of equality. In a 1948 talk from Flint, he said, "I know the problem of the man or woman who works for wages or on a salary."[43] In another 1948 talk, he said, "Men and women who are employed in productive, worthwhile occupations are happier, better citizens, and they add strength to our entire nation."[44] Her speechwriting was important as the governor did not read the speeches before going on the air.[45]

In a revealing speech, Applegate wrote a radio speech that Sigler presented to the Michigan Federation of Women's Clubs on November 15, 1947. In it, the work of the women's club was recognized. The governor cited the many years that women's clubs devoted to changing the state's "antiquated" child labor laws. They lobbied many legislators for their cause. The governor said, "This year—largely because you kept at it, and interested more and more people in the need for constructive regulation of child labor—the state legislature adopted what many people consider to be one of the best laws of the kinds in the nation."[46]

After Sigler was not re-elected, Applegate approached the coverage of the women's clubs just as she had the Michigan legislature. When she arrived in Miami, there were nearly 1,000 organizations that she covered with about half actively involved in community activities.[47] Applegate was prepared to report on the clubwomen beat. She had noted the activities of the women in their interactions with the governor in Michigan before she was hired by the *Miami Herald*.

In 1954, Applegate wrote a two-part series about a home for the disabled. She visited the home and described the setting and the people. Her first story begins:

> The power of women working as a unified group is being recognized more and more. Their material contribution to their communities is recognized in their various projects—school equipment, nurseries, building beautification, etc. More intangible is the influence they exert in civic matters, which sometimes manifests itself in tangible ways. The expanded program at the Florida Farm Colony is one of these. The Florida Federation of Women's Clubs supported the appropriations bill passed by the 1953 legislature.[48]

The 1953 legislature appropriated much more than was originally requested after being lobbied by the women's organization. The superintendent of the home thanked the women for their help and asked for continued support, saying "because a word from you can mean a great deal."[49] In the second article, Applegate again pointed out the significant work that the club women did. She wrote about the work of the Junior League women to raise money to buy occupational therapy equipment and other women's groups who were putting together a survey to learn the needs of children in the state.[50]

Tackling Issues Through Club Work

The work of women's clubs set the foundations of communities and began addressing social ills and inequities. Often, their power lied in promoting issues that were based on their roles as mothers or other feminine endeavors, such as garden clubs. This was not threatening to the male structure. While it could be viewed as reinforcing women's traditional roles, it also could be viewed as women using power that currently existed for them. After all, who decided that news about the welfare of children was "soft news,"—less important than the city council meetings? Members of the PTA might not have been vocal in fighting for equality for themselves, but they certainly could fight the equality of their daughters. That was the power of motherhood. And the coverage of those PTA meetings and activities were covered by women's page journalists.

A 1963 *Miami News* story about a national PTA convention focused on a resolution to reach out to students from lower socioeconomic communities and those with disabilities.[51] Another 1963 story, also based on a report from the national PTA convention in the *Fort Lauderdale News,* centered on the low expectation that some educators had for girls. The report encouraged educators to raise their standards for girls.[52] It was stories like these that appealed to women in a way that was less radical than the representation in other ways—it was framed by motherhood.

The prominent women's club leaders became more involved in the educational meetings as the years went by. They were often held up as examples of what other women could achieve. At an annual meeting, Jane Natt was a featured speaker who addressed ways to "make club news vital." While mentioning that she was a wife and a mother, an advance article noted her paid work as head of Mrs. Natt's Bakery. In addition, she was a past president of the Miami Chamber of Commerce Women's Division.[53]

These women's page journalists respected the work of women in these organizations. In 1963, Applegate wrote a feature package about volunteers in Miami and noted that the work of these women was saving the community millions of dollars. She wrote, for example, that the 15,000 hours of work put in by 150 auxiliary members at a local hospital the year before had saved $20,000.[54] She also outlined the numerous fundraisers that these volunteers put together from door-to-door requests to charity balls. Applegate wrote, "Their efforts have built and equipped hospitals, helped lame children walk, kept orchestras afloat and servicemen overseas in touch with their families."[55] In Applegate's typical journalistic fashion, the package was not just a celebration of volunteers—she also wrote an article focusing on the problems. She wrote about volunteers who were poorly trained or violated ethical guidelines. She also advised how to avoid problematic volunteers.[56]

Marginalized Populations

Helping marginalized groups was a common cause for women's organization. According to a history of the Florida Federation of Women's Clubs, one of the chief concerns of its members was the welfare of children. The members supported the Proposed Juvenile Court Amendment to the Florida Constitution, which was intended to establish a statewide uniform of juvenile courts in the 1950s.[57] The organization also passed a resolution urging the legislature to appropriate funds for an industrial school for "delinquent negro girls" that had been built in Ocala but had not been funded for maintenance, operation, and staffing.[58] Other 1950s issues the club supported were crowding in mental hospitals, the dangers of comic books, and fears of nuclear destruction. In the 1960s, the women continued to fight for the Everglades and against a rising crime rate.

The League of Women Voters in Florida was a non-partisan and active group. *St. Petersburg Press* publisher Nelson Poynter's wife was president of the League in 1939.[59] The group was open minded in regard to race relations. According to Mrs. Poynter (later Stephenson):

> I can recall that I refused to have meetings where segregation was apparent. I felt that meetings should be open to all women and many of hotels and clubs at that time discriminated against blacks and Jews. Also, I said no luncheon meetings, teas, dinners—anything that would cost any woman admission. We usually would meet and have study groups in the Times building.[60]

The League sent its first registered lobbyist, Maxine Baker, to Tallahassee in 1949—she was the first woman lobbyist in the state.[61] This was a foreshadowing of later lobbying efforts with city councils and school boards.

The main women's page writer for the Associated Press during the 1950s was Dorothy Roe, who had a journalism degree from the University of Missouri and a background in hard news. At the wire service, she covered the work of women's clubs and their work in the growing cities and suburbs. For example, in 1952, she wrote about women's clubs and their role in traffic issues.[62] She noted that local chapters were responding to problems outlined at a meeting of the American Transit Association. Roe wrote, "While the gentlemen are sweating it out, women's clubs around the country are putting their minds to the matter, working with municipal committees and appealing to their own millions of members to do their parts in untangling the scrambled streets."[63]

Libraries

As noted earlier, club women were often the reason that libraries developed. Women's page journalists frequently championed this cause. In South Florida, it was a women's page journalist who worked to establish the library system. Helen Muir had been a women's page journalist and editor at the *Miami News* and the *Miami Herald* in the 1940s and 1950s. She arrived in Miami, after previously working at a newspaper in her native New York, to take over publicity duties from the previously mentioned Dorothy Roe at the Roney Plaza Hotel. In the mid-1930s, she received a call from the *Miami News* to take over Jane Woods's position at the newspaper, who was leaving to marry Henry Reno.[64] (Jane and Harry Reno were the parents of the future US Attorney General Janet Reno.)

Muir was a strong journalist, but her real calling may have been libraries. Growing up in New York, she had often frequented the free libraries. When she relocated to Coconut Grove, she found a private library where she was charged $5 per book. A public library, on the other hand, sent out a bookmobile into lower-income neighborhoods. When her four-year-old daughter, Melissa, was killed after being hit by a car, libraries became a kind of memorial. At first, Muir donated books to the library in her late daughter's name. It led to her becoming the children's book editor at the *Miami Herald*. She was then appointed to the City of Miami library board. In later years, she helped to establish a county library. She was aided in her work by the women's clubs of Miami, which beginning in the 1930s began fundraising efforts ranging from house tours to fashion shows.[65]

Environmentalism

Garden clubs are easy to dismiss as frivolous organizations. Yet, many of these and other women's organizations made significant contributions to the environment—in a time before the environment was even discussed. After all, the Environmental Protection Association was not even created until 1970. Again, women found this power in a way that was not as threatening. One of the most powerful voices about environmental issues was Rachel Carson, author of the 1962 book *Silent Spring*. The book warned of the dangers of pesticides, especially DDT. In one of her few speeches, and one of her last, to the Garden Club of America, she warned, "These are large problems, and there is no easy solution."[66] The women were listening to the message, but she was quickly attacked by the chemical companies. She was called "hysterical" and "a priestess of nature."[67] Yet, in 1992, a panel of experts selected *Silent Spring* as the most influential book of the past 50 years.[68]

One of the most obvious examples was the campaign to save of the Everglades, the largest subtropical wilderness in the United States. Many became aware of the need to protect the Everglades after reading Marjory Stoneman Douglas's *Everglades: River of Grass*, published in 1947.[69] (Stoneman Douglas was the first female reporter at the *Miami Herald*.) It has been written that her book on the Everglades "became the bible of the

Florida environmentalists, much the way that *Silent Spring* inspired the national environmental movement."[70] A club member herself, Douglas described a women's club as "a self-produced university … a small, respectable pot, boiling away unnoticed, a stirring of minds, a spirit of inquiry, a new awareness of ideas."[71]

Juvenile Justice System

The issue of juvenile crime was another important issue for women's organizations. In 1964, a central issue of the PTA Convention resolutions urged educating youth on hazards of smoking, efforts to assure equal opportunity for all children, and strengthening programs to combat venereal disease. The organization also sponsored a pilot conference of "Judicial Concern for Children in Trouble," cosponsored with National Council of Juvenile Court Judges in Marianna, Florida.

This could also be looked at as helping women in their transition into the public sphere as numerous studies and experts were announcing that the children of working women were becoming juvenile delinquents. Applegate was praised for an article on juveniles and shoplifting by a Miami probation officer. He wrote to Applegate's managing editor thanking the reporter for "not only covering the troublesome problem of shoplifting, but offering direct advice to parents who are having this difficulty."[72]

Applegate was a member of the Children's Home Society.[73] Her managing editor said of Applegate, "She has a feeling for service to others which she translates into meaningful articles based on painstaking study and research."[74] As Dorothy Clifford, the women's page editor at the *Tallahassee Democrat* and a Junior League president, said, there was no stigma against being involved in community organizations that would later be an issue for journalism objectivity.

Covering Society and Social Class

Critics have noted that early feminist leaders focused on middle-class women at expense of marginalized women. Later, many in the movement worked to address those in working-class communities. The women in the upper class were rarely considered a part of the movement. As Douglas noted: "Here's the dirty little secret about sisterhood. It was easy to feel sisterhood with those 'beneath' you or lateral to you in class."[75] She went on to explain the uncomfortable feeling that moneyed women would understand the concept of inequality. This may have been different for women's page journalists who had often covered the events of high society and got to know the women behind the wealth. After all, many women's pages had a heavy dose of society news that dominated content for many years. These journalists truly knew women from cross-sections of their communities.

These women journalists sought to redefine society news. Castleberry said, "I looked at society with a small 's' instead of a capital 'S' which didn't always please my bosses."[76] She changed the definition of "society" to include "all humanity—the social structure of the community."[77] The club training meetings would become more inclusive in later years. As Castleberry described in Dallas, the training sessions became a "framework of sisterhood" that included about 500 women of all ages, ethnicities, backgrounds, and interests. The meetings resulted in connections that likely would not have taken place otherwise. Castleberry said she remembered watching immediate change take place:

> Marvelous things happened, such as the year that I seated the president of the Junior League next to the woman from South Dallas who lived in a housing project and whose eight children were sleeping on the floor because they had no beds. And by the end of the day, the president of the Junior League not only provided beds for the children, she had provided medical care for one of the children in need. So what it really did—what I found out very early on was that women, underneath the top service, speak the same language.[78]

These are the kinds of views many women's page journalists shared. In a 1967 presentation, Anderson told other women journalists to "de-emphasize society activities ... and emphasize events and features of interest to the whole community."[79] It was a topic that Anderson and Maggie Savoy had been trying to change for years—one that they had uncovered in a study they undertook for the Associated Press Managing Editors (APME). In a summary of the research, Savoy wrote in a letter, "generally speaking the boss paid little attention to his society page as long as he wasn't heckled by some of his wife's friends."[80]

One of the most significant society writers in the women's pages was Eleanor Page Voysey at the *Chicago Tribune*. She covered her beat for more than 45 years. Page considered the high society of her city to be different from other places. She said that New York high society was determined by money while, in the south, a family name determined a person's place in society. Yet, in Chicago, "only charity work had the power to allow someone to know everyone and go everywhere." For her, society was defined by what the person contributed.[81] She was as intimidating figure—to both competitors and colleagues. She once told a shorter assistant struggling to match Page's brisk, long-legged walk down North Michigan Avenue, "You'd better take a bus." She often covered women in politics and social events. For example, she wrote about Chicago residents who went to events at the Arlington races and other local parties.[82] Other stories were about political meetings and fundraisers. One story by Page included information about Alice Roosevelt, a woman running for statewide office and the head of the Republican Party's women's division.[83] She did cover high society in Chicago's black community. Copies of these articles are kept at a Chicago Museum.[84]

Kathryn Robinette joined the women's pages of the *Palm Beach Post* in 1966. As a society reporter, she often attended several parties during a single evening. She was known for her accessibility and a tight writing style. She was clever, too. She once asked in a 1988 column: "If too many cooks spoil the soup, what will 32 ball chairmen do to the Palm Beach party scene?"[85] She often covered galas, such as the International Red Cross Ball in Palm Beach. It was founded by Marjorie Merriweather Post, who made her home at Mar-a-Lago in Palm Beach. One of Robinette's favorite events to cover was this ball. One year, Robinette had assigned photographers from the *Post* to cover the event, and she told the two men to rent tuxedos because the ball was "white tie." (The term is used to describe the dressiest of formal events.) They arrived, dressed head to toe in white—including white shoes. According to her husband, "Kathryn almost died."[86]

In Houston, Betty Ewing reported from up to three parties a night. Those parties were largely fundraisers for groups such as the museums, the Houston Grand Opera, the Houston Symphony, and Friends of the Zoo. As these organizations grew, more benefits and fundraisers were established. She said, "I would go out and make friends with people involved."[87] With all those organizations, it was a challenge determining which events to attend. Ultimately, her decision making came down to which event had the best story. She said, "You have to pick the best, the most important. And, how many people is this going to effect. It's got to be well written. If you can attract the readership, then it's good for the people putting on the benefit."[88]

This is not to imply that Ewing spent most of her time in higher society. As her friend and former *Chronicle* television critic Ann Hodges said: "She knew everybody, from those at the top of the social ladder to the janitors. She treated them all alike." In fact, Ewing said she considered her column to be a feature column rather than a society column. She often wrote about the wives of local leaders and celebrities. She did so in a manner that highlighted the accomplishments of these women—even if the news angle began in their roles of wife or mother. For example, she wrote about Martha Sanford Dodds—the wife of Dr. Barry Munitz, the interim chancellor of the University of Houston. Ewing noted that prior to their move to Texas, Dodds had been an English teacher at a Chicago-area high school where she taught professional football players Ray Nitschke and Ed O'Bradovich. Dodd's work in organizing parents in the fight over the closing of a neighborhood—a fight covered by *Good Housekeeping*—was also noted by Ewing.[89]

In 1947, Savoy became women's editor at the *Phoenix Gazette* and she penned the column "Around Town." After 10 years at the *Gazette*, Savoy moved to the *Arizona Republic*. While at the *Republic*, Savoy wrote the column "Savoy Faire." Her editor J. Edward Murray wrote that, "Maggie used her daily society column to stir a social conscience in the movers and shakers."[90] She was known for covering women in her column from different social classes.

Most black newspapers offered a society page or at least a column. For example, groundbreaking journalist Dorothy Gilliam got her start as a society writer for the black newspaper the *Louisville Defender* in the 1950s.[91] In the late 1960s, the *Oakland Tribune* covered as many social events about white women as black women. According to the newspaper's executive editor Paul Minolas, "A major proportion of our community is Negro and we consider it proper to include news about them."[92]

Notes

1. Dorothy Roe, *The Problem With Women is Men* (Englewood Cliffs, N.J.: Prentice-Hall, 1961), 123.
2. Karen J. Blair, *The Clubwoman as Feminist: True Womanhood Redefined, 1868–1914* (New York: Holmes & Meier Publishers, 1980), 25.
3. Anne Firor Scott, *Making the Invisible Woman Visible* (Urbana: University of Illinois Press, 1984), 283.
4. Roe, *Problem With Women*, 125.
5. Roberta Applegate, "Association News and the Club Editor," undated speech, Coral Gables, Papers of Roberta Applegate, National Women and Media Collection, State Historical Society of Missouri.
6. Jacquelyn Masur McElhaney and Pauline Periwinkle, *Progressive Reform in Dallas* (College Station, Texas: Texas A & M Press, 1998), 15.
7. Nellie Roberson, "The Work of Women's Organizations," *The Journal of Social Forces*, November 1922: 50.
8. Blair, *Clubwoman as Feminist*, 101.
9. Carmen Morrina, "*The League Goes to War*," The Junior League of Miami, accessed June 25, 2018, http://www.jlmiami.org/our-history/.
10. Marie Anderson, "Commencement Speech," Marie Anderson's papers, Box 3, National Women and Media Collection, State Historical Society of Missouri.
11. Several letters from Pancoast to Anderson are included in Marie Anderson's papers, Box 3, National Women and Media Collection, State Historical Society of Missouri.
12. Roe, *Problem with Women*, 124.

13. A. Lanethea Mathews-Gardner, "The 1950s, Women, Civic Engagement, and Political Change," presented at American Political Science Association, Chicago, Illinois, September 1, 2004, 13.
14. Pauline Periwinkle, *Dallas Morning News*, June 4, 1900. Cited in McElhaney, *Progressive Reform*, xvi.
15. Anne Firor Scott, *Natural Allies: Women's Associations in American History* (Urbana: University of Illinois Press, 1991), 3.
16. Lanethea Mathews-Gardner, "The 1950s, Women, Civic Engagement, and Political Change," American Political Science Association Conference, Chicago, Illinois, September 2004, 3.
17. Mathews-Gardner, "1950s, Women, Civic Engagement," 34.
18. Mathews-Gardner, "1950s, Women, Civic Engagement," 15.
19. Jessie H. Meyer, *Leading the Way: A Century of Service* (Lakeland, Florida: Florida Federation of Women's Clubs, 1994), 168.
20. Doris Greenberg, "Treaty is Back by Women's Clubs," *New York Times*, April 30, 1949.
21. Mary Irving, "She Says 'No More,'" *Miami News*, May 19, 1963.
22. Lois Cress, "Women Engineers: We Need More," *Denver Post*, June 16, 1963.
23. Lois Cress, "Women of the Year," *Denver Post*, October 1, 1961.
24. Vivian Castleberry, "Women in Journalism Oral History Project," Washington Press Club Foundation, transcript, Session 2A, 58.
25. Maggie Kennedy, "Solution Simple as ABCD," *Dallas Times Herald*, May 17, 1970.
26. "Class for Clubwomen," *Time*, September 30, 1946.
27. Pauline Mandigo, "Good Public Relations," *General Federation of Women's Clubs*, December 1950, 12.
28. "Herald Extends Club Invitation," *Miami Herald*, September 13, 1953, Papers of Marie Anderson, National Women and Media Collection, State Historical Society of Missouri.
29. Dorothy Jurney, "Autobiography," n.d., 2, Papers of Dorothy Jurney, National Women and Media Collection, State Historical Society of Missouri.
30. Eleanor Dixon and Roberta Applegate, "Keeping Clubwoman Happy," *Matrix*, n.d., 8–9.
31. Ibid.

32. "Inside Story for Women's Club Reporters," *St. Petersburg Times/Evening Independent*, n.d., Papers of Florence Burge, University of Nevada, Reno, 82-36/II/1.
33. Roberta Applegate speech, n.d., 1.
34. Dixon and Applegate, "Keeping Clubwoman Happy," 8.
35. Edee Greene, "Let's Get Together," *Fort Lauderdale News*, September 11, 1961.
36. Ibid.
37. Paul Myhre letter to Edee Greene, March 12, 1965, Penney-Missouri papers, National Women and Media Collection, State Historical Society of Missouri.
38. Paul Myhre letter to Edee Greene, January 22, 1965, Penney-Missouri papers, National Women and Media Collection, State Historical Society of Missouri.
39. Julia Bristol, "Women's Editor: Edee Greene Created a Section Even She Can Read with a Relish," *Editor & Publisher*, February 23, 1963, 13.
40. Judith S. Houssell, "Let Us Help You: Cincinnati Teaches Black Women How To Report Club News," *Matrix*, Summer 1970, 13.
41. Beverly Smith, "Introduction of Roberta Applegate," Papers of Roberta Applegate, National Women and Media Collection, State Historical Society of Missouri.
42. Roberta Applegate, "Kim Sigler Was My Boss," 1948 speech, 4, Papers of Roberta Applegate, National Women and Media Collection, State Historical Society of Missouri.
43. Kim Sigler television address, October 22, 1948, Flint, Michigan, 7, Papers of Kim Sigler, Bentley Historical Library, University of Michigan, Box 2.
44. Kim Sigler, WKAR Broadcast, "Employment Talk," October 5, 194, Papers of Kim Sigler, Bentley Historical Library, University of Michigan, Box 2.
45. Heidi Bright, "Always a journalist – Roberta Applegate," *Update Faculty*, Kansas State University, n.d., 6.
46. Governor Kim Sigler to the Michigan Federation of Women's Clubs, November 15, 1947, Papers of Kim Sigler, Bentley Historical Library, University of Michigan.
47. Roberta Applegate, "Association News and the Club Editor," undated speech, Coral Gables, Papers of Roberta Applegate, National Women and Media Collection, State Historical Society of Missouri.
48. Roberta Applegate, "'Children' at Florida Farm Colony Range from 6 to 60," Miami Herald, October 14, 1954.

49. Ibid.
50. Roberta Applegate, "Emphasis at Florida Farm Colony Placed on Rehabilitation, Training," *Miami Herald*, October 15, 1954.
51. Joan Nielson McHale, "Open New Doors for All Students," *Miami News*, May 23, 1963.
52. Joan Nielson McHale, "'We Don't Expect Much of Women' Says PTA Speaker," *Fort Lauderdale News*, May 23, 1963.
53. "Clubwomen are Invited to Sixth Herald Press Conference at 10 Monday Morning," *Miami Herald*, October 28, 1951.
54. Roberta Applegate, "Volunteers: They Knock on Many Doors and They Save You Millions of Dollars," *Miami Herald*, May 26, 1963.
55. Ibid.
56. Roberta Applegate, "Misfits: Some Volunteers 'Take Over' Job," *Miami Herald*, May 26, 1963.
57. Jessie Hamm Meyer, *Leading the Way: A Century of Service* (Lakeland, Florida: Florida Federation of Women's Clubs, 1994), 168.
58. Meyer, *Leading the Way*, 169.
59. Arnetta Brown, *Recollections: A History of the League of Women Voters in Florida, 1939–1989* (St. Petersburg, Florida: League of Women Voters of Florida Education Fund, 1989), 3.
60. Brown, *Recollections*, 4–5.
61. Brown, *Recollections*, 21.
62. Dorothy Roe, Associated Press, "Parking Problems May Fall to Women," *Adrian (Michigan) Telegram*, May 20, 1952, Dorothy Roe Papers, National Women and Media Collection, State Historical Society of Missouri.
63. Ibid.
64. Helen Muir "oral history," Society of Women Geographers, Helen Muir Papers, University of Miami Special Collections, 6.
65. Marie Anderson, *Julia's Daughters: Women in Dade's History* (Miami, Florida: Herstory of Florida, Inc. 1980), 79.
66. Al Gore, "Introduction," in Rachel Carson, *Silent Spring* (New York: Houghton Mifflin Company, 1994), xx.
67. Gore, "Introduction," xvi.
68. Gore, "Introduction," xxv.
69. Marjory Stoneman Douglas, *The Everglades: River of Grass* (New York: Rinehart & Company, 1947).

70. Jack E. Davis, "Up From the Sawgrass: Marjory Stoneman Douglas and the Influence of Female Activism in Florida Conservation" in *Making Waves: Female Activists in Twentieth-Century Florida*, eds. Jack E. Davis and Kari Frederickson (Gainesville, Florida: University Press of Florida, 2003), 147.
71. Davis, "Up From the Sawgrass," 154.
72. Jack V. Blanton letter to George Beebe, September 18, 1961, Papers of Roberta Applegate, National Women and Media Collection, State Historical Society of Missouri.
73. Eleanor Ostergaard, "Roberta was Born to Her Job," *Miami Herald*, August 23, 1957.
74. "Herald Club Editor Receives Women's C of C Award," *Miami Herald*, August 23, 1957.
75. Susan Douglas, *Where the Girls Are*, 225.
76. Castleberry, "Women in Journalism," Session 2A, 60.
77. Castleberry, "Women in Journalism," Session 4, 160.
78. Castleberry, "Women in Journalism," Session 3, 130.
79. "Penney-Missouri Workshop is Another Classic Event," *Southern Advertising and Publishing*, April 1967, 15–16.
80. Maggie Savoy letter to Malcolm Mallette and Marie Anderson, January 14, 1969, Papers of Marie Anderson, National Women and Media Collection, State Historical Society of Missouri.
81. James Janega, "Eleanor Page Voysey, 88; Longtime Tribune Society Set the Standard for Covering Elite," *Chicago Tribune*, May 5, 2002.
82. Eleanor Page, "Arlington Races Share Spotlight with Visitors," *Chicago Daily Tribune*, July 5, 1952.
83. Eleanor Page, "Meet the Women Leaders at the Convention," *Chicago Daily Tribune*, July 7, 1952.
84. A collection of Page's columns, which covered the black community, are available at the Chicago History Museum.
85. Kimberly Wilmot Voss, "Kathryn Robinette: Redefining Palm Beach Society," *Tustenegee* 8, no. 1: 9.
86. Thom Smith, "Society Editor Remembered for Her Common Touch," *Palm Beach Post*, July 30, 1997.
87. Betty Ewing, "Oral History," Betty Ewing Papers, 1972–1992, Texas Woman's University, Denton, Texas, 23.
88. Ewing, "Oral History," 22.

89. Betty Ewing, "UH Interim Chancellor Has Made Several Smart Moves," *Houston Chronicle*, September 6, 1977.
90. J. Edward Murray, "Untitled," in *Anyone Who Enters Here Must Celebrate Maggie*, ed. Jim Bellows (Los Angeles: Ward Ritchie Press, 1972), 19.
91. Kay Mills, *A Place in the News: From the Women's Page to the Front Page* (New York: Columbia University Press, 1990), 179.
92. "Pages for Women," *Time*, May 19, 1967.

4

Recognizing the Soft News of the Women's Pages

When it came to the women's pages, there were rich examples of "soft news" that appealed to female readers. ("Hard news" is usually defined by the content of the front pages: conflict, crime, politics, timeliness, among others.) Just because the sections contained largely "soft news" does not make them less relevant. As Kay Mills wrote: "Soft news? Hard news? Where did these terms come from? The sexual implications fairly leap from the page."[1] And in doing so, the definition reinforces the idea that women's interests are somehow lesser. The four Fs of family, fashion, food, and furnishings impact our lives each day and thus should be taken seriously. The women's pages also reveal the process of social change for women and the development of feminism. The soft news content of the women's pages of newspapers deserves a re-examination by historians.

Local Women's Page Columns

Most women's pages featured local columns, usually by a reporter on the women's page staff. At first glance, it might be easy to dismiss them as frivolous personal takes on dating or entertaining. And while they did usually contain a mix of observations and humor, they also addressed

K. W. Voss, *Re-Evaluating Women's Page Journalism in the Post-World War II Era*,
https://doi.org/10.1007/978-3-319-96214-6_4

issues that their readers would certainly consider newsworthy, even if not fitting into the category of hard news. They ranged from slice-of-life or humor columns to advice columns, but they could also be as specific as sewing and quilting columns or beauty columns.

Slice-of-Life and Humor Columns

Reporter Marj Heyduck began her column, "Third and Main," at the *Dayton Journal Herald* in 1944 and it ran for more than two decades. The name was a reference to the center of town. Some columns were personal such as one about her mother for Mother's Day and memories of her being a "sassy teen" and another for Christmas when a neighbor shoveled her driveway.[2] Most of her observations were local. Yet, she also covered national news, including food conferences, fashion shows, and political conventions. A Penney-Missouri Award winner, she also spoke at American Press Institute events. Collections of Heyduck's columns resulted in three books that are still available online.

Dottie Lebo wrote a humor column, "Home at Heart," for the women's pages of the *Sunday Patriot-News* in Harrisburg, Pennsylvania, from 1957 until 1972. She wrote from her home while she raised her children. When on deadline, she typed her column on a 1940s Underwood behind a closed door. She wrote about the challenges of the local homemakers including carpools, layaway plans, and S&H green stamps. She also wrote about current events such as President Kennedy's assassination, the Apollo moonwalk, and the Beatle's invasion of America. There were also lots of stories about her family. Years later, her daughter collected the columns in a book. She wrote, "She is among the generation of mothers who raised the nation's baby boomers: a fifties Mom, but one who could not and would not conform to the era's rigid standards for housewives."[3]

In 1959, Edee Greene began her witty column, "AhMen" at the *Fort Lauderdale News*. She covered numerous topics from local issues like co-education[4] to journalism trends.[5] Greene often wrote about her own family and the parenting skills of her friends. In one 1960 column, she told the story of a rebellious teenage son and his guest. Greene wrote about his mother, "Being a forthright woman she straightened him out about the rights of teenagers and the responsibility of guests."[6] She wrote about her fellow women's page editors in 1961—and the meetings of the Florida Women's Press Club.[7] In another column, she wrote about gender and education.[8]

In Glendale, California, women's page editor Betty Preston Oiler wrote a column that regularly featured her own family, including the wedding of her step-daughter and the birth of her first grandchild. In one column, she writes of her spouse: "My husband is interested in another woman. It's the usual story. She's younger than he is. Much younger. And she plays the wide-eyed innocent bit right up to the hilt." She went on to conclude that he would eventually realize that he could never keep up with that young woman's pace: "There will come a time when he'll realize that he needs me. The time came quicker than I anticipated." Oiler revealed the kicker: "'Here,' her husband said, coming across the room with four-month-old Toby in his arms, 'you take your granddaughter, she's wet.'"[9]

Maggie Savoy's columns in Arizona also addressed the development of women's issues that predated the women's liberation movement. She addressed a labor issue on January 25, 1959. Her column featured a debate regarding a law that limited women to working shorter hours. She wrote: "A man can work as long as he likes. A woman has limited hours. This sounds protective. Yet career girls and professional women—such as accountants, bank employees, scientists, other women in many professions—feel it is discriminatory."[10] The column went on to cover a roundtable on the issue. Other columns addressed women's health issues,[11] financial advice,[12] and profiles of community leaders.[13] She also covered social activities and often took a news angle. For example, in her coverage of one gathering, she quoted Douglas McKay on his views on the Republican Party: "They forgot the women. They're the best campaigners in the world—they get excited, go out and pound pavements."[14]

Savoy was also active in environmental and preservation causes and wrote a column about business overtaking the environment and the resulting ugliness. The column led to so much reader reaction that she called for a meeting of local leaders to address the issue. The result was the creation of the Valley Beautiful Committee. The Committee focused on clean-up programs and fundraising programs to bury power lines.[15] She also advocated saving trees and plants rather than losing the natural areas to construction.[16] Savoy shared her concerns about the environment and urban poverty at the 1967 Penney-Missouri Awards workshop for women's page editors. She said:

> In the midst of our nation of plenty arise the ghetto and slums of the city. Ironically, the nation spends millions to shoot for the moon, but it is unable to alter the poverty of one-quarter of its population. The poor in their cages get poorer and they become embittered, apathetic and angered. The Horatio Algers of our generation have moved to the suburbs and left their poorer cousins in the city. Herein lies a pivotal problem of our century.[17]

Sewing and Quilting Columns

Many newspapers—especially those in the Midwest—had a quilting column beginning in the 1920s. The column included both quilting advice and a pattern. The most significant column was the one that ran in the *Kansas City Star*, which first appeared on September 22, 1928. Typically, a block of the quilt image ran in the newspaper and readers had to send in a nickel or dime to receive the actual pattern. Among the popular designs were those by Edna Marie Dunn. Her work was impressive. She edited and drew hundreds of quilt patterns that the *Star* printed. (She only signed four of her early designs and ended up the newspaper's anonymous editor for the next 30 years.) One researcher wrote, "Over the years, her quilt illustrations seem to reflect the time she had to devote to the drawing."[18]

Women's page editor Ethel Taylor ran a knitting column in her section in the *Van Nuys News* in the 1960s. The *Pittsburgh Press* included a column about knitting in the 1960s. The author, Pat Texler, also authored booklets, such as "Pat's Guide to Interchangeable Yarns."[19]

Beauty Columns

Many women's pages had beauty columns, usually written by a local reporter. The columns included stories about new products, cosmetic trends, and skin problems. Often the columnists answered readers' questions—including some that addressed significant issues—including one letter writer who asked how to cover bruises after her husband hit her.[20] Eleanor Hart wrote the Glamor Clinic column at the *Miami Herald* in the 1960s with most columns focusing on weight loss and makeovers. The black newspaper *Chicago Defender* ran the syndicated "Glamour Clinic" column written by Gerry Masciana, who ran a modeling and charm school.

Advice Columns

A staple of women's pages were advice columns. It is easy to dismiss these columns, but an examination of the columns shows some progressive ideas. It was a place to demonstrate a voice of authority. If there was little equality in terms of pay or promotions, women did have the moral authority that allowed them to give advice about relationships and household issues. This was especially important as male experts were reinforcing women's traditional roles, as was explored by Barbara Ehrenreich and Deirdre English in their book, *For Her Own Good: Two Centuries of the Experts' Advice for Women* in 1978.[21] (It was reissued in 2005.) They noted in the introduction that physicians such as stress expert Dr. Hans Selye warned that women working outside the home would run the risk of heart attack: "Some cardiologists even claimed evidence of an 'epidemic' of heart disease among women supposedly liberated by feminism."[22]

Eppie Lederer took over the syndicated Ann Landers column housed at the *Chicago Sun-Times* in August 1955. (Interestingly, she was rejected for a local political position for being too outspoken.) At one point she was getting about 2,000 letters a day—nearly a third was from teenagers. A survey in the late 1950s found that 85 percent of all female readers read the column daily compared to 45 percent of the male readers. As an example of how influential her column was, consider her December 1971 column about cancer, a topic that was rarely spoken about at the time. She pointed out the statistics—of the 200 million Americans alive, 50 million were likely to develop the disease—and the lack of governmental dollars spent on cancer research. She urged her readers to contact their senators to support a cancer research bill pending before Congress. It was estimated between 300,000 and 1 million letters came in from Ann Landers readers. She was on hand when President Richard Nixon signed the National Cancer Act.[23]

In 1959, Abigail Van Buren (author of "Dear Abby") wanted to pull her column from the *Miami News* and run it in the *Miami Herald* next to her sister's column (Ann Landers). *Miami News* Editor Jim Bellows came up with a plan—he would run a local advice column and it would eventually compete with the sisters' work. He recruited reporter Agnes Ash to pen the column, "Jane Dare."[24] During its run, progressive topics were addressed including the issue of opinionated women. In a 1963 column, a reader (Mad in Miami) wrote in about a male friend of her husband who regularly puts down women. The woman argued with the man and now her husband thought she should apologize. Dare responded, "You may not have behaved strictly as would a gracious hostess but under the circumstances, as a reluctant one, could hardly be expected to offer profuse apologies."[25] (Dear Abby later returned to the *News*.)

Many newspapers ran the column "The Women Alone," written by Helen Gurley Brown. Her 1962 book *Sex and the Single Girl* had caused a sensation. The book encouraged women's independence—and a little contradiction thrown in. For example, she advised that a woman have an apartment of her own and that she have a job that interests her. Yet, she also recommended that she not have an ounce of "baby fat."[26] While the argument has been made that much of the advice was based on attracting a man's attention, it should also be noted that the advice did encourage women to be economically independent and aware of current events.

Her newspaper column encouraged similar independence. In a 1963 column that ran in the *Miami News*, a reader who was a widow wrote that her children were angry with her because she had turned down a marriage proposal. Gurley Brown encouraged the widow to stand her ground. She wrote, "As for her children, they'll have no choice but to have their teeth recapped when they grind them down over this mother who may sound frivolous but who very much knows her own mind."[27]

Another popular syndicated columnist in the women's pages was Erma Bombeck, who wrote "At Wit's End." The column became syndicated in 1965, running three times a week in hundreds of newspapers across the country. In it, a writer noted that the message was, "housework, if it is done right, can kill you. It was that the women who kept house in the happy hunting ground called suburbia were so lonely that they held meaningful conversations with their tropical fish."[28] Bombeck's humorous voice was important to note for her ability to satirize housework. Her funny jabs at the monotony of cooking, cleaning, and child-raising allowed homemakers to recognize some of the difficulties they faced without disparaging them.

Her approach to women's roles in society appealed to many suburban women. She had put herself through school and had a career before she had children. She believed that feminism and being a housewife could co-exist. Bombeck recalled going to hear Betty Friedan speak and that she scolded the audience for finding housework funny rather than demeaning. Bombeck's view was "first we had to laugh; the crying had to come later."[29] It was a slight that she did not forget in later years. Bombeck said of Friedan and other militant feminists: "These women threw a war for themselves and didn't invite any of us. That was very wrong of them."[30]

Her view about Friedan did not mean that she was not an active feminist—especially in later years. In 1978, she began a two-year national tour in favor of the ERA. She recalled a lieutenant governor of a southern state patting her on the head and said she should be home having babies. Her response was, "My babies were old enough to vote against him."[31] She said she took the defeat of the constitutional amendment hard and she had little respect for younger women who opposed the ERA.[32] She was able to have an impact by allowing her voice to be one of a mother and homemaker. As her fellow columnist Ann Landers said of Bombeck, "She is savvy and sophisticated enough not to come across as too savvy and sophisticated."[33]

A 1951 industry study found that the advice columns were the most widely read part of the women's pages.[34] Dorothy Dix (Elizabeth Meriwether Gilmer) was one of the best-known columnists whose work ran in the women's pages—syndicated in more than 250 newspapers. She wrote that she never missed a deadline in more than 50 years and that she wrote every word herself. In a 1947 letter to Dorothy Jurney, Dix wrote that she received letters from every rank of society. Some letters she answered personally and others she answered in her column. She said there was no question that she was not asked. This included "one from the enterprising girl who sent ten cents with the request that I give her the formula for sex appeal and tell her how to look hot and keep cool."[35] She said that she had seen an increase of letters from men—especially those returning from war with questions about getting a job or a divorce. Request for relationship advice was common, especially from those young people who had married during the war. These women "find themselves with no money, no jobs, tied down with babies they don't want, bitterly disenchanted with each other and trying to find a way out of a marriage that never should have taken place."[36] It has been said that "her importance in setting the tone for the future columnists cannot be exaggerated."[37] Beatrice Fairfax was another popular advice columnist whose work ran in the Hearst newspapers. (The byline was actually used by several women writers, although Mary Manning is most often associated with the pen name.)

A 1953 university thesis looked at several advice columns in the women's pages. The author examined the columns from Mrs. Mayfield's Mailbag (*Rocky Mountain News* and syndicated), Martha Carr's Opinion (*St. Louis Post-Dispatch*), Mary Haworth's Mail (*San Jose Mercury*), and The Good Neighbor/Anita Day Hubbard (*San Francisco Examiner*). Letter writers were concerned about family relationships, confessional secrets, and occasionally household queries. In addition, Dorothy Ricker wrote the weekly advice column "Teenage Mail" from 1952 to 1984, which usually ran in the women's pages. It ran in dozens of newspapers and addressed the issues of smoking, dating, and friendships.

Embracing the Four Fs

As mentioned earlier, the content of the women's pages was often described as the four Fs: family, food, fashion, and furnishings. It was usually done in a demeaning way, as if these topics are not significantly important to most people. However, these concepts impact our everyday life. A closer examination of the four Fs reveals a perspective that can easily argue the women's page editors were doing all they could to elevate the significance of the topics to something more than fluff and filler.

Family

Of the four Fs—family, fashion, food, and furnishings—the one that is most shockingly diminished is "family." The women's section pushed the issue of family—especially that of motherhood—forward as a newsworthy subject. Whether a mother worked outside of the home or not was not a debatable issue for women's page editors who wanted both groups as readers. Consider the welcoming tone of Penney-Missouri Award Director Paul Myhre in a letter to Beverley Morales after learning she had been fired from the *Sun-Sentinel*: "My guess is that you grabbed a better job somewhere else—which your talents certainly would attract—or you have just decided to give housewifing a whirl?"[38] His approach mirrored the views of the Florida's women page editors who saw being a homemaker as a "job."

Family—or more often mothering—was taken seriously in the women's pages. One women's page story, written by the Associated Press women's reporter Joy Miller, addressed the need for parents to discipline their children.[39] In a 1956 *Miami Herald* series, Roberta Applegate addressed "disturbed children" and what parents could do to help them. In an approach that was ahead of its time, she urged against a stigma of mental illness. She also quoted experts who rejected a current theory that espoused poor parenting as a cause for mental illness.[40] In Los Angeles, Maggie Savoy wrote about the importance of parental involvement in a child's education.[41]

In the women's pages of the *Seattle Post-Intelligencer*, Bobbi McCallum wrote a series in 1966 about infertility, at a time when the topic was not typically discussed. She reported about developing medical procedures for couples trying to conceive featuring the views of several doctors. At the time, the topic was controversial, and the Federal Drug Administration had not approved the hormones involved in the treatment.[42] In another article, she interviewed a marriage counselor who addressed emotional problems related to infertility.

Often, McCallum wrote about the changing definition of family. She wrote a four-part series on adoption that was progressive for the time. The first article featured the story of Beth, a young woman who was giving up a baby for adoption. The 17-year-old was from Wyoming but was staying at a home for pregnant, unwed women in Seattle. The lead was a direct quote referencing the adoption paperwork the young mother would have to sign: "All parental rights and interests. Interests? How can I relinquish all interest in the first baby I've given birth to?" The story went on to describe the decision making that she had to go through after first ignoring that she was pregnant. Although the father offered to marry her—she did consider it—she said as a high school student she knew she was too young. Following the baby's birth, Beth was looking at her future differently. She said, "I've changed a lot—grown up. I'm going to plan my future, finish school, get a job, save some money."[43]

The second story was about a couple unable to conceive children and had decided to adopt. The story described the lengthy process that couples must go through in order to adopt. It also featured the stigma that the family faced because their children were adopted. The mother, Joan Diederich, described the reaction of some people: "They always bring up the adopted kids who have gone wrong. They make you defend your decision to adopt."[44]

The third story featured what would be considered controversial at the time—the adoption of a child from a different race. In the story, McCallum references an adoption agency that found that "mixed-race babies" were the most difficult to place. In this story, a Seattle couple, the Hagan family, was adopting a baby that was half Caucasian and half African American. The couple, who already had biological children of their own, said they were looking to expand their family and did not care about the racial background of the child. The father, a professor at the University of Washington, said of his new son: "He's part of the family and they'll stand up for him. We feel he'll be better off growing up with our love and support than without it."[45]

The next and final story was a continuation of the Hagan adoption along with the reaction from friends and family. Some family members were shocked and bothered by a mix-race baby. They soon came around after meeting the young child, Erin. Friends also made some offending statements. The Hagans said they had anticipated some negative reactions and they hoped their son would face a more positive environment—but they were realistic. Professor Hagan said: "Some social workers think by the time Erin is a teen, racial problems will be worked out. But we're not betting on that."[46]

A month after the series ran, McCallum wrote a story about a foster family who took care of disabled children after raising their own biological children. McCallum described the many doctor's visits and other additional work that the foster children needed but that it was worth the inconvenience. The foster mother was quoted as saying: "There are too many children in institutions right now. They need people like us to love them."[47]

The *Seattle Post-Intelligencer* wasn't the only paper whose women's section dedicated considerable coverage to family issues. Jean Otto, the women's page reporter in Appleton, Wisconsin, wrote a seven-part series in 1965 about unwed mothers. She addressed women's pregnancies, parental involvement, concerns of the state, the father's involvement, and society's stake in the children.[48]

Covering families and writing about parenting came naturally for many of the women's page editors. Several, such as Beverley Morales and Edee Greene, raised children while working at the newspapers. Jurney believed being a wife and mother allowed female reporters to place more emphasis on human concerns.[49] Greene regularly wrote about her family and the challenges of parenting a rebellious teenage son.[50] At the *Milwaukee Journal*, Hagen was also covering social issues for the women's section including a story about a group formed to defend the rights of children.[51]

In Hawaii, women's page reporter Pat Millard's baby daughter Heather was "adopted" by the newspaper to better understand child development through news stories in the early 1960s. Stories started when she was a newborn and each milestone was documented. Heather was used as the example, and a pediatrician or other child development expert was consulted. Stories included Heather's colic and other childhood illnesses, as well as taking swimming lessons. Millard's editor Drue Lytle wrote,

"Little Heather has become a widely-known character around town."[52] Tragically, she drowned in the family pool when she was 18 months old. This too did not go unaddressed by the newspaper.

Miami Herald women's page editor Marie Anderson was 55 years old when she got her first taste of motherhood. It was thanks to her relationship with the Missouri School of Journalism. Dean Earl English had heard from a priest in Honduras about a young woman, Zulay Domínguez, in his community who showed journalistic promise. The priest sent her to the United States with the intent of her studying at the University of Missouri. Those plans did not work out and after a few months in Kansas City, English contacted Anderson, knowing that the *Miami Herald* would be a good place for a young journalist to be trained.

In January 1971, Anderson picked up Domínguez from the airport. She helped Domínguez find a place to live and found her an internship at the *Miami Herald*. Through some confusion in translation from Spanish to English, Domínguez came to call Anderson "mom." The name stuck and over the years, the relationship grew so that Anderson was known as Domínguez's American mother. Anderson was a witness at her surrogate daughter's wedding when she became Zulay Domínguez Chirinos. She got to know Domínguez Chirinos's children. "She was there for all the rituals," Domínguez said. "She was the American mom I needed."[53] (Domínguez Chirinos is now a member of the editorial board at the *Miami Herald*.)

Relationships like Anderson's demonstrated that while some of the women's page editors did not marry, their lives did reflect the "spinster" stereotype of the time. In Jurney's case, her marriage ended in divorce. She had met someone else and filed the paperwork to end the marriage. Her husband, Frank, fought the divorce, and the case made it to the state's Supreme Court where he won. Greene was also divorced, although she had three children. She later married for a second time to a fellow journalist, who also had three children. Greene was living a true-life "Brady Bunch." Stories of her blended family were often featured in her column. Greene later noted in a letter to Myhre that she had eleven and a half grandchildren: "You see he has three children and I have three but we BOTH claim all the grandchildren."[54]

As divorce laws were changing across the country, there were often series about the topics in the women's pages. Marian McBride was a women's page reporter for the *Milwaukee Sentinel* from 1963 to 1970. In her reporting, she often wrote about the activities and research about the Wisconsin Commission on the Status of Women. In 1968, she wrote a series called "Wisconsin Women, Know Your Rights," which was largely based on the Commission's work, as well as input from two local lawyers. It was later republished in a booklet.[55] It began: "Sex discrimination still exists in many alleys of American life. But often only ignorance of the law leads women to deprivation or loss. Knowing her rights is just as important as having them."[56] The article was done in a question-and-answer format, which addressed state law regarding women. For example, women could serve on juries in Wisconsin. This right differed state by state. It also noted that a husband must provide for his family, and if he does not, a wife could charge items of support to his accounts. Women with questions were directed to Legal Aid or the district attorney's office. The booklet also noted that a wife did not need her husband's consent to work outside of the home, yet if she works in the family business, her husband did not need to pay her.[57]

In 1975, Pat Millard of the *Honolulu Advertiser* women's pages wrote a series about recent changes in divorce laws and interviewed numerous lawyers as she researched the subject. "Islanders seem to think of divorce as easier to get since the 'no-fault' divorce law has been in effect," she wrote, "but members of the legal profession see just as much red tape and divorce as traumatic, emotionally and financially as it ever was."[58] In another story in the series, she explained that while divorce laws may have been simplified, there were still complications. "Splitting up the financial relationship a couple develops during their marriage is not that simple, say attorneys," she wrote.[59] The series had a significant impact. According to an editor, "The Family Court had it reprinted verbatim. They give it to every couple contemplating divorce." Further, the articles were cited in an academic journal about the changing divorce laws in the state.[60]

When Marjorie Paxson was hired by Gannett, she recalled a company policy that paid for the relocation of a spouse. "It struck me that I don't have a spouse but I have a very nice sister-in-law," she said, "so I asked the corporate personnel officer—I said, 'Well, you would pay for a spouse to visit the new location.' 'Oh, yes.' And I said, 'Well, I don't have a spouse, would you pay for my sister-in-law to help me move?' There was a pause for a minute and then he said yes."[61]

These anecdotes show that women's page editors viewed "family" in several different ways. And when it came to covering traditional families, Jurney urged managing editors to allow women's page editors to reach out to middle-class women who may not have been part of the club-women community. Jurney described the work of these homemakers:

> She fixes breakfast, she washes clothes, she dresses the children, cleans the house, does the dishes, makes lunch, irons the clothes, makes supper, makes light snacks, makes beds, dusts, mops, sweeps, mends old clothes, washes windows, scrubs the kitchen, works in the yard, shops for groceries. That is far different from your wife with her committees, the Girl Scouts, the charity drives, the Red Cross, the concerts and the library.[62]

Fashion

Fashion is easy to dismiss as fluff, but it held an important role. While men dominated the news and sports positions, the fashion beat was a place for women to find their niche. In building her journalism career, Gloria Biggs covered fashion for *Hollywood Citizen-News* and *Western Family Magazine* as a freelancer in the early 1950s.[63] The American Press Institute's 1951 industry publication *Fashion in Newspapers* revealed this concept: "No aspect of the news is further from the comprehension of the average male editor than fashion."[64] This concept put women in a unique role at most newspapers where their voice was the authoritative one. They were the ones who could dictate the fashion business in their communities. This often meant approaching fashion writers from women's magazines. For example, Jurney was able to hire a fashion writer away from *Mademoiselle*.[65]

Fashion helps define a time period—whether it was the end of an era of wearing gloves and hats, which represented a period of fashion conformity, or the reluctant acceptance of women wearing pants in public as a victory regarding gender equality.[66] In recent years, more fashion options are available because the dominance of department stores was reduced and discount retailers took hold before online shopping became common. Yet, prior to the end of home economics classes that taught sewing as an important skill, people (typically women) would tailor their own clothes, and women's pages of newspapers and women's magazines included sewing patterns. Readers who could not purchase the runway clothing described by fashion editors could create their own version. Prior to the introduction of clothing as individual expression, which coincided with cheap materials and production, most women outside of higher social economic classes did not use fashion to make an individual statement—the goal was to fit in, and the voices of fashion editors were important in achieving that goal.[67]

Likely the most significant newspaper fashion journalist of the 1950s and 1960s was fashion editor Eugenia Sheppard at the *New York Herald Tribune*. Known for her crafty writing skills, she described the 1957 European fashion shows and the use of buttons and bows: "It's all terribly cute, but like giving a girl candy when she craves steak." She wrote of designer Lanvin-Castillo's new extra-short skirt length, "Pretty sexy for a tall girl, but it may make a short one disappear altogether." She responded to Jean Dessès's "dovetail look": "Dresses have always been inspired by birds. I think it's time somebody came right out and told this nice guy to switch to biology or some other ology. Anything but birds."

Beginning in 1956, Sheppard wrote a thrice-weekly column, "Inside Fashion." She was known for revolutionizing fashion journalism by adjusting its focus from fabric to the people who designed and wore it. According to the *New York Times*, Sheppard "became known for her breezy writing style, a personalized approach to fashion and her ability to spot trends even before the trend-setters realized they were setting them." Gail Sheehy, who worked for Sheppard, described her editor as "fiercely competitive."[68] Yet, Sheppard was also supportive of her reporters and was not afraid to give designers her opinions. Designer Bill Blass wrote that she had given him some of the toughest and most important advice of his career. She told him that he should stop trying to produce clothes for the middle of the country and stick to the New York women who made him famous. He wrote that it was difficult to hear but that she was correct.[69]

Many women's page editors recognized that fashion was big business. *Washington Star* fashion editor, and Penney-Missouri Award winner, Eleni Epstein called the fashion industry a worldwide multibillion-dollar business. "Whole economies were and are predicated on the fashion business," she said. "[T]he fashion industry is part of history itself."[70] And, clothing is often the most obvious indication of social status.[71] This concept has been echoed by fashion critic Teri Agins:

> For all its glamour and frivolity, fashion happens to be a relevant and powerful force in our lives. At every level of society, people care greatly about the way they look, which affects both their self-esteem and the way other people interact with them. And it has been true since the beginning of time that people from all walks of life make the effort to dress in style.[72]

At the South Florida *Sun-Sentinel* in 1961, Beverley Morales noted her new approach to fashion coverage consisted of "tossing out Dior and other big-name fashion lights in the waste basket, on the thought that no one knows Dior but everyone has a closet full of clothes." She planned to do articles about what was in those closets.[73] The *Miami Herald* localized a national wire story from *Women's Wear Daily* about clothes that were poorly made. The story led to piles of letters from readers with similar complaints; subsequently, a story about the local complaints ran in the women's section.[74]

A 1961 article in the *Fort Lauderdale News* women's pages focused on the latest trend in sweaters and how to care for them.[75] In another 1961 story, the reporter wrote about a Fort Lauderdale consignment shop. She reported that the store allowed women without the means for new ball gowns to have a cheaper option; her list of customers and contributors was "a closely guarded secret."[76] In 1963, the *Miami Herald* women's section featured a story about the fashion designs of students at Miami-Dade Junior College.[77] Two photographs accompanied the article, with one of the designs featuring a pantsuit—a style that would be debated for years. In 1965, the *Miami Herald* included a wire story about the Paris fashion shows. The big news was that Yves St. Laurent was going to let reporters into his fashion shows after barring them the previous year.[78]

Trend reporting could be found much earlier, though, as well. Aileen Ryan began covering fashion for the *Milwaukee Journal* in the 1920s. It was the era of the flapper, and the exposed knees were shocking communities. These working woman "wore lipstick and bobbed her hair, and her clothes differed dramatically from those of the previous generation."[79] The change was not lost on Ryan who persuaded her editor to allow her to create a shopping column with the creative title of "Sinful Susan's Shocking Shopping." It was full of racy content. For example, in the column, Ryan wrote about cigarette holders for women, perfumed cigarettes, false eyelashes, fancy garters, and feminine flasks for bathtub gin.[80]

Miami Herald women's page journalist Jo Werne combined her hobby with her work, and it led to the 1973 Penney-Missouri Award for fashion writing. A reporter on numerous beats, she had been sewing for years. Raised on an Ohio farm, she joined the 4-H when she was nine years old and given the choice of a project. Her options were to learn to sew or raise a hog. She chose the former. Her handmade bean bag won a blue ribbon, and her interest was sparked. She described her hobby as "therapy, after pounding a typewriter all day long." Her award came after her search for inexpensive fabrics. In researching, she discovered a booming polyester knitting industry in Miami.[81] The work resulted in the article, "Polyester: A New $70 Million Business." In it, she described what polyester is and how it was made. She visited the fabric mills and interviewed the workers. A Penney-Missouri judge, a senior editor at *Time Magazine*, wrote of her "reporting colorfully on the sociology of the Cuban work forces. The result is a very human dimension."[82]

Social change also was represented in the women's page fashion coverage. In a 1969 story, Epstein was quoted as saying that in Washington, DC, women would wear pants on the street but not to the office.[83] As social change occurred, it was reflected in the clothing worn by working women. This can be seen in the often heated debate about women being allowed to wear pants to work in the early 1970s. It was a symbolic gesture about the changing role of women in American society. It took a formal grievance in 1971 for the women on the classified ad staff of the *Detroit Free Press* to be allowed to wear pants.[84] Sally Raleigh at the *Seattle Post-Intelligencer* was especially proud of her victory, following a series of memos with male executives, requesting the right for women at the newspaper to wear pantsuits to work.

This issue would arise years later for Paxson when she took over as publisher of the *Muskogee Phoenix* in 1980. On the first day of work, Paxson learned about one of the former male publisher's policies. He turned and looked at her and said, "You might as well know that I have a policy that women can't wear pants." "What?!" she replied, surprised.[85] Although Paxson had planned to look "every inch the lady publisher" and had purchased a number of skirts, she decided to wear her lone pantsuit to the office on day two. The next day she arrived at eight o'clock, wearing her pantsuit. Purposely wanting to draw attention to her clothing, she entered the building through the press room, then walked through the composing room, and finally made her way through the news room before reaching her office.

By noon, the former publisher's secretary was in Paxson's office. "Everybody is asking if there's been a change—if they can wear pants?" the secretary asked. That afternoon Paxson gathered the department heads together to officially announce a change that the dress code had changed. Employees could wear pants, she told them, and it did not really make any difference to her what either the men or women were wearing, "as long as they were neat, as long as they were clean, and as long as they were dressed appropriately for the job they were supposed to do for the *Phoenix*."[86] That evening many of the females went shopping, and the next day 29 of the 45 women working at the newspaper arrived wearing pantsuits. "That story got around town very quickly," Paxson remembered.[87] Shortly thereafter she was shopping at Sears when the clerk looked down at the name on Paxson's credit card. She looked up at Paxson. "Are you the new lady at the paper?" she asked. Paxson replied affirmatively. "I'm so glad you let them wear pants," the woman responded.[88]

In Seattle, Bobbi McCallum wrote about fur expert Florence Balut. The story began, "The Master Furriers Guild of America's 'Man of the Year' is a Dietrich-voiced, vivacious grandmother of five with a flair for fashion." The story goes on to note her interest in animal preservation including working with the US Department of the Interior.[89] Unlike today, when the question of fur is typically either for or against, the topic was more nuanced. While Balut was a furrier, she also spoke out about balancing the needs of the animals. She described the environmental impact on a small Alaskan island, "We take just enough to keep the herd balanced. If we didn't, the food on the island couldn't support the herd and they'd all starve."[90] The story was more than the fluffy fashion features that some historians have described.

Women's pages also became instrumental in their coverage of the national and international fashion shows—moving into what was once the exclusive territory of women's magazines. During *Milwaukee Journal* women's page editor Aileen Ryan's first trip to New York, the fashion capital of the country, she made fashion journalism history. It was 1931 and at that point only magazine reporters and buyers were allowed into the fashion shows. Ryan would not accept that policy. She knocked on as many as 12 showroom doors a day and got access to about a third of them. She recounted that no one had heard of the Milwaukee newspaper, but she eventually prevailed and sent clips of her stories to those New York designers. Ryan said that eventually "the New Yorkers began to understand the value of what I was doing."[91] Ryan continued to fight for more access each year, and she slowly was able to get access for her photographer, too. This meant other newspapers had to buy their fashion photographs from the *Milwaukee Journal*. In 1937, images from Ryan's trips to the fashion shows in Europe became the first color photos in the *Journal*.[92] Women page editors from across the country soon followed her example.

Drue Lytle covered fashion for her Hawaii newspaper, traveling the world covering the glamorous shows and writing daily stories. She explained in a letter, "I'll never understand the press weeks in New York where they crowd you so hard you don't do them justice."[93] She also covered fashion when designers visited Honolulu such as when "Couture International" held a fashion show in 1963. Lytle wrote that the 100 pieces featured on the runway were valued at more than $17,000.[94] In 1966, she spent 10 days in New York covering fashion shows and another week covering shows in Europe, including London and Paris. She also covered everyday local clothing.[95]

Food

In 2004, *American Journalism Review* featured an article about the importance of one of the four Fs: "Food journalism, once a throwaway compendium of recipes and 'what's hot' articles, has gone upscale. Newspapers and magazines are dedicating top talent to the food beat, and they are hungry for sophisticated stories with timely angles."[96]

Food stories and recipes have been found in newspapers as early as the 1880s, according to digitized projects. The food pages were often a mix of food news and lighter features. Their importance to their communities was truly showcased during World War II when rationing changed the options available to American home cooks. The limits on meat, sugar, and coffee meant creating more imaginative recipes. After the war, the increase in mass-produced canned food meant new products and questions from consumers. Later came the popularity of TV dinners and an interest in French cooking—all topics covered by newspaper food journalists.

Food has long been a significant issue in political, social, and economic ways. For example, during times of war, women were often lectured about rationing as their way of serving their country. Roberta Applegate wrote a speech for Michigan Governor Kim Sigler in the years before she came to the *Miami Herald* demonstrating how important homemakers were to the food industry. "Never, in the history of our nation," she wrote, "has it been more important that women—as citizens and as homemakers—take an active interest in governmental issues."[97] One way for the women to do this was to take part in the president's program to save food, especially grains. She wrote, "This state food committee is counting on the housewives of Michigan, even more than on the hotel and restaurant operators to translate its programs into action."[98]

For decades, questions about home cooking were answered by the food editor who worked in the women's pages. They helped track down lost recipes and aided in planning a holiday menu. The newspaper food editors were important to their communities as they wrote about food trends, popular recipes, and local restaurants. These food editors exchanged recipes with readers, explained new dishes and products, and warned about new nutrition studies and technology. They worked with top chefs and home cooks. They practiced good journalism while keeping advertisers at bay in the 1950s and 1960s.[99]

The food industry featured meetings for food editors where the journalists learned about new products and new techniques in food. It also gave the women a chance to socialize and network at a time when they were excluded from other journalism organizations. A primary reason, though, the food editors went to the conferences was to take part in the reporting contests, and their newspapers regularly publicized the works of the winners in their pages. If there was any question about who was doing the food writing, consider the name of the honor: the Vesta Award. It was named for the mythical goddess of home and hearth. The food sections were evaluated on the service to readers, journalistic writing, originality, timeliness, and thoroughness.[100] Awards were given in different circulation categories and black-and-white versus color pages. A newspaper professional was among the group judging the entries.[101]

The food editors were a busy group. Dorothy Dean (a pen name) received more than 20,000 calls each year at the *Spokesman-Review*.[102] Dean served readers of the *Spokesman-Review* for 45 years. The Dorothy Dean Homemaker's Service included weekly cooking demonstrations, a test kitchen, and monthly recipe leaflets. Many readers subscribed to the Dorothy Dean leaflets and regularly received recipes to be included in a treasured green three-ring binder. Readers adored the food editors. In October 2010, the *Spokesman-Review* honored the 75th anniversary of Dorothy Dean. Numerous readers responded with their memories. One reader wrote, "When I am fresh out of ideas, I still refer to her recipes." Another fan wrote: "When I married in 1956, the only thing I could cook was fudge. A cookbook was a necessity and shortly I obtained my Dorothy Dean cookbook, which I continue to rely on to this day."[103]

At the *Seattle Post-Intelligencer*, it took four home economists to answer readers' questions and requests. A former food editor recalled, "Readers would call and say, 'I want a nice meatloaf recipe.'" The home economist would then go through the files at the newspaper and mail the recipe to the caller.[104] This was standard practice at newspapers across the country where women's page journalists had a direct connection with the residents in the communities they covered.

Marion Olive Prior Ferriss Guinn was likely the first food editor at the *Seattle Times*, writing under the pen name Dorothy Neighbors, which was used from 1927 until 1980. Guinn was hired by the *Times*, after graduating from the University of Washington in 1929 with degrees in journalism and home economics. During World War II, Guinn presented a number of "Housewives Go to War" programs advising women of ways to help the war effort.[105] According to an article in the *Times*, "She was at times youthful, at times matronly but always cheerful, competent and hospital."[106]

At the *Seattle Times*, the recipe files have been saved and are now in the Special Collections at the Seattle Library. According to Jodee Fenton, managing librarian at the Special Collections: "Those recipes are very much of their time, which is what made me think that the collection has a real role in the history of eating. What was good? What did we desire? The recipes are a very important piece of social history." Some of the recipes reflected the times and others are still being made today. Dean readers were offered Swedish meatballs, Patio Lickin' Chicken, and zucchini-nut cookies. Neighbors' recipes included poached red snapper, shrimp risotto, and molded aspic with artichoke remoulade.

Women's page editors took food coverage seriously. They often tested recipes, researched industry trends, and attended food conferences. For example, Edee Greene attended the 1970 Food Editors Conference in San Francisco.[107] Convenience also became an issue as married women with children joined the labor force in unprecedented numbers. (The number of fast-food restaurants nearly tripled during the 1960s.)[108] Women's pages responded with articles about how to eat healthy and how to make food quickly. Jurney thought the Associated Press was especially strong in its food copy. She encouraged the managing editors to allow women's page editors to be creative in page design. "It is so important to use attractive pictures of food with food copy," she requested of the editors. "Don't worry about getting people into these pictures."[109]

Furnishings

After World War II, suburban communities across the country grew quickly. And all those new homes were soon filling up with appliances. In the five years following the end of the war, not only did consumer spending increase 60 percent, but the amount spent on household furnishings and appliances rose 240 percent. In some ways, this consumer growth was a political issue. According to historian Elaine Tyler May, this was a way of winning the Cold War. She wrote that in President Richard Nixon's vision:

> The suburban ideal of home ownership would defuse two potentially disruptive forces: women and workers. In appliance-laden houses across the country, working-class as well as business-class breadwinners could fulfill the new American work-to-consume ethic. … The family home would be the place where a man could display his success through the accumulation of consumer goods. Women, in turn, would reap rewards for domesticity by surrounding themselves with commodities. Presumably, they would remain content as housewives because appliances would ease their burden.[110]

Dorothy Dawe was the assistant women's page editor at the *Milwaukee Journal* from the 1920s through the 1940s with most of her coverage focused on furnishings.[111] She was hired after Aileen Ryan, the section editor, convinced the managing editor that furnishings were news.[112] According to Ryan, who worked with Dawe for many years: "Dorothy Dawe had a completely advanced perspective. She was a real pioneer."[113] Dawe was a Milwaukee native and a Marquette University graduate who worked at the *Milwaukee Journal* for 19 years at a time when homes were changing. She reported on new developments in technology that impacted lighting and electrical sockets in houses.[114] She wrote stories about uniquely designed homes, such as a 1928-built brick bungalow on the south side of Milwaukee that was updated with a wood-burning fireplace in 1946.[115] She wrote about the scarcity of available furniture in the immediate post-World War II years—before the consumerism of the 1950s kicked in.[116]

Her obituary noted that Dawe had "done much to build interest in homes and changing periods of decoration." Upon hearing of her death, the American Furniture Mart named its annual award for best furnishing writing in her honor. An industry spokesperson noted, "Dorothy's reports in the home furnishing field set the pace for the basic judging requirements of the greatest good for the greatest number."[117]

Following in Dawe's footsteps was Lois Hagen, a University of Wisconsin graduate. Hagen was born in Westby, Wisconsin, in 1918. After graduation, she worked as a journalist at *Time* and the Associated Press before spending the bulk of her career at the *Milwaukee Journal*, which she joined in 1947. Initially, she covered fashion and wrote general features before taking on the furnishing beat, which included carpets, fabrics, tableware, and accessories.[118] She covered everything from new kinds of furniture, such as those introduced at the semi-annual "Good Design" exhibit at Chicago's Merchandise Mart,[119] to trends in design, such as the overuse of the term "contemporary" in 1950s furniture descriptions. She quoted an expert, "I like my milk homogenized but I don't know about my furniture."[120] She also often interviewed people about their homes and how the rooms were decorated.

She won a Penney-Missouri Award for writing and reporting in 1965. It was for a 12-part series on historic houses in Virginia. The series contained rich descriptions and detailed histories of homes that went back for generations. In one article, she wrote about historic Shirley mansion near Richmond. The mansion had been the home of the Carter family since 1723, where Ann Hill Carter, mother of Confederate Gen. Robert E. Lee, was married in the building to Henry "Light Horse Harry" Lee.[121]

While in Miami, Jurney said she was "dismayed" how few women read the *Herald* and how many were unfamiliar with the reporters' bylines. She said she found that one of the topics readers wanted was not being covered in the women's section—news about home furnishings. Her solution? "We assigned one of our best women writers to that field—to write about Miami homes and to report the news of home furnishings available in Miami stories," she told managing editors. "We sent this reporter to the home furnishings market to write about the coming trends in furniture. It is now one of the THE big sections of the paper."[122]

An article in the *Tallahassee Democrat* profiled an interior decorator and her work. The reporter emphasized the professionalism of women who decorate houses.[123] It is worth noting that while women were often the ones making the economic decisions, they often could not get credit in their own names. Michigan Representative Martha Griffiths, who worked to get the ERA passed by Congress, wrote to a Miami woman explaining the difficulty of women to get credit. She wrote, "some lenders will not permit a wife—regardless of her income—to open a charge account, borrow money, or buy a car in her own name."[124]

Conclusion

The soft news of the women's pages was as important as the hard news of the front pages to readers. Stories about the four Fs addressed the moments of everyday lives. Recipes were requested and clipped. The columnists—both local and national—gave readers a voice. The letter exchanges served as an early version of social media as advice was sought and given. While this content was important, it was not the only women's news in the sections. The next two chapters document the topics that went beyond the typical soft news and added stories about health, politics, and economics.

Notes

1. Kay Mills, *A Place in the News: From the Women's Page to the Front Pages* (New York: Columbia University Press, 1990), 110.
2. Marj Heyduck, *Best of Marj: Favorite 'Third and Main' Columns* (Dayton, OH: Dayton Newspapers, 1962).
3. Dottie Lebo, *Home at Heart* (New York: iUniverse, Inc, 2007), xxii.
4. Edee Greene, "Jane Breaks Out of Co-Education," *Fort Lauderdale News*, September 20, 1961.
5. Edee Greene, "Newshens Fly Nest to Cluck," *Fort Lauderdale News*, September 18, 1961.

6. Edee Greene, "Fidel's Frolicking to Rock 'n Roll Beat," *Fort Lauderdale News*, September 21, 1960.
7. Edee Greene, "Newshens Fly Nest to Cluck," *Fort Lauderdale News*, September 18, 1961.
8. Edee Greene, "Jane Breaks Out of Co-Education," *Fort Lauderdale News*, September 20, 1961.
9. Betty Preston, "Beware of the Other Woman! She's a Bundle of Charm," *Glendale News-Press*, March 13, 1970.
10. Maggie Savoy, "Is Law Discriminatory?" *Arizona Republic*, January 25, 1959.
11. This column addressed alcoholism and motherhood. Maggie Savoy, "Here's Some Good Advice," *Arizona Republic*, January 28, 1959.
12. Maggie Savoy, "Duck the Quick Stock Tips," *Arizona Republic*, January 26, 1959.
13. Maggie Savoy, "He's Paying American Back," *Arizona Republic*, January 5, 1959.
14. Maggie Savoy, "She'll Bake Him 'Cake Of Year,'" *Arizona Republic*, January 31, 1959.
15. Mary Ellis Carlton, "Take a Look at Your City," *Long Beach Independent*, February 12, 1961.
16. Clare Boothe Luce, "Untitled," in *Anyone Who Enters Here Must Celebrate Maggie*, ed. Jim Bellows (Los Angeles: Ward Ritchie Press, 1972), 18.
17. Jeannette Medith, "Attack City Problems, Penney Writers Told," *Columbia Missourian*, March 17, 1967.
18. Barbara Brackman, *Women of Design: Quilts in the Newspaper* (Kansas City, Missouri: Kansas City Star, 2004), 6.
19. Pat Trexler, "Pat's Pointers," *Pittsburgh Press*, March 20, 1966.
20. Annette Blaugrund, *Dispensing Beauty in New York and Beyond* (Charleston, South Carolina: History Press, 2011), 161–173.
21. Barbara Ehrenreich and Deirdre English, *For Her Own Good: Two Centuries of the Experts' Advice for Women* (New York: Anchor, 2005).
22. Ehrenreich and English, *For Her Own Good*, xiii.
23. Rick Kogan, *America's Mom: The Life, Lessons, and Legacy of Ann Landers* (New York: William Murrow, 2003), 103–104.
24. Jim Bellows, *The Last Editor: How I Saved the New York Times, the Washington Post, and the Los Angeles Times from Dullness and Complacency* (Kansas City, Missouri: Andrews McMeel, 2002), 80.

25. Jane Dare, "Husband Insists I Apologize," *Miami News*, May 23, 1963.
26. Helen Gurley Brown, *Sex and the Single Girl* (New York: Barnes and Noble Book, 2004 reprint), 10.
27. Helen Gurley Brown, "Widow Prefers Her Solitude," *Miami News*, May 23, 1963.
28. John Skow, "Erma in Bomburbia," *Time*, July 2, 1984, 2.
29. Skow, "Erma in Bomburbia," 8.
30. Ibid.
31. Ibid.
32. Ibid.
33. Skow, "Erma in Bomburbia," 10.
34. Wayne A. Danielson, "A Value-Analysis of Advice Columns in Newspapers" (master's thesis, Stanford University, 1953), 1.
35. Dorothy Dix letter to Dorothy Jurney, October 10, 1947, Papers of Dorothy Jurney, National Women and Media Collection, State Historical Society of Missouri.
36. Ibid.
37. Danielson, *Advice Columns*, 4.
38. Paul L. Myhre letter to Beverley Morales, October 6, 1961, Papers of the Penney-Missouri Awards, National Women and Media Collection, State Historical Society of Missouri.
39. Joy Miller, "Swat Your Kinds When They Misbehave," *Miami Herald*, May 20, 1963.
40. Roberta Applegate, "Parents Much Face Child's Behavior Problems as Readily as Physical Ones," *Miami Herald*, May 23, 1956.
41. Maggie Savoy, "Head Start Specialist Deals with Parental Involvement," *Los Angeles Times*, November 6, 1969.
42. Bobbi McCallum, "New Hope for Childless," *Seattle Post-Intelligencer*, January 31, 1966.
43. Bobbi McCallum, "The Day Beth Gave Up Her Baby," *Seattle Post-Intelligencer*, August 11, 1968.
44. Bobbi McCallum, "For Us Adopting Is No Charity," *Seattle Post-Intelligencer*, August 12, 1968.
45. Bobbi McCallum, "Brother's Face Is Brown," *Seattle Post-Intelligencer*, August 13, 1968.
46. Bobbi McCallum, "Love of Irish for Part-Negro Baby," *Seattle Post-Intelligencer*, August 14, 1968.

47. Bobbi McCallum, "Triple Tragedy: Don't Turn Away," *Seattle Post-Intelligencer*, September 8, 1968.
48. Jean Otto, *First Love: Memoirs of a First Amendment Freedom Fighter* (Oak Park, Ill.: Marion Street Press, 2008), 65.
49. Dorothy Jurney, "Talk at Carolina Symposium," 4, Papers of Dorothy Jurney, National Women and Media Collection, State Historical Society of Missouri.
50. Edee Greene, "Fidel's Frolicking to Rock 'n Roll Beat," *Fort Lauderdale News*, September 21, 1960.
51. Lois Hagen, "New Group to Defend Rights of Children," *Milwaukee Journal*, July 27, 1971.
52. Drue Lytle letter to Paul Myhre, February 8, 1963, Papers of the Penney-Missouri Awards, National Women and Media Collection, State Historical Society of Missouri.
53. Author's phone interview with Zulay Domínguez Chirinos, August 15, 2007.
54. Edee Greene letter to Paul Myhre, 1967, Papers of the Penney-Missouri Awards, National Women and Media Collection, State Historical Society of Missouri.
55. "Our History," Wisconsin Women's Network, accessed June 27, 2018, http://www.wiwomensnetwork.org/.
56. Marian McBride, *Wisconsin Women: Know Your Rights* (Milwaukee, Wisconsin: *Milwaukee Sentinel*, 1968).
57. Ibid.
58. Pat Hunter, "'No fault' divorce – It Still Isn't Easier," *Honolulu Advertiser*, April 7, 1975.
59. Pat Hunter, "'Financial Results in a Divorced Can Be a Disaster," *Honolulu Advertiser*, April 8, 1975.
60. Calvin G.C. Pang, "Slow-Baked, Flash-Fried, Not to be Devoured: Development of the Partnership Model of Property Division in Hawaii and Beyond," *University of Hawaii Law Review*, 1998.
61. Marjorie Paxson, "Women in Journalism Oral History Project," Washington Press Club Foundation, transcript, Session 4, 106.
62. Dorothy Jurney, "Remarks of Dorothy Jurney," Associated Press Managing Editors Annual Convention, November 17, 1960, 4.
63. Gloria Biggs Biography, *Penney-Missouri Banquet Program*, n.d., Papers of Gloria Biggs, National Women and Media Collection, State Historical Society of Missouri.

64. Garrett D. Byrnes, *Newspapers in Fashion* (New York: Columbia University Press, 1951), 1.
65. Dorothy Jurney to Paul Myhre, February 9, 1965, Papers of the Penney-Missouri Awards, National Women and Media Collection, State Historical Society of Missouri.
66. Kimberly Wilmot Voss, "Who's Wearing the Pants? How *The New York Times* Reported the Changing Dress of Women," *Media Report to Women*, Spring 2011.
67. Elizabeth Cline, *Overdressed: The Shockingly High Cost of Cheap Fashion* (New York: Portfolio, 2012).
68. Gail Sheehy, *Daring: My Passages, A Memoir* (New York: William Murrow, 2014).
69. Bill Blass, *Bare Blass* (New York: Harper Collins, 2002).
70. "Eleni Epstein Knows Who She is, Honey," *Washington Times*, November 16, 1983.
71. Katherine C. Grier, "Review of Fashion, Culture, and Identity by Fred Davis," *Winterthur Portfolio* 28, no. 1 (Spring 1993): 104.
72. Teri Agins, *The End of Fashion: How Marketing Changed the Clothing Business* (New York: William Morrow, 1999), 7.
73. Beverley Morales letter to Paul Myhre, June 15, 1961, Papers of the Penney-Missouri Awards, Western Historical Manuscript Collection, University of Missouri.
74. Marjorie Paxson, "Penney-Missouri Awards Banquet," University of Missouri, March 31, 1966, 5. Papers of the Penney-Missouri Awards, National Women and Media Collection, State Historical Society of Missouri.
75. Grace Whipple, "Pamper Us, Beg Yarns," *Fort Lauderdale News*, September 19, 1961.
76. Pat Palmer, "She Sells Only Bargains," *Fort Lauderdale News*, September 18, 1961.
77. Eleanor Ratelle, "Young Miami Designers," *Miami Herald*, May 20, 1963.
78. Herald wire service, "St. Laurent to Show After All," *Miami Herald*, 1965.
79. Linda M. Scott, *Fresh Lipstick: Redressing Fashion and Feminism* (New York: Palgrave Macmillan, 2005), 166.
80. Robert Wells, *The Milwaukee Journal: An Informal Chronicle of Its First 100 Years* (Milwaukee, Wisconsin: Milwaukee Journal, 1981), 146.

81. Jo Werne Biography to Paul Myhre, 3, Papers of the Penney-Missouri Awards, National Women and Media Collection, State Historical Society of Missouri.
82. Chris Porterfield, "Practicality, Significance Prevail Over Less Urgent, Familiar Ideas," *Penney Press*, March 1973, 6.
83. "Who's Wearing the Pants Now?" (Long Beach) *California Independent*, January 13, 1969.
84. "Union Fights for Pants suits," *Placement & the Personnel Marketplace*, November 23, 1970, 10.
85. Paxson, "Women in Journalism," Session 4, 118.
86. Ibid.
87. Ibid.
88. Paxson, "Women in Journalism," Session 5, 120.
89. Bobbi McCallum, "Seal'd for Delivery," *Seattle Post-Intelligencer*, July 25, 1968.
90. Ibid.
91. Wells, *Milwaukee Journal*, 224.
92. Jacquelyn Gray, "Journal Got a Quick Start on Fashion," *The Milwaukee Journal*, March 31, 1995.
93. Drue Lytle letter to Paul Myhre, March 4, 1967, Papers of the Penney-Missouri Awards, National Women and Media Collection, State Historical Society of Missouri.
94. Drue Lytle, "Fashion Group Presents Couture Internationale," *Honolulu Advertiser*, December 9, 1963.
95. Drue Lytle, "Swimwear Named For Duke," *Honolulu Advertiser*, August 23, 1961.
96. Doug Brown, "Haute Cuisine," *American Journalism Review*, February/March 2004.
97. Governor Kim Sigler speech to Michigan Federation of Women's Clubs, November 15, 1947, 1, Papers of Kim Sigler, Bentley Library, University of Michigan.
98. Sigler, speech, 4.
99. Kimberly Wilmot Voss, *The Food Section: Newspaper Women and the Culinary Community* (Lanham, Maryland: Rowman and Littlefield, 2014).
100. "Journal Wins Award at Food Conference," *Milwaukee Journal*, September 28, 1969.

101. "Vesta Award to Journal Food Writer," *Milwaukee Journal*, September 24, 1965.
102. Laura Crooks, "Our Very Own Kitchen Queen," *Spokesman-Review*, October 19, 2005.
103. "Reader Memories: Nobody Compares to Dorothy Dean," *Spokesman-Review*, October 20, 2010.
104. Nancy Leson, "Recipe Box: Seattle Newspapers Have Historic Perspective," *Seattle Times*, October 18, 2011.
105. Carole Beers, "Marion Ferriss Guinn, 85, was 'Dorothy Neighbors' at *Times*," *Seattle Times*, January 28, 1994, http://community.seattletimes.nwsource.com/archive/?date=19940128&slug=1891967.
106. Sharon Boswell and Lorraine McConaghy, "Homeward Bound," *Seattle Times*, June 2, 1996.
107. Edee Greene to Paul Myhre, September 15, 1970, Papers of Penney-Missouri Awards, National Women and Media Collection, State Historical Society of Missouri.
108. Susan Strasser, *Never Done: A History of American Housework* (New York: Random House, 1982), 283.
109. Dorothy Jurney, "Remarks by Dorothy Jurney," The Associated Press Managing Editors Convention, Williamsburg Virginia, November 17, 1960, Papers of the Penney-Missouri Awards, National Women and Media Collection, State Historical Society of Missouri.
110. Elaine Tyler May, *Homeward Bound: American Families in the Cold War Era* (New York: HarperCollins Publishers, 1988), 164.
111. "Dorothy Dawe, Writer, Dead," *Milwaukee Journal*, October 4, 1947.
112. Wells, *Milwaukee Journal*, 341.
113. "Former Editor Tells Dorothy Dawe Story," *Milwaukee Journal*, January 11, 1972.
114. Dorothy Dawe, "What's to Come in Lighting Shown in New York Exhibit," *Milwaukee Journal*, December 13, 1945.
115. Dorothy Dawe, "Story of a Typical Milwaukee Bungalow Changed into Appealing Modern Home," *Milwaukee Journal*, November 10, 1946.
116. Dorothy Dawe, "There's Hope of New Accessories, Metal Pieces," *Milwaukee Journal*, January 13, 1946.
117. "Dorothy Dawe Press Award," *Milwaukee Journal*, January 3, 1949.
118. Lois Hagen, "Brussel's World Fair Through American Eyes," *Milwaukee Journal*, June 5, 1958.

119. Lois Hagen, “Cream of Home Furnishings,” *Milwaukee Journal*, January 20, 1950.
120. Lois Hagen, “Ignorance Makes ‘Contemporary’ A Bad Word,” *Milwaukee Journal*, June 16, 1958.
121. Lois Hagen, “James River Plantations,” *Milwaukee Journal*, May 11, 1965.
122. Dorothy Jurney, “Remarks of Dorothy Jurney,” Associated Press Managing Editors Annual Convention, November 17, 1960, 5.
123. “She’s a Designing Woman,” *Tallahassee Democrat*, September 12, 1965.
124. Martha Griffiths letter to Catherine Dutch, October 10, 1972, Papers of Martha Griffiths, Bentley Historical Library, University of Michigan.

5

Women's Pages Cover Another F

The women's pages of newspapers have been long defined as the four Fs—family, fashion, food, and furnishings—as detailed in the previous chapter. While these topics were often reduced to "fluff" in the eyes of critics, they certainly were areas that touched the everyday lives of readers. The women's pages and the women who ran them also began to grapple with another F—feminism—that was confronting society. The fight for women's liberation had been around for generations. The dismissive coverage of the women's movement on the front pages of newspapers since its inception with the convention at Seneca Falls in 1848 through the efforts to pass the ERA in the 1970s has been well-documented.[1] Women's liberation leaders often turned to creating their own publications to reach receptive females audiences, ranging from Susan B. Anthony and Elizabeth Cady Stanton's more radical *The Revolution* to Lucy Stone's moderate-leaning *Women's Journal*.[2] Unfortunately, the suffrage press had minimal effect in reaching mass audiences with most only reaching a few hundred readers.[3] The women's sections of the nation's metropolitan newspapers, on the other hand, became the one place where women could find news about women's issues. And even if those sections didn't act as lightning rods for activism, they at least weren't addressing them derisively. More effectively, it could be argued, they were a place for a more nuanced dialogue and exploration.

K. W. Voss, *Re-Evaluating Women's Page Journalism in the Post-World War II Era*,
https://doi.org/10.1007/978-3-319-96214-6_5

Feminism as a Process

The label "feminist" was a loaded one for some people. Many women were most familiar with the concept by media representations that were rather extreme. It took time for even forward-thinking people to understand women's liberation. As an example, journalist Bill Moyers was a guest speaker at the 1971 Penney-Missouri workshops and began his speech by announcing that he was a newly recruited member of the movement. He told of his conversion after a conversation with his nine-year-old daughter. She said that she wanted to be a nurse when she grew up. When asked why she did not aspire to be a doctor, she replied: "Oh, Daddy, don't be silly. I'm a girl." It led Moyers to ponder: "I know there are thousands of women who are doctors. But what invisible inheritance in our society has been working upon the consciousness of a nine-year-old girl to cause her to see her potential as limited by the accident of being a female child."[4]

The use of the terms "women's libber" or feminism as part of self-identification was a difficult one for some women—despite the fact that their actions would have put them in that category. Susan Douglas has written that the media's representation has "turned feminism into a dirty word, but they also made feminism inevitable."[5] The mediated concept of feminism was not one that some women's page editors were particularly ready to embrace. For example, in her later years, Edee Greene said, "I've been described as a women's libber. I don't think I am."[6] She was likely objecting to some of the methods and images associated with the women's movement. Greene's work and impact, however, fit many of the goals of the women's movement, as did her own philosophy. Greene was known for collecting giraffe figures, making the comparison that "you have to stick your neck out to accomplish anything."[7]

Another women's page editor who wrestled with the association to feminism was Gloria Biggs. She was the women's page editor at the *St. Petersburg Times* when she was tapped to oversee the women's section of the new Gannett newspaper, *TODAY*, in Cocoa in 1966. The following year, she gave a speech to Gannett editors that was also published in the Gannett newsletter on how to attract female readers. It was rather stereotypical advice as she recommended that content should be centered on information, appearance, people, and emotion. She concluded with, "I'd like to emphasize that I'm not a feminist. … I'm happy to have men run the show." Years later, she wrote a note on that speech to a friend: "I weep when I read the lines about not being a feminist but then realize that in 1968 that's the way it was and the way I thought I was supposed to say I was!"[8]

Part of the conflicting feelings about the term may have been about the good and bad of Betty Friedan. The outspoken feminist undoubtedly changed American society. Her activism was vast—from her book *The Feminine Mystique* to the creation to the National Organization for Women to her regular voice speaking out for women's causes. Yet, she could be brash and, at times, her style offended others. Friedan, whose mother had been a women's page editor in Peoria, Illinois, was a regular speaker in Florida in the 1960s and 1970s. Marie Anderson, who self-identified as a feminist, wrote on August 22, 1969: "And there are not too many women who will put up the good fight. And most of them get lumped under Betty Friedan's umbrella, which is unfortunate."[9] Yet, someone had to be the media face of the movement. As Anderson went on to write: "Then there are those who don't want to fight. That's all right, too, I guess, but I can't imagine why someone wouldn't want to be considered a person even if she didn't want to do anything all day but dust the figurines and thaw the frozen dinner."[10]

The book certainly moved many people, but the fact was that society was going to be slower to change. And while Anderson was clearly a feminist, it does not mean that the content of her section always reflected that. An example can be found in a series in spring 1970 called "How to Get a Teenage Boy." The reporter, Ellen Peck, instructs young women to promote their femininity and hide their intelligence. The series got at least one angry letter from a reader—addressed to "Dear Sirs." Ann E. Heffernan wrote:

> Now really, isn't it about time we stopped feeding this propaganda to our kids? What is wrong with our society that men are so unsure of themselves that they must be raised from the cradle on daily portions of ego building? Why can't our girls be natural, and happy with what they have to offer?[11]

Anderson responded to Heffernan by letter about two weeks later. She wrote: "I ruefully admit that I agree with you. The series was highly recommended and I did not take the time to read it myself. This was my error and I apologize."[12] Heffernan noted in her letter that she would likely be dismissed as a "weirdo feminist."[13] Likely the term's "weirdo" association meant that women avoided it while still taking part in feminist campaigns.

The above example does not mean to imply that Anderson tended to ignore or shy away from content that would be considered friendly to the women's movement. On the contrary, she wrote a weekly column called "Monday Musings" in which she frequently addressed issues such as gender discrimination. In a 1964 column, she addressed the need for women in management: "A female company manager might not be as laughable as it sounds. You can't deter a dedicated woman and the company might gallantly show her more respect than they've customarily shown."[14] She questioned the sexist advertising of airlines: "Airlines need a male equivalent of those bunnies they carry if they want to cater to their growing female passenger trade."[15] She wrote about birth control in 1966: "If there were fewer unwanted babies who get a bad start in life, we might not have so many grown-ups who come to a bad end."[16]

A 1970 column addressed the case of jockey Barbara Jo Rubin. The young woman had been banned from her position in South Florida due to her gender after the male jockeys had threatened to strike. She later went on to win her first race in Charles Town, West Virginia. Anderson wrote, "If Jockey Barbara Jo had been a Latin, Jew or black, it is doubtful that she would have been deprived of her right to work. But she was just a woman."[17] It turned out that the jockey was Jewish, and a reader chastised Anderson for not double-checking this fact and accusing her of spreading hate.[18] Anderson responded:

> I am highly in favor of eliminating all bigotry and discrimination—against Latins, Jews, blacks, Catholics, Poles and anybody else, including women. My point was that most of the others mentioned have been fighting this discrimination for years and through organization have managed to eliminate much of it, not all. Women, however, until just recently have not been organized to fight this discrimination, hence Barbara Jo had no one to help her fight her battle.[19]

Phoenix and Los Angeles women's page editor Maggie Savoy was an outspoken feminist who sought to explain women's issues in a media environment that was often hostile to the message. Her method of defining a woman's right for equality was a complex one—changing based on the audience. In her newspaper column, Savoy wrote about the need for gender equality and for the end to negative liberation stereotypes. She also wrote about how she explained women's liberation to men:

> Depending on the inquisitor I answer variously. If he's intellectual, I remind him: 'Our brains weigh the same; it's our paychecks that are slim and unladylike.' If he's a politician, I simply remind him: 'We outnumber you.' If he said—and some still do—'Women's place is in the home,' I brighten. 'It's so wonderful we want to share it. Here's my dishrag.'[20]

Feminism and Family

Women's lives outside of the home were often a complicated topic for journalists to cover. As early as 1914, an announcement for a meeting included the headline: "What is Feminism? Come and find out."[21] Historian Nancy Cott has noted that in its early American use, the word "feminism" had a shock value. In the early years, those who considered themselves feminists were looking for more than just the right to vote—they wanted equality in numerous areas. Cott noted that a speaker at the time said "all feminist were suffragists, but not all suffragettes are feminists."[22] By 1920, women had the right to vote. The fight for more rights for women would ebb and flow in the ensuing decades. By 1960, the word "feminism" was being used again.

The 1960s media's representation of feminism often labeled activists as "anti-family." This had to be jarring for women who saw themselves as mothers and believers in women's rights. For example, Miami women's page journalist Helen Muir had a substantial newspaper career before she left to have her daughter Mary. Fourteen months after the birth, the *Miami News* asked her to write a column. When she told her mother-in-law about her job offer, the response was "Oh, it would kill Bill." The reason, her mother-in-law believed, was that her son might think he was unable to support his family by himself. When Muir asked her husband if that was the case, he said, "Hell, no." Muir took on the column.[23]

These women were learning to negotiate a new place in society and had few role models. They were not necessarily leaving the workforce after marrying and if they did, they were likely to return after their children went to school. According to Elaine Tyler May:

> Less noted but equally significant, the men and women who formed families between 1940 and 1960 also reduced the divorce rate after a postwar peak. Marriages forged in the late 1940s were particularly stable. Even those couples who eventually divorced remained together long enough to prevent the divorce rate from rising until the mid-1960s. Contrary to fears of observers at the time, the role of breadwinner and homemaker were not abandoned; they were embraced.[24]

The role of homemaker has been overly simplified in many popular culture references, as represented by the high-heel wearing, pearl accessorized June Cleaver on the television show *Leave It to Beaver*. The show, which ran from 1957 to 1963, helped to shape the image of middle-class America. These images do not represent the complex role of taking care of the home that home economists had developed over the decades. Women's page editors would have appreciated the work of homemaking—their sections featured articles about easing the work, and advertisers featured products to make their lives easier. Several editors were trying to balance work and family—Edee Greene and Beverley Morales had children, for example. Many of the women also employed housekeepers—so they would have seen housework as a job. Muir noted that her housekeeper was with her family for two decades.[25] In Miami, Dorothy Jurney included news of her housekeeper, Katherine Johnson, in the annual "Jurneys' Jurnal," which was sent to friends and family at Christmas. She wrote of spending Thanksgiving with Johnson:

> Katherine has been an important part of the Jurneys' household since Spring. She sees to it that household chores are dispatched in a most efficient manner. It is her easy manner, thoughtful ways and good cooking which make for gracious living in the household.[26]

The easing of household work, whether due to housekeepers or appliances, allowed more women to get out of the home. Women's page journalists took notice and told the stories of women's activities. This was represented by a 1963 *Miami News* profile of Flora Supworth, a mother of two teenagers who at 40 years old was graduating from college. While the story, written by Billie O'Day, quickly mentions that Supworth was a wife and mother, the main focus was her achievements. She had decided to finish her degree after deciding she wanted to help teens in a local detention center. Supworth was quoted as saying:

> I'm not knocking organizational work—it's creative, too. And women in organizations accomplish plenty. But the higher you go in work like that, the further you're removed from the work. You end up sitting at head tables with a hat on your head. That's not for me.[27]

Beginning of Social Change

In the late 1960s, *Louisville Courier-Journal* women's page editor Carol Sutton said that her supervising editors did not challenge her changes to the section's content, although "sometimes I'd see an eyebrow arched."[28] It was the beginning of the women's liberation movement and the students on the local college campuses were becoming active. Sutton sent reporters to cover those activities and did a lengthy story about the women's movement to lead the front of her section. A male editor asked her if she was not overplaying the story. Sutton responded: "No, I think we're on the threshold of the largest social change you'll ever see in this country." He looked back startled and said "O.K."[29]

A criticism of the first and second waves of the women's movements was the focus on white, middle-class women. While that is a valid criticism, there are numerous examples of women's page coverage that included working-class women and women of color. In a 1958 *Miami Herald* women's page series, Roberta Applegate wrote a series on young Miami families and featured junior executives and hotel workers.[30] The *Miami Herald's* 1962 women's page featured a series on families whose relatives were on trial in Communist Cuba. Another series that year featured leaders in the

Miami African-American community.[31] In a 1967 presentation to women's page journalists, Anderson told the audience to "de-emphasize society activities … and emphasize events and features of interest to the whole community."[32] In 1969, Florida *TODAY* featured a report about the thousands of hungry people in Brevard County. In reaction, Biggs organized a group called Stop Gap to help them. She was its first chairman and then a board member.[33]

Some of the most visible battles of the civil rights movement were sit-ins at lunch counters refusing to serve African Americans in 1960. After having been refused service at the lunch counter of a Woolworth's in Greensboro, North Carolina, African-American college student Joseph McNeill returned the next day with three classmates to sit at the counter until they were served. They were denied service. Soon more students, black and white, joined in the protest which led to an article in the *New York Times*. The sit-ins spread across the country to de-segregate lunch counters. They caused then-presidential candidate John F. Kennedy to send a telegram to the sit-in students in Atlanta stating, "They have shown that the new way for Americans to stand up for their rights is to sit down."[34]

While policies against racial segregation were changing, policies that excluded women—especially during lunch hour—were not being challenged. For example, in Friedan's meetings with her editor for *The Feminist Mystique*, she was removed from the male-only lunch room of the Plaza Hotel. By 1969, Friedan led a fight for women to eat lunch at the same New York restaurant. The fight to eat lunch at the Oak Room of the Plaza Hotel, which had a policy against women in the room from noon until 3 p.m., occurred on Abraham Lincoln's birthday. Numerous journalists covered the event. This did not mean that change was immediate. Note the 1971 policy for the Gulf + Western Industries (the future Viacom Company) Luncheon Club:

> The intention of the Gulf + Western Luncheon Club is to keep it as much as possible a men's eating club. Therefore, only when having lunch with outside parties, whose group may include a female executive, will women be considered acceptable as luncheon guests. Under no circumstances are members to invite their secretaries to lunch, and only senior executives may invite their wives, when and if such a situation is absolutely necessary. There will be no exceptions to the above.[35]

The women's page editors were aware of the inequities and, in Florida, some women were tired of being excluded from male-only lunches and clubs. In 1969 in Miami, Roxcy Bolton led the fight to allow women to eat lunch at Jordan Marsh and Burdine's.[36] At the time, a sign noted that the restaurant was "men only" during the lunch hour at Burdine's. Bolton protested the policy—an act that was covered by the *Miami Herald*. Her request, described as "friendly persuasion," led to the store taking the signs down but not changing the policy. The story led to a letter from a reader to the store, noting: "The 'men only' signs are, of course, an insult to the women making up the bulk of Burdine's customers. They are a further insult to the business woman who is in equal need of a place to take clients and meet associates for a quick lunch."[37]

In Fort Lauderdale, Greene and Virginia Shuman Young, the first female mayor of the city, fought against the proposed male-only policy for the Tower Club at the top of the Landmark Bank building. Greene said, "When we heard it was going to be a restaurant for men, we told the owner that if he tried it he'd have two grandmothers picketing on the sidewalk."[38] These women understood that it was their roles as grandmothers that gave them a certain amount of clout in taking a stand—maybe more than their roles as journalist and politician.

Covering Career-Minded Woman

While some of the women's page journalists struggled with embracing feminist terminology, few of them needed the women's liberation movement to enlighten them. They could easily cater to the women who stayed at home but also celebrate and champion those who left the house for paid work. While clearly there was home-based content, there were also stories about women who worked outside the home or volunteered. As early as the mid-1940s, the *Milwaukee Journal* women's section included a series of articles about working women called "proof of the pudding careers for women." The twelfth in the series, published in 1946, featured the story of Dr. Lois Brancel, a chiropodist—one who specializes in human feet—who was also a married mother of two boys.[39] Another 1946 article, the eighteenth in the series, profiled an occupational therapist,

Marjorie Taylor. She was quoted as saying, "The need for trained occupational therapists in both civilian and military institutions is greater today than at any time in the past, even though there have never been enough young women to fill the available positions."[40]

In 1947, the Milwaukee newspaper printed a booklet called *Career Women*.[41] It was a reprinting of a series of vocational articles that had previously run in the women's pages. Unlike the assumed history that encouraged most middle-class young women to stay at home, these articles encouraged young, educated women to find careers—including mothers. Among the suggested careers was news photography and included an interview with Barbara Horner, a photojournalist with the *Green Bay Press-Gazette*. Another suggestion was becoming a reporter with the warning, "The reporter must remain on the job while a story is breaking, even if that means missing a cocktail party or being late for a dinner date."[42] A final suggestion was to become a doctor with the headline, "Women Doctors Marry but Continue Practices, Too." In the article, it is noted that at the time, there were only eight female doctors in the state.[43]

Vivian Castleberry also was routinely featuring stories about working women in the women's section of the *Dallas Times Herald*. For example, she profiled a geologist who shared the same view on finding power in saying anything as long as she was ladylike. The story was centered on the Dallas woman's new position with the Deep Sea Drilling Project headquartered in California. Dr. Betty Lee Gealy was making what she considered a controversial move by leaving her husband behind—a Southern Methodist University professor—and taking their four children across the country. For her, it was a matter of using her skills and training. Castleberry quoted Gealy at length:

> I have never been able to find a career outlet in Dallas. I could have, you understand, if I had been willing to play the game by artificial rules that are set up. I could have affected the outward appearance. I could have worn the tweed skirts and the flat-heeled shoes and, maybe, even have kept my mouth shut. But I cannot deny my femininity. I like being a woman. This created a dichotomy. I am a woman in what has been a man's field. Nobody has suffered the bitter consequences of this more than I.[44]

Two years later, Castleberry wrote about Navy Captain Rita Lenihan who was visiting Dallas on a recruitment visit for the WAVES. She said, "All you have to do is tell a woman she's needed and she can't wait to fill that need." Castleberry outlined the discrimination Lenihan had experienced in her career. The officer had repeatedly applied to graduate school at Georgetown University but was rejected each time because of her gender. Eventually, she talked her way into a class.[45]

Castleberry assigned a reporter to profile a nun, Kay Poirot, who had recently left the sisterhood. After serving from 1953 to 1968, she left and married a high school boyfriend. She had become a nun to make a difference but felt that she could do more outside of the church. "My problem was the frustration of knowing you can do so much more without the framework or system of the sisterhood," she said. "When you are a nun, you can get so involved in an institution like a school or a hospital that you never know what people's problems really are."[46]

The women's pages became particularly adept at writing stories about working women not as "firsts," but simply as women who held jobs outside of the home. One example can be found in a 1960s *Miami Herald* series on women who worked at Cape Canaveral. With the space race running on the front page of newspapers across the country, more attention was paid to Patrick Air Force base. For the women's pages, this would have been a natural way to find a female angle.

The five-part series featured the stories of four women who, Applegate wrote, "are working to unlock the secrets of space."[47] Eleanor Livingston was the deputy chief of the community relations branch. Prior to this position, Livingston was a medical and science writer in New York. (The article did point out she was married.)[48] The next article told the story of Dorothy Laidlaw, who had been a contract expert at the base for a decade. She was one of three women in this position. Applegate noted that Laidlaw was married and that her housework load was easier because they lived in a trailer.[49] The third woman was June Luther. She was a missile mathematician who worked in computer language.[50] The final story featured Ollie Porto, a secretary to the base manager. Her supervisor was quoted as saying: "Ollie is the catalyst that holds us together here. I don't know what we'd do without her."[51] Each of these women was recognized for their work—without focusing on the fact they were female.

The women's pages regularly featured stories about women with careers outside of the home—especially when the careers were non-traditional. In 1963, the *Fort Lauderdale News* featured a short article about a young woman who worked at a stable and it noted that it was an unusual occupation for a female.[52] In 1967, a profile in *TODAY* featured a woman who was a postal carrier.[53] A 1971 *Palm Beach Times* story profiled Eleanor Thorton, MD, an emergency room physician. With little chance of being accepted to medical school in the United States, she had gone to Germany to study because in that country one-third of the medial students were female.[54] A sidebar to that story, written by a male doctor, described the difficulties that women medical students faced in the United States due to the prejudice by male administrators. In comparison with other countries that had a significant percentage of women in their medical schools, only seven percent of the student body was female in the United States, the story said. Only South Vietnam, Madagascar, and Spain had a smaller proportion of women doctors. The writer cited a survey done of medical school deans and their attitudes toward female students. One dean quoted in the story said, "I just don't like women—as people or doctors—they belong at home cooking and cleaning, certainly not as medical colleagues."[55]

In Detroit, Jurney assigned a collection of stories about women and working conditions in the workplace.[56] The series included charts that documented pay inequities and the lack of women in management position. One of the stories addressed a General Motors program that encouraged women to enter male-dominated fields like engineering.[57] Several other stories pointed out that not all businesses welcomed policies that forced the hiring of women. One executive said, "We're being forced to play the number game with women."[58] Yet, the tone of the series was that the changes would occur so society needed to prepare for them. Reporter Helen Fogel wrote, "It is a fact that the women's movement and women's demands for equality, both of which seemed laughable to many a few short years ago, are laughable no longer."[59] A concluding story in the series addressed how businesses would react to more women in the workforce. Fogel wrote:

> It may take all of America's celebrated business and industrial know-how to implement a regulation that looks far into the future where traditional sex roles are erased, at least in the work world, and to implement it with today's women who grew up in a society that taught her success beyond her home is unfeminine.[60]

In Fort Lauderdale, Florida, some women journalists took a stand when the city advertised for a public relations position and specified that it must be a male. According to Marjorie Paxson, the reason was that a woman could not accompany the male city commissioners on civic trips. She said, "I don't know who they were more worried about—a woman or the city commissioners."[61] The local Theta Sigma Phi chapter went to speak to the city officials and the policy was changed. None of the women wanted the position—it was the principle. It was that kind of story that Paxson said the women's pages should cover. She used her position as a keynote speaker at a banquet of the 1966 Penney-Missouri Awards to spread this message:

> As women's editors, we have a lot of very precious white space at our disposal every day. It's time we started putting some hard news into that valuable space. It's time we accepted the responsibility of making our readers aware.[62]

Covering Reproductive Issues

If there was a topic of interest to women that wasn't being covered in the news sections of the newspapers around the country, it was women's reproductive rights. But before the concept of reproductive issues could become part of coverage in the women's pages, sex needed to be introduced. Women's page journalists were some of the first to begin the dialogue. This was at a time when Lucy and Dezi Arnez slept in separate beds on television and the use of the word "pregnant" on the air was prohibited, so Lucy was described as "expecting."

Miami Herald women's page editor Dorothy Jurney was encouraging women's page editors all over the country to cover sex in their sections. The concept of birth control was one that many women like Jurney had addressed in her own life. Jurney married engineer Frank Jurney in 1940 when she was 31 years old. Right before they married, Frank informed his future wife that he did not want her to work. She responded that she did not want any children and work was really more important to her than getting married.[63] Obviously, she must have used some form of birth control.

While Jurney encouraged reporters to use good taste in writing about the topic, she said her female readers appeared to be less "squeamish" than male readers. At the *Miami Herald*, she ran stories in the early 1950s on the Kinsey Report on sexuality and women, the largest study ever conducted on human sexual behavior. This would have been significant to her readers as it cleared up long-held myths about female frigidities. As *Time* magazine noted about US women, "They are by no means as frigid as they have been made out, and their sex lives often become more satisfactory with age." Until that study, psychiatrists and some gynecologists had estimated that between one-third and two-thirds of the American women were frigid.[64]

The *Miami Herald's* women's section also covered issues of childbirth, which won Penney-Missouri awards and again allowed Jurney to encourage other women's sections to follow suit with similar stories. Jurney was recognized for her photo package about Cesarean birth in 1958.[65] In 1963, Applegate also would be recognized for her story "How Sage Are Caesarian Births?" in the *Miami Herald*.[66]

Ann Landers's column regularly addressed sexual questions—so much so that in 1963 she had enough material for a book. She wrote that she got hundreds of letters each week from teens who were having sex. The book *Ann Landers Talks to Teen-Agers About Sex* often offered frank, progressive advice. For example,

> For too many years the subject of sex among teenagers was soft-pedaled. There was a widely held theory that frank discussion might excite undue curiosity. 'Don't give the kids ideas' is the way it was put. Well, the kids

> already have ideas, and many of them have put the ideas into practice. … I am a strong advocate of open discussion—and the more open the better.[67]

Marie Anderson also assigned stories about reproductive rights. A 1969 *Miami Herald* article detailed how the introduction of the birth control pill changed the way young people looked at contraception. Although the expert quoted described the University of Florida as being progressive because it no longer expelled pregnant students, the article also included information that upheld traditional values. The expert was quoted further as saying that if students who were not engaged and wanting birth control pills through the student health center, they had to get permission from their parents.[68] In an interesting anecdote, it also noted that pregnant students would no longer get kicked out of the dorms to serve as a cautionary tale. A physician from the student health center said, "If anything, it causes a strengthening of other girls' moral stand and gives them pause to think."[69]

By 1970, Katharine Stokes, a women's page journalist at the *Ft. Lauderdale News*, suggested several women's liberation friendly story topics that her newspaper had used. One was a three-part series on rape. The first installment featured the stories of rape victims, followed by interviews of convicted rapists in the second story. The final story in the series featured interviews with judges, doctors, and psychologists regarding rape laws. Another story was about the availability of birth control pills to single women. In the story, two female single reporters went to different doctors to investigate the availability and found it was easy to get. A third suggestion was a different take on reproductive options. She had compared a male having a vasectomy to a female having a sterilization operation. She interviewed a man who had a vasectomy about his experiences and also spoke with doctors and medical associations.[70]

A 1971 *Palm Beach Times* article took on the importance of the need and ability of nurses to distribute information about family planning and birth control to women in lower socioeconomic communities.[71] Also in 1971, Anderson was profiled by the national industry publication *Publishers' Auxiliary* in which she mentioned her support of "population control." The use of the term allowed the concept of birth control to be a patriotic issue rather than a women's issue.[72]

Some women's sections also addressed the abortion debate. It was at a time when the country was debating legislation involving abortion. In 1967, "unjustified abortion" was a felony in 17 states—including Florida. At this time, many Cuban refugee doctors who had been providing abortions in Havana were doing the same in Miami. According to a *Time* magazine article, approximately 30 abortion mills paid off officials and took in $20 million.[73] Anderson encouraged women's page journalists to tackle the topic in her 1970 talk at the Penney-Missouri workshop. "If we are producing unwanted babies, what about abortion?" she asked. "Legally women can dye their hair, bulge their busts or slice off their bosoms, but you can't tamper with the reproductive apparatus."[74]

Covering the ERA and Women's Equality

Social movement leaders need the media to spread their messages. The media, of course, frames the messages in ways that can reinforce the importance of that message or in ways that can dismiss that message. Numerous studies have looked at the intersection of the media and the women's liberation movement.[75] Most of these representations were negative. For example, in a study of the print media's framing of the women's movement from 1966 to 1986, researchers Laura Ashley and Beth Olson found that the coverage of feminists often delegitimized their goals. On the other hand, anti-feminists were described as well organized and attractive.[76]

Support for the legislation was complicated for some women. Marie Anderson, herself a wealthy woman and a former Junior League president, recalled trying to explain women's issues. She told a *Fort Lauderdale News* reporter, "I once asked some Junior League members their thoughts on the ERA. They felt it was a threat to their way of life. They have never come in contact with discrimination."[77] Yet, wealth did not necessarily protect women from being treated unfairly. For example, Rep. Martha Griffiths, who worked to get the ERA passed by Congress, wrote to a Miami woman explaining the difficulty of women to get credit. She wrote, "Some lenders will not permit a wife—regardless of her income—to open a charge account, borrow money, or buy a car in her own name."[78]

It was within this frame that the fight for the ERA was also presented in many states—including Florida. There were mediated protests, marches, and rallies. Celebrities made appearances. Each side organized by color—green for the pro-ERA group and red for those opposed. The media treated the assertions of each side equally and did not analyze the truth of the claims. In a talk to Knight Ridder newspaper executives, Jurney addressed the myths that poor reporting was perpetuating. She cited a newspaper article in which the reporter did not question a John Birch Society speaker about her statements against the ERA, asserting there was no inequality. For example, Jurney said, the speaker "fails to point out that there is a discriminatory practice applied against women who want to join the military. A woman has to be a high school graduate; a man does not; a woman has to score 40 points higher than a man in qualifying exams."[79]

As the women's liberation movement gained momentum, women's page editor Maggie Savoy became even more outspoken. In 1969, she wrote about the clichés that limited women's opportunities in a profile of Elizabeth Duncan Koontz, head of the women's bureau. For example, one was the view that a woman's place was in the home. Savoy quoted Koontz's response: "That's not where she is. Rising costs of living, rising rates of divorce, desertion, separation and widowhood put nearly half the women between 18 and 65 in the labor force and the percentage rises rapidly." Koontz went on to describe the need for work training for women: "A secretary makes $2.50 an hour. The girl who repairs the typewriter makes $8.50."[80] In another 1969 story, she mocked a chauvinist speaking at a fundraiser by listing direct quotes from his offensive talk. For example, he said, "I will gladly admit that women are superior to men, only to stop them from believing they are our equals."[81]

Through the year of 1970, Savoy regularly addressed the issues of the women's movement. In February of that year, Savoy wrote about a woman, Jo Ann Evans Gardner, who was active in NOW. Savoy quoted the psychologist Gardner: "I'm a fighter, an assertive female and that doesn't go over so well. When I suddenly realized I hadn't been assertive enough, I started picketing for women's liberation. And I've never been happier in my life."[82] In May of that year, she wrote another column explaining feminism: "Now, fellas, I know this whole lib thing comes as a shock. Who needs another revolution? This one for heaven's sakes, threatens apple pie. Don't worry, men. Apple pie will not disappear. You may have to bake it."[83]

In June 1970, Savoy again wrote about NOW noting that the organization had 90 chapters and 6000 members. The article was largely a profile about a San Francisco businesswoman Aileen Clarke Hernandez who was taking over the helm of NOW. She described the anger that women felt over inequities they suffered. Hernandez was quoted, "We want to free women from the bonds and stereotypes they're in so they can participate equally, if they chose, in business, government, institutions."[84] Later that month, Savoy wrote about women finally becoming members of the business organization Town Hall—a tradition that women had been fighting for 33 years. Savoy wrote: "The walls of Town Hall crumbled Monday—without a shot. That super-prestigious bastion of all-masculine intelligentsia integrated, as 15 members—all women—were ushered to the speaker's table."[85] At a meeting for a Phoenix Business Association during that same year she introduced herself as, "a bra-wearing, dues paying member of women's liberation," which was a movement that was "rational, sane, logical and overdue."[86] A colleague wrote of her: "Maggie really wanted to liberate. Not only women's liberation, which she supported with the rollicking zest of having long been liberated, but men's liberation, too."[87]

In a 1970 article Savoy wrote for the American Society of Newspaper Editors, she took editors to task for not fully explaining the issues central to the women's movement. She wrote: "Blunt fact: American women are second class citizens. They want a fair shot at the starting line. Like other minority groups—they are the fighting victims of stereotyping, myths, mis- and un-truths, attitudes, prejudices, chauvinism."[88] She challenged male editors to catch on to the issues. She asked them, "Do you duck the responsibility of helping your women's editor achieve excellence for her 51 percent of your readership? Or do you just listen to one, two or a dozen irate society women and sign, 'Don't rock the boat.'"[89] So outspoken was Savoy that when the feminist organization KNOW, Inc.[90] issued a short list of "Reporters You Can Trust," her name was on the list.[91] After her death in 1970, Associated Press reporter Kelly Tunney predicted, "I imagine her in the hereafter reminding St. Peter that women are equal spirits, that there should be more blacks in the heavenly chambers, that women should be allowed to wear pantsuits to prayer."[92]

Political spokesperson Liz Carpenter described Castleberry as the "godmother of the women's movement in Dallas."[93] Castleberry has said, "I was a feminist before there was such a thing,"[94] and "I entered the feminist movement before there was a feminist movement."[95] While other women's page editors were conflicted about the term, Castleberry embraced it and lived by its principles. She served as a mentor for other young women at the newspaper and in women's organizations. Longtime Dallas feminist Virginia Whitehill said Castleberry was one of the two most important women in Dallas.[96] Carpenter also said Castleberry was "beloved" in Dallas because "she made all the difference" as the "godmother of the women's movement in Dallas."[97]

In Seattle, women's page reporter Susan Paynter's covered reproductive issues, rape hotlines, and the ERA, all by focusing on the local YWCA, which later split off to become a women's health center. "I got so many stories out of that place. That's where I would go to report on so many issues. Or, I'd find people there." She also got contacts for her coverage for the ERA and other legislation aimed at equality for women. After her twelve-part series about the ERA ran in the newspaper, it was reprinted in a tabloid size. It was in such demand that it was reprinted three times. "Of course, I got letters saying that I should die, and I should burn in hell, and other people were lighting candles for my soul," she said. "I didn't get death threats that I remember, just people said that I should be dead."[98]

The women's page coverage of the ERA led to what was widely known in Seattle as the "Amazon memo." After women's page editor Sally Raleigh told managing editor Lou Guzzo that her section was going to run the ERA series, she was warned that there needed to address the potential significant downsides to the legislation. He said that he "really feared that there were some real risks to our society if women had equal rights because we could be 'creating a generation of Amazons.' Those were his words.

There could be no retreating. We'd be out there with our freedom, and what if we didn't like it? What if it destroyed families, and people didn't stay in family units and raise their children anymore?"[99] Paynter continued to write about women's issues, but not without its problems. She said in an oral history: "Out of all the years of writing such controversial things about gay marriage and gun control and abortion and job issues and violence and all the things I've written about, I never got so much angry mail as I got whenever I would write about women working versus women not working."[100]

Community Projects

Despite their typical mixed feelings about the term "feminist," there is little question that the work of the women's page journalists would fall under the umbrella of issues and projects that feminists were embracing. These women were keenly aware of social problems in their communities, and they frequently used their position to shine a light on the problem and, at times, worked at finding solutions.

In one example, the *Miami Herald's* women's page addressed the needs of widows in a 1959 six-part series written by Roberta Applegate. According to Census figures at the time, twelve percent of adult women were widowed, and the Florida retirements would have meant it was a good part of the readership. Applegate interviewed many widows and spoke with guidance counselors, and legal and sociology experts. Titled "What would you do if your husband died?" it was syndicated through United Features to women's pages across the country.[101]

In another example, Edee Greene establishing a domestic violence shelter for women. Greene, along with a group of others, established the shelter in a four-bedroom house in July 1974. Greene was spurred to further action after a woman came to the door with her children. She had been brutally beaten by her husband. Because the shelter was not then licensed, her children were put into foster care. The separation from her children was too much and she returned to her husband. A week later, he shot and killed her in front of their children. The tragedy led to a 62-bed emergency crisis center.[102]

Part of the catalyst for the shelter was a Fort Lauderdale task force, Community Service Council, headed by Greene. The committee did a survey of Florida courts to find out which judges addressed domestic violence. They found that it never happened. Said Greene, "It did not occur to them that these women were scared to death."[103] Today, the center is a prototype for domestic violence shelters across the country. Bonnie Flynn, who had headed the non-profit in later years, said of Greene, "I certainly consider her one of the most important supporters of women's advocacy and women's rights in the county."[104]

In the ensuing years, a more visible women's liberation movement would spread across the country and included Florida. One of the most visible women to lead the movement was Roxcy Bolton—a regular confidant of Marie Anderson at the *Miami Herald*. Bolton, at one point a national board member of NOW, advocated for numerous women's issues in the 1960s and early 1970s. She worked to open male-only lunch counters in Miami, established women's shelters and rape crisis centers, and passed better legislation in rape cases.[105] Bolton faced an uphill battle in gaining support for the ERA in Florida. After all, it took until 1969 for Florida to get around to ratifying the 19th Amendment, which had given women the right to vote in 1920. In recognition of the 30th anniversary, both houses finally symbolically ratified the amendment.[106] By the time the state would come to national attention for its battle to ratify the ERA, there were no longer women's pages to offer support, as will be addressed in the final chapter. The result was a very different representation of women's issue.

Take, for example, Elizabeth Whitney's *St. Petersburg Times* Sunday magazine piece in January 1969 called "The Status of the Sexes." She later recalled that her male editor did not want to run the essay but that his boss, Anne Rowe, overruled him.[107] It's difficult to image Rowe allowing the kind of coverage that appeared in a 1975 *St. Petersburg Times* story about a debate and parade in Tallahassee on the ERA. The story was written by a male reporter who observed in the story that ERA supporters wore "tiny ERA tee-shirts without bras." He also included this detail in the story, using an anonymous source: "'I usually don't like parades, but this one is okay,' said one spectator as the bra-less marchers passed by."[108]

Notes

1. Rodger Streitmatter, "Slowing the Momentum for Women's Rights," in *Mightier Than the Sword: How the News Media Have Shaped American History*, 4th ed. (Boulder, CO: Westview Press, 2016), 30–44.
2. Martha Solomon, ed., *A Voice of Their Own: The Woman Suffrage Press 1840–1910* (Tuscaloosa, AL: University of Alabama Press, 1991).
3. Streitmatter, "Slowing the Momentum," 39.
4. Bill Moyers, 1971 Penney-Missouri Magazine Awards Luncheon, November 3, 1971, New York, New York. Available in papers of James Cash Penney, Southern Methodist University, Dallas, Texas.
5. Susan Douglas, *Where the Girls Are: Growing Up Female With the Mass Media* (New York: Three Rivers Press, 1995 reprint), 10.
6. Deb Kollars, "Retirement to Punctuate Lifetime of Language," *Miami Herald*, June 1, 1986.
7. Ibid.
8. Gloria Biggs, "To Catch a Woman," Editorially Speaking, Gannet Group of Newspapers, Vol. 25, 1967, 21, Papers of Gloria Biggs, National Women and Media Collection, State Historical Society of Missouri.
9. Marie Anderson, "Letter to Elinor," August 22, 1969, Papers of Marie Anderson, National Women and Media Collection, State Historical Society of Missouri.
10. Ibid.
11. Ann E. Heffernan letter to the *Miami Herald*, April 8, 1970, Papers of Marie Anderson, National Women and Media Collection, State Historical Society of Missouri.
12. Marie Anderson letter to Ann E. Heffernan, April 17, 1970, Papers of Marie Anderson, National Women and Media Collection, State Historical Society of Missouri.
13. Ann E. Heffernan letter to the Miami Herald, April 8, 1970, Papers of Marie Anderson, National Women and Media Collection, State Historical Society of Missouri.
14. Marie Anderson, "Limb Limbo," *Miami Herald*, September 21, 1964, Papers of Marie Anderson, National Women and Media Collection, State Historical Society of Missouri.

15. Marie Anderson, "Look Ou-u-u-ut!" *Miami Herald*, October 31, 1966, Papers of Marie Anderson, National Women and Media Collection, State Historical Society of Missouri.
16. Marie Anderson, "It's a Sticky Situation," *Miami Herald*, August 22, 1966, Papers of Marie Anderson, National Women and Media Collection, State Historical Society of Missouri.
17. Marie Anderson, "Too Bad Jo's Just a Girl," *Miami Herald*, July 1970, Papers of Marie Anderson, National Women and Media Collection, State Historical Society of Missouri.
18. Mrs. L.V. Olson letter to Marie Anderson, July 15, 1970, Papers of Marie Anderson, National Women and Media Collection, State Historical Society of Missouri.
19. Marie Anderson letter to Mrs. L.V. Olson, July 27, 1970, Papers of Marie Anderson National Women and Media Collection, State Historical Society of Missouri.
20. Maggie Savoy, "Man's Primer to Womlib," *Los Angeles Times*, November 29, 1970; also in Jim Bellows, *The Last Editor: How I Saved the New York Times, the Washington Post, and the Los Angeles Times from Dullness and Complacency* (Kansas City, MO: Andrews McMeel, 2002), 110. This anecdote was repeated in Savoy, "Maggie Savoy: A Woman's Voice," *ASNE Bulletin*, November–December 1970, 8.
21. Nancy Cott, *The Grounding of Modern Feminism* (New Haven, CT: Yale University Press, 1987), 12.
22. Nancy Cott, *Grounding of Modern Feminism*, 15.
23. Helen Muir "oral history," Society of Women Geographers, Helen Muir Papers, University of Miami Special Collections, 8.
24. Elaine Tyler May, *Homeward Bound: American Families in the Cold War Era* (New York: Basic Books, 1988), 5.
25. Helen Muir, Alison Owen, ed., *Baby Grace Sees the Cow: A Memoir* (The Prologue Society, 2004), 82.
26. Dorothy and Frank Jurney, "Jurneys' Jurnal," Miami, Florida, December 25, 1955, Papers of Dorothy Jurney, National Women and Media Collection, State Historical Society of Missouri.
27. Billie O'Day, "Mom Will Wear the Cap and Gown," *Miami News*, May 19, 1963.
28. Interview with Carol Sutton, University of Louisville. Oral History Project, July 21, 1982, CD #1, Part 2.
29. Ibid.

30. "Herald's Women Writers Again Are Judged the Best," *Miami Herald*, September 14, 1958.
31. "Herald Women Earn Awards By the Dozen," *Miami Herald*, September 9, 1962.
32. "Penney-Missouri Workshop is Another Classic Event," *Southern Advertising and Publishing*, April 1967, 15–16.
33. "Gloria Biggs Named *Times* Publisher," (Cocoa, Florida) *Today*, March 1, 1973.
34. Juan Williams, *Eyes on the Prize: America's Civil Rights Years 1954–1965* (New York: Penguin, 1988), 135.
35. David N. Judelson memo to executives, July 13, 1971. Papers of Betty Friedan, carton 27, folder 720. Schlesinger Library.
36. Barbara J. Love, ed., *Feminists Who Changed America* (Urbana, IL: University of Illinois Press, 2006), 48.
37. "Rocxy Bolton, A Force for Equality," The Florida Memory Blog, State Library and Archives of Florida, http://www.floridamemory.com/blog/2018/03/28/roxcy-bolton-and-the-womens-movement-in-florida/.
38. Susan Gillis, *Fort Lauderdale: The Venice of America* (Charleston, SC: Arcadia Publishing, 2004), 135.
39. Clarice Rowlands, "Chiropodist Enjoys Life, Home, Work," *Milwaukee Journal*, March 17, 1946.
40. Clarice Rowlands, "Numerous Jobs Await All Graduate Therapists Now," *Milwaukee Journal*, April 21, 1946.
41. *Career Women: A Series of Vocational Articles* (Milwaukee, WI: Milwaukee Journal, 1947).
42. *Career Women*, 31.
43. *Career Women*, 72.
44. Vivian Castleberry, "New Address: Ocean Floor," *Dallas Times Herald*, October 31, 1967.
45. Vivian Castleberry, "Navy Ahoy," *Dallas Times Herald*, September 8, 1969.
46. Ann Worley, "Habit: Keeping House," *Dallas Times Herald*, May 17, 1970.
47. Roberta Applegate, "Care Canaveral: A New World," *Miami Herald*, July 3, 1960.
48. Roberta Applegate, "Ellie Knows Her Space Facts – From Monkeys to Catnip," *Miami Herald*, July 4, 1960.

49. Roberta Applegate, "Her Missile Base Work's a Huge 'Clean-Up' Chore," *Miami Herald*, July 5, 1960.
50. Roberta Applegate, "June Tells Missiles Where to Go," *Miami Herald*, July 6, 1960.
51. Roberta Applegate, "Ollie's a Housekeeper – for Cape Canaveral," *Miami Herald*, July 7, 1960.
52. Associated Press, "This Groom is a Girl in Stable Occupation," *Fort Lauderdale News*, May 24, 1963.
53. Sheila Clark, "Here Comes the Mailman – Only It Isn't a Male," (Cocoa, Florida) *TODAY*, February 26, 1967.
54. "At Age 35, She Decided to Go to Medical School," *Palm Beach Times*, September 21, 1971.
55. "Whether Men Like It or Not, More Women to Become M.D.s," *Palm Beach Times*, September 21, 1971.
56. Dorothy Jurney note, October 9, 1988, about *Detroit Free Press* order for stories. Papers of Dorothy Jurney, National Women and Media Collection, State Historical Society of Missouri.
57. Helen Fogel, "GM and Women Today," *Detroit Free Press*, April 1972.
58. Helen Fogel, "GM Executive Looks at the Impact of Women Workers," *Detroit Free Press*, April 1972.
59. Helen Fogel, "Putting New Rules into Effect," *Detroit Free Press*, April 1972.
60. Helen Fogel, "U.S. Industry, Women Head for New Era," *Detroit Free Press*, April 1972.
61. Talk by Marjorie Paxson, Penney-Missouri Awards Banquet, March 31, 1966, 4, Papers of the Penney-Missouri Awards, National Women and Media Collection, State Historical Society of Missouri.
62. Ibid.
63. Dorothy Jurney, "Women in Journalism Oral History Project," Washington Press Club Foundation, Session 1, 23.
64. "5,940 Women," *Time*, August 24, 1953.
65. "Herald's Women Writers Again are Judged the Best," *Miami Herald*, September 14, 1958.
66. "First Prize for Miss Applegate," (Lansing, Michigan) *State Journal*, September 26, 1963.
67. Ann Landers, *Ann Landers Talks to Teen-Agers About Sex* (Englewood Cliffs, NJ: Prentice-Hall, 1963), 28.

68. "Campus Attitudes on Student Sex Change," *Miami Herald*, July 13, 1969.
69. Ibid.
70. Katharine Stokes, "The Best Story Ideas, 1970," Penney-Missouri Awards Workshops, Papers of the Penney-Missouri Awards, National Women and Media Collection, State Historical Society of Missouri.
71. "There's More to Life Than Having Babies," *Palm Beach Times*, September 21, 1971.
72. Carl G. Miller, "Marie Anderson: Winning Awards Had Become a Habit," *Publishers' Auxiliary*, June 12, 1971, 11.
73. "The Desperate Dilemma of Abortion," *Time*, October 13, 1967, 4.
74. "Penney-Missouri Awards Tenth Anniversary, 1960–1970, program," Box 4, Papers of Marie Anderson, National Women and Media Collection, State Historical Society of Missouri.
75. See Patricia Bradley, *Mass Media and the Shaping of American Feminism*, 1963–1975 (University Press of Mississippi, 2003); Susan Brownmiller, *In Our Time: Memoir of a Revolution* (New York: Random House, 1999), 136–166; Laura Ashley and Beth Olson, "Constructing Reality: Print Media's Framing of the Women's Movement, 1966–1986," *Journalism and Mass Communications Quarterly*, Summer 1998: 263–277.
76. Ashley and Olson, "Constructing Reality," 263–277.
77. Susan Sachs, "Dean Sees Herself as Late Starter," *Fort Lauderdale News*, June 27, 1973.
78. Martha Griffiths letter to Catherine Dutch from Miami, Florida, October 10, 1972, Papers of Martha Griffiths, Bentley Historical Library, University of Michigan.
79. Dorothy Jurney, untitled talk to Knight Ridder newspaper executives, Point Clear, Alabama, 1976. Papers of Dorothy Jurney, National Women and Media Collection, State Historical Society of Missouri.
80. Maggie Savoy, "Woman Power Still in Fog Clichés," *Los Angeles Times*, November 24, 1969.
81. Maggie Savoy, "Marquis Mocks Feminine Mystique," *Los Angeles Times*, November 20, 1969.
82. Maggie Savoy, "Psychologist Wants Equal Status NOW," *Los Angeles Times*, February 22, 1970.
83. Maggie Savoy, "Women's Lib and Adam's Rib Face to Face," *Los Angeles Times*, May 17, 1970.

84. Maggie Savoy, "NOW Lib Group Leader Too Busy to Be Angry," *Los Angeles Times*, June 3, 1970.
85. Maggie Savoy, "Women Capture Town Hall Without Firing Shot," *Los Angeles Times*, June 10, 1970.
86. Maggie Savoy, "Untitled," in *Anyone Who Enters Here Must Celebrate Maggie*, ed. Jim Bellows (Los Angeles: Ward Ritchie Press, 1972), 91.
87. Ibid.
88. Savoy, "Maggie Savoy: A Woman's Voice," *ASNE Bulletin*, November–December 1970, 8.
89. Savoy, "A Woman's Voice," 11.
90. KNOW, Inc., was a feminist organization that owned its own press and would print women's liberation news. Judith Hole and Ellen Levine, *Rebirth of Feminism* (New York: The New York Times Book Co., 1971), 272.
91. KNOW, Inc. "Reporters You Can Trust," Papers of Catherine East, Box 16, folder 34, Schlesinger Library, Harvard University.
92. Kelly Tunney, "Untitled," in *Anyone Who Enters Here Must Celebrate Maggie*, ed. Jim Bellows (Los Angeles: Ward Ritchie Press, 1972), 31.
93. Vivian Castleberry, "Women in Journalism Oral History Project," Washington Press Club Foundation, Introduction, transcript, Session 1.
94. Vivian Castleberry, "Biographies of VFA Fabulous Feminists: Vivian Castleberry," Veteran Feminists of America, accessed May 10, 2018, http://www.veteranfeministsofamerica.org/stories/fabulous-feminist-bios/vivian-castleberry/.
95. Barbara J. Love, ed., *Feminists Who Changed America 1963–1975* (Chicago, IL: University of Illinois Press, 2006), 77.
96. Joyce Saenz Harris, "They Were There," *Dallas Morning News*, February 15, 2004.
97. Anne Kasper, Introduction, "Women in Journalism Oral History Project," Washington Press Club Foundation.
98. Susan Paynter oral history with Maria McLeod, "ERA Oral History Interview," Washington State Historical Society, transcript, May 22, 2008, 11, http://www.washingtonhistory.org/files/library/Paynter.pdf.
99. Paynter oral history, 13.
100. Paynter oral history, 21.
101. United Features Syndicate letter to editors, n.d., Papers of Roberta Applegate, National Women and Media Collection, State Historical Society of Missouri.

102. “Saving Lives … One at a Time,” Women in Distress of Broward County, 2003 Annual Report, http://www.womenindistress.org/Docs/02706AnnualReport.pdf.
103. Jennifer Ordonez, “For This Women’s Rights Pioneer, a Life of New Frontiers, Even at 80,” *Miami Herald*, November 14, 1993.
104. Ibid.
105. Love, *Feminists Who Changed*, 48.
106. “Better Late …” *Time*, June 6, 1969.
107. Elizabeth Whitney, “Swamp Sales to Out-of-Towners Was Story of a Lifetime,” *St. Petersburg Times*, February 18, 1990, 5.
108. Wire Reports, “2,000 Marchers Call on Senate to Approve ERA,” *St. Petersburg Times*, April 15, 1975.

6

Quilted News: Creating a New Definition of News

The newspaper industry has long given more value to hard news or what can be defined as news based on institutions in the public sphere, such as the government, economy, and law. In journalism history, these were topics outside the women's section—that's where soft news stories, or feature stories, were located. The difference had major implications within the industry. As media historian Kay Mills has written: "Hard news and soft news were by no means gender-free terms. Instead, they evoked rich gender implications."[1] Media researcher Zena Beth McGlashan has noted, "'important' reporting often has been considered as coverage of immediate, breaking and 'exciting' stories such as wars and riots, a definition of 'real' journalism too ingrained in our consciousnesses to be easily replaced."[2] Yet, much of the assumption of "hard news" as more important is a concept developed by the male-dominated industry. When it comes to readership surveys, results show that readers—especially women—like a mix of both kinds of news.

At the *Washington Post*, in the late 1940s and early 1950s, women's page editor Marie Sauer said she was trying to create a balance in her content for those who did not want to give up their wartime jobs and those who wanted to stay at home and "resented the belittling of their child-rearing role."[3] To do this, Sauer featured stories about activities and

K. W. Voss, *Re-Evaluating Women's Page Journalism in the Post-World War II Era*,
https://doi.org/10.1007/978-3-319-96214-6_6

interests for women such as sports, politics, and aviation that were not considered feminine. She also included the results of surveys that examined gender issues. A headline in the March 4, 1950, issue was "Women claim equal courage with men, survey discloses."[4] According to Sauer, "Even though at that time, they (women) weren't ready to be president, the most important issues to them were peace, budget balancing, honesty and efficiency in government, equal pay for equal work. … Hard news or soft news? I felt that women wanted both."[5]

Communication researchers have noted that soft news "does not necessitate timely publication and has a low level of substantive informational value (if at all), i.e. gossip, human interest stories, offbeat events."[6] This concept of hard versus vs. soft news has also been explored from the role of the journalist in defining what topics are newsworthy.[7] In addition, researchers have found that it is not just a topic that places it in a soft or hard category; the framing of the story—or how the story is told—should also be considered.[8]

Several communication scholars have noted the gender-based aspect of news—that hard news was significant while soft news was less important. The consensus was that women journalists were often limited to soft news while men reporters were geared toward the "more important" hard news.[9] In journalism history, these were topics outside the women's section where the supposed soft news, or feature stories, was located.

The baby boom and consumerism spurred an advertising explosion in the 1950s for newspapers, with much of that directed at appliance and home goods sales. That meant bigger women's sections with more room for women's news. Some of it was the traditional fare of the fours Fs—but there were also more substantial articles. For example, Marie Anderson and Dorothy Jurney ran progressive articles about political and social issues, features about professional women, and Eleanor Roosevelt's daily "My Day" column. They also were able to "have a good deal of impact by covering such issues as housing needs in the black community."[10] In the 1950s, they ran stories on opportunities for women workers,[11] problems facing widows, and foster care issues.[12]

Some critics have expressed their concerns over progressive news being located near recipes in this section,[13] feeling that it diminished women's issues. Anderson, however, was not bothered by this. This is likely because she saw these things as intertwined. The correspondence between Jurney and Anderson revealed these sensibilities, as they were prone to address job inequities for women followed by mentions of gardening and what dish had been recently served within the same letter.[14] In another letter, Jurney included a 1970 magazine advertisement for a resort. In the ad, a young couple stands in the water holding hands. His pants are rolled up and hers aren't. Jurney wrote to Anderson, "It's bad enough these people have to push sex at the exclusion of everything else but why do they have to have a pix where he has the sense to roll up his pants and she hasn't?"[15]

Mixing Soft and Hard News

The content of the women's pages frequently balanced these dueling but compatible ideas of news within these sections, both within and between stories. It was possible to have a story on beauty tips across from one on workplace discrimination, and it was also possible to profile a working mother, intertwining the challenges and rewards of motherhood with employment issues. The idea of having both is something that the industry overall has not embraced in the years after the end of the women's pages. There was a revival of the section in the 1990s—led in large part by the *Chicago Tribune*. A *New York Times* article noted that the revival of the sections "has helped to rekindle the old back-pages debate: Do women really need a separate press? Or shouldn't editors treat women as if 51 percent of the population were not a 'minority concern'?"[16] A reader responded in a way that many women's page editors would have appreciated. She noted that she was insulted that the section she enjoyed reading was considered the "ghetto." She concluded, "This female Harvard Law School-graduate, Columbia Ph.D-holding tenured professor in her mid-50's is interested in fashion and brides and recipes and all those bad old things."[17]

Former women's page editor Koky Dishon addressed the National Conference of Women's Editors in 1971 with the intent to point out shortcomings of the sections and to suggest changes. She criticized the emphasis on furnishings and fashions. "The mythical women at which this women's section is targeted at is really very easy to describe," Dishon said. "She fits the all-American dream which I and other women's editors should have challenged many years ago."[18] She also said that in order for change to be made, male editors needed to allow women editors more flexibility. She said, "After talking to so many women in the last couple of years at papers of all sizes, I believe that the majority of caretakers of these pages find themselves boxed in—trapped by a system that may have once suited them well but is no longer flexible enough to let them do a good job of newspapering."[19] She concluded by saying that the sections should not eliminate food, fashions, and furnishing stories but also cover current issues important to women.

A close read of the women's sections at papers across the country paint a broader portrait of news being presented to their readers. There were stories about family, food, fashion, and furnishings, but there were also stories about woman's equality, education, health, politics, race, and more. And it can be argued that even within the easily overlooked stories of society, gossip, or homemaking that the women's page reporters were giving their readers news that went beyond the conventional definitions of "soft news," even if it did not meet the traditional definitions of "hard news."

Society Coverage

For much of contemporary American journalism history, women's pages and society sections were often used interchangeably. While the society aspects were undoubtedly elitist, they did offer some journalistic lessons. As Dishon wrote, "As we wrote about weddings and births and debutante balls, we learned about the importance of rites and rituals in people's lives."[20] Edee Greene pointed out that writing up engagement and wedding announcements provided "invaluable training in accuracy."[21] For many young women, society writing was a foot in the door of a newspaper at a time when other sections were not hiring women.

For much of women's page history, society coverage was of the upper class, but it was beginning to change in the 1960s. In a 1964 *Editor & Publisher* feature on Marie Anderson, she said that women's sections were covering less society news and more hard news. She said, "We need to operate a little more like the city desk."[22] In a 1967 presentation also covered by *Editor & Publisher*, Anderson told women's page journalists to "de-emphasize society activities and emphasize events and features of interest to the whole community."[23] She said the trend in women's pages was to play down society news.[24]

Vivian Castleberry had been following that concept throughout the 1960s in Dallas. "I looked at society with a small 's' instead of a capital 'S' which didn't always please my bosses," she said.[25] She changed the definition of "society" to include "all humanity—the social structure of the community."[26] Castleberry worked to include parts of the community and topics that had been ignored in the past. She said: "I always felt more comfortable in the hovels of South Dallas and in West Dallas where there was only Spanish spoken … I don't understand Spanish, but I often felt more comfortable in that setting than I did in the glitzy Four Hundred kind of country club, Petroleum Club milieu."[27] When she did occasionally attend society events, her discomfort showed. At one party, her society editor approached her and told her to "Please wipe that expression off your face."[28]

Gossip Coverage

One of the most well-known gossip writers was Jeanette Walls. In a book about her career, Walls shared a story from 1968 in which Truman Capote had heard that former First Lady Jackie Kennedy was going to marry Aristotle Onassis. According to Walls, the *Washington Post* women's page journalist Maxine Cheshire actually had the story before Capote, but her editor Ben Bradlee instead stopped publication of the story. Cheshire recalled Bradlee saying: "I really don't believe she's going to do it. I don't believe she's going to do it."[29] Cheshire was known for her solid and timely reporting. She was the first to report that Kennedy was pregnant with John Jr. She also was the first to report that President Johnson rejected the portrait done by Peter Hurd. Chesire said, "We're expected to get scoops and not be scooped."[30]

Homemaking Columns

Many newspapers had a housekeeping column. The *Chicago Daily News* had a household hints column that led to a 1933 book. It began by thanking its readership: "This goes out with a vote of thanks to the thousands of housewives who graciously contributed their culinary and general household discoveries."[31] There were chapters about the kitchen, laundry, wardrobe, and sewing. The editors were expected to know a little of everything. Maude Coons, who started at the *Omaha World-Herald* as the household editor in 1936, answered between sixty and seventy-five questions from callers each day, she estimated. Sometimes the questions veered from fashion and food into other areas, as some callers "really were just lonely and wanted to talk."

Likely one of the most successful homemaking columns began at the *Honolulu Advertiser*, which eventually led to national syndication as "Hints from Heloise." During a Honolulu cocktail party, the column's eventual creator Eloise Cruz mentioned to guests that she wanted to start a newspaper column for housewives to exchange household hints. She got the idea from a group of friends who gathered regularly to discuss running their households more efficiently. When she first mentioned her idea at the party, a man laughed in response and made a bet that she could not get a newspaper job because she was "nothing but a housewife."

The next day she went to the offices of the *Honolulu Advertiser*. She persuaded the editor to try her column, then called "Readers' Exchange," for a 30-day period for no pay. Her first column appeared in February 1959. She worked on a card table in her bedroom and taught herself to type while going through stacks of mail, which she got a lot of from readers. When she offered a free pamphlet about how to do laundry, she received more than 100,000 requests. In 1960, Eloise changed the column's name from "Readers' Exchange" to "Hints from Heloise." She liked the alliteration and added an H to her own name. From then on, she was known only as Heloise.[32] Cruz's description of her column promoted it as advice for the "the everyday housewife with children, tired working mothers, office girls and those others who just never find the time to get everything done. You never will … don't think you can."[33]

Expanding the "Fs"

Dorothy Jurney said in a 1978 speech that the roles of wife and mother in the lives of women added to their journalistic abilities—allowing them to place more of an emphasis on human concerns. "These experiences do not rob an able woman journalist of traditional news concepts," she said. "Rather they add dimension. She sees news value in many areas that seldom occur to a man to be important."[34] Family—or more often mothering—was taken seriously in the women's pages.

They also covered different kinds of families. On Mother's Day in 1968, Kathryn Robinette assigned a story about foster mothers for the *Palm Beach Post-Times*. For the story, the reporter interviewed officials about the more than 200 foster children in the community and their needs. She also profiled three foster mothers and described their approaches to parenting. One mother said: "You can't holler and scold with children like these. I found it much easier to talk to them quietly and not be angry."[35]

There were several women's page editors who did not marry, including Marie Anderson, Billie O'Day, and Marjorie Paxson. They did add to conversations about relationships. In a speech to female high school students, Anderson said, "Marriage, of course, is a fine institution and I don't want to knock it but don't get upset if you don't make it."[36] In that same speech, she encouraged the students to develop their own skills—and be independent. "Don't go to college just to find a husband," she said. "Be selfish about it. Learn things for your own good … It's good insurance to be able to do something on your own."[37] Anderson had a community of friends she socialized with regularly. "I don't mind being alone," she said. "I have lots of friends I feel I can communicate with if I want to."[38] In her retirement, Anderson and Jurney went on trips to China, Egypt, and India.[39] Jurney often spent weeks in the winter with Anderson in Florida.[40] In 1979, the two friends took a three-week vacation to New Mexico and Nevada.[41]

Fashion journalism often revealed current social issues. For example, after a young boy was punished at his school for not cutting his hair—which violated a dress code—Houston fashion reporter Judy Lunn wrote a three-part series about dress codes. She began by looking at history and the restriction of Puritan dressing. "There's nothing new about dress codes," she wrote. Her story went on to address clothing and social class, historical dress, and social issues.[42] Another story addressed the five-year-old Houston boy and the school's decision to punish the child for having longer hair. His parents explained that he had a "mal-formed" head and thus longer hair prevented him from looking different from other children. The case went to court: *Billy Epperson v Pasadena School District.* The American Civil Liberties Union represented the family, although the lawyer admitted that the organization had not won a case regarding dress codes in the federal district. "They maintain schools have the right to make those decisions," he stated. However, the child was allowed back to school the following year when the court ruling came down in the summer.[43]

The coverage of food also addressed social issues. For example, Carol Sutton wrote about poverty for articles that ran beginning on Thanksgiving Day in 1972 for her Louisville newspaper. The series, "Hunger in Kentucky," chronicled four families struggling to feed their children.[44] It was illustrated with the photo of the inside of the empty refrigerator from an elderly woman's home. Sutton said at that point she felt empowered to stretch the content of her section.

Finally, furnishings coverage could also go beyond decorating trends or architecture. For example, a 1965 *Miami Herald* story addressed how to prepare a house for fumigation. Next to a photo of a house that had been invaded by termites under a nylon tent, the story listed the preparation needed before fumigation began. In the case of one of the reporter's sources, the family needed weeks of work—including removing 300 orchids. According to the article, this was a problem for thousands of Dade County families each year.[45]

Adding E for Education

One topic regularly in the women's pages was education. Sometimes it was due to reporting about PTA activities as noted in the coverage of club women. There were also numerous news stories and features about education. This was especially true in the *Fort Lauderdale News*, which included several school and educational policy stories. A 1961 *Fort Lauderdale News* story addressed the educational problems that children had when they had poor eyesight. According to the article, one in four children did poorly in school because they could not see the blackboard.[46] A 1963 story in the same newspaper addressed a program to make sure that children's speech skills were adequate. It was based on educational policy set by the state, as the news value.[47]

The value of the fine arts in schools was frequently highlighted. In a 1965 *Miami Herald* story, a music camp for high school was highlighted. The orchestra camp featured some famous conductors who were there to teach the students responsibility along with musical skills. One conductor lectured the students that one violin player does not make an orchestra but, as a group, the students can create a symphony.[48]

Adding H for Health

Health-related stories were commonly found in the women's section, especially topics that tended to make male reporters or editors uncomfortable, such as the pregnancy and birth control stories addressed in the previous chapter. In 1968, the *Miami Herald's* women's section included a series on menopause. The reporter focused on the physical changes a woman faces and on how these changes might impact a marriage. She concluded the series on a positive note: "This is the time to expand horizons—to take that trip, take that course, join that club, or even, for the woman, start that career she always wanted."[49]

In her first interview since leaving the White House, Dr. Janet Travell sat down with women's page journalist Vera Glaser. Travell was the first female White House physician, hired by President Kennedy, and she remained for the Johnson administration. The profile, which ran in 1965 in the *St. Petersburg Times*, did not focus on her gender but rather the work she did in the medical field. Glaser noted that Travell was hired because she was the only doctor who was able to ease the president's agonizing back pain. Glaser did not shy away from tough questions, asking the doctor about the president's assassination. She wrote of the doctor's response, "Let's skip that."[50]

Adding P for Politics

The women's pages also addressed political issues—especially if a "women's angle" could be found. A 1958 women's page article profiled Marion Martin, who was the nation's only woman commissioner of a state department of labor. She had been in that position in Maine for the past 11 years. She was in Miami to address the Florida Industrial Commission's Workmen's Compensation Conference. In the story, Roberta Applegate included a quote from Martin that may have spurred some women into action: "Labor-management relations after all are just human relations and the woman in the household is the one who resolved conflicts." The same techniques a woman uses to solve family quarrels are used in labor and management conflicts.[51]

A 1959 *Miami Herald* story featured the views of a Republican committee woman, Claire B. Williams, and her views on woman in politics. Williams, of St. Petersburg, said she was insulted by statements made by male politicians about the woman's vote. "As if we weren't human beings, too," she said. She was particularly irritated by the stereotype assigned to the woman voter. "It's insulting to women to say a candidate must have dimples and wavy hair to appeal to the women," she said. "We look for the same thing men do and so often we're better informed."

She also said that a woman was not ready to be president. Not for a stereotypical reason, but that the path to the presidency needs to be in place. She said that women would not be ready until there were more women in Congress and more women governors.[52] Several years later, the *Sun-Sentinel's* Beverley Morales addressed the stereotype of women voting for candidates based on their handsome appearances. She urged her female readers to use their political power. In her column, she wrote: "Women now hold the balance of voting power in Florida and in the nation. They outnumber men, 107,000 to 97,000 on Broward County's voter books, for example. ... They could change the face of the nation if they cared to."[53]

A 1964 *Miami Herald* story, edited by Anderson and Paxson, profiled five women who would play major roles at the upcoming Republican Convention. Although this story by the Associated Press addressed the hard work of the women, the writer also described the women as "good-looking," illustrating the mixed messages that the sections conveyed. While the story did not challenge the status quo, there was a recognition of inequality. For example, it included this line: "Since little girls rarely dream of growing up to be president—they know it's a waste of imagination, at least right now—they are taking on more important political jobs every year instead, to show they are here to stay."[54]

Another story in that same issue, a UPI wire story, profiled Katie Louchheim, the top-ranking woman in the State Department. She was known for taking new approaches to governmental programs. A colleague said: "Sometimes the State Department gets used to doing things a certain way. Then someone like Mrs. Louchheim walks in, does things a little differently, and injects new life into the job."[55]

In 1959, the *Miami Herald*'s women's section included a column by Vera Glaser about women and politics. She addressed the increasing role of women in elected positions and their role as voters in the 1960s. She wrote: "There will be a marked increase in the number of women serving in public office from city halls to the United States Congress. This trend can be seen from year to year now." She concluded by pointing out that by 1970, there will be more than five million more women of voting age than men.[56]

A 1965 article by Glaser ran in numerous Florida's women's pages, including the *St. Petersburg Times* and the *Miami Herald*, that profiled twelve female lawmakers. The story begins, "There are only a dozen lady members of the 89th Congress, but they're cooking up enough in their legislative skillets to make the nation healthy, wealthy and wise."[57] The story outlined the different policies that the women were championing including the nation's military and space projects.

There were also subtler examples of content addressing increased roles for women. A 1970 column in the Florida *TODAY* women's section addressed how local women felt about the Vietnam War and gave examples of residents who were writing to the president.[58] The women's columns were moving from traditional activities to those in the public sphere. These women may not have been career women, but neither were they prevented from having any voice outside of the home.

North Dakota women's page editor Doris Eastman went to the 1959 Columbia University seminar—like several of the top journalists of the time. It impacted the content of her section and focused more on politics. In her oral history, she said: "Before women started to get into politics in larger numbers, the women's desk at the *Forum* covered their activities, but we discovered them so completely, it was decided that they were getting put in with the rest of the politicians in the city and the state desks handled the stories."[59] She also covered the wives of politicians, including Mrs. Rockefeller and Mrs. Romney. Eastman said: "Mrs. Nixon was easy; I covered her three times, and she was gracious and talked about her family and life in the White House and rigors of the campaign, but she wouldn't discuss politics. Her quote was 'That's Dick's field.'"[60]

Adding R for Race

Prior to the civil rights movement, newspapers routinely ignored issues in the black community; instead the newspaper itself was segregated—news about the black community was found in the "black pages." (For many years, some newspapers had "black pages" just as they had "women's pages.") The *St. Petersburg Times* struggled with its decision to continue with the segregated section. Eventually, some more militant leaders in the black community called for an end to the section in St. Petersburg. Leaders of the National Association for the Advancement of Colored People came to the newspaper to argue against the elimination. The newspaper took the debate public. Letters came in overwhelmingly to kill the section, and it was eliminated in 1967.[61]

At the *St. Petersburg Times*, black brides were given the option of having their photo run in the women's pages or the black pages. Most brides chose the black page.[62] As mentioned in an earlier chapter, other newspapers typically did not include black brides until women's page editors fought for a policy change. That was not, however, the only occasion that the women's pages addressed the black community. Many, in fact, covered the black community to some degree.

In the 1950s, Jurney's section at the *Miami Herald* included stories about people and activities in the black community at a time when the main news section of the newspaper largely ignored issues affecting the African American community. For example, a story about the upgrading of housing in an African American community ran in the women's section, rather than the city section.[63] She said she attempted to cover the civil rights movement, but her hands were tied by management who did not want such news in her section, and she did not feel as though she could rebel.[64] She recalled: "I had grown up in a time when you called the boss Mister. Respect for the boss and his way of doing things. I worked for some men that I thought were not very smart and I resented that very much."[65]

In early 1962, Applegate wrote a series on African Americans in Miami that ran across the country. "I was frankly amazed that the reaction has been so one-sided: favorable," she wrote to her managing editor about the reaction she had received to the series.[66] She received one negative letter and no negative phone calls. She noted a local businesswoman said, "It was the most forward looking and helpful series she had read." Several others also noted how powerful the series was. She also mentioned one of the sources she had spoken to from the "Central Negro" district. He had been leery of the story but called her after it was published to tell her: "I really enjoyed it. You sure covered the waterfront."[67]

Maggie Savoy often addressed racism, sexism, and economic inequities. According to Reva Berger Tooley, whom Savoy handpicked to replace her as the *Arizona Republic's* women's page editor, Savoy pushed to get photos of black brides into the paper's society section. Tooley wrote: "It was a time when nobody talked of civil rights. Maggie fought there for women—not women Panthers or women Chicanos or women's rights—just women who were struggling to be just a little bit bigger than society wanted them to be."[68]

The Penney-Missouri Award workshops attendees had begun discussing improving the coverage of the black community in the 1960s. The 1968 workshops featured a speech by Ponchitta Pierce, a New York editor of *Ebony* magazine, in which she encouraged the women to consider black audiences and to feature more coverage of the black community. "Far too often the press acts and talks about Negroes as if Negroes do not read the newspapers or watch television, give birth, marry, die and go to PTA meetings," she said. "Some newspapers and stations are beginning to make efforts to fill this void but they have a long way to go."[69] Pierce later became a judge for the Penney-Missouri Awards.[70]

The national media began to cover the practice of segregation in the south following the 1954 Supreme Court ruling in *Brown v Board of Education* requiring the desegregation of schools. Litigation seeking the desegregation of schools in the Miami-Dade County was first filed in 1956. As a result, a law was passed that allowed parents to enroll their child in any school in the district as long as they provided the transportation. The first sign of integration was in September of 1959, when twenty-five black students began attending Orchard Villa Elementary School.

While schools were becoming integrated and laws provided for equality in employment, neighborhoods remained segregated. Miami was one city where this issue was coming to the forefront, and it was in the women's section that the newspaper found a way to involve readers. The women's section featured a column by local reporter Eleanor Hart called "Column with a Heart." She generally approached it as an advice column, taking letters from readers and addressing their questions and issues in the weekly column, using anonymous names for the letter writers.

By the summer of 1966, some readers were beginning to question neighborhood segregation and broached the topic with Hart. Letters began appearing in Column with a Heart on July 22, 1966, and Hart allowed the debate to continue until September 25, 1966, when she issued an editor's note to conclude the conversation. It began with a letter from Idealist. She was a white Miami resident who wrote that her religion advocated the support of civil rights. (The headline indicates the author is male, but Hart's notes confirm the letter writer was female.) She was in favor of integration and went to an integrated church. She was now moving to a new, segregated neighborhood and was considering selling her current house to a black couple. Her neighbors were angry about her decision. Idealist wrote:

> If a Negro family were to move next door to me, I'd welcome them, regardless of what these same friends would think. But the truth is, I will still be living in an un-integrated neighborhood, leaving behind me a lot of unhappy and angry people. Yet, if I refuse to sell to a Negro, I will be perpetrating the unreasonable, unjust system of segregation that exists in most of our city today. Please advise.[71]

Hart responded: "You can't 'please' all factions. Whatever your decision, someone will 'dissent.' Your dilemma is one that other residents in this area are facing. We welcome their comments." Letters poured in and resulted in five more columns about the topic.

A week later, Hart ran four letters in response—two in support of integration and two against. The first was from Caucasian Who Favors Integration, who noted that Idealist should sell her house to a family of good character regardless of skin color. Hart bolded the following from the letter:

> The reason so many people are against integration is that they are ignorant of the Negro. Should Idealist sell her house to a Negro family, I'm sure her neighbors will find that the Negro isn't as different from his white brother as the bigots, trouble-makers, etc. would have us believe.[72]

The next letter came from 16-year-old Tomorrow's Adult, who advised Idealist to sell her home to a black family. He or she wrote, "Maybe Idealist can open other people's closed doors." A third letter writer took the opposite approach, citing racial stereotypes. A fourth letter writer from Fort Pierce noted that the government could force integration in business and schools but that a home was a man's "castle." Be Considerate wrote: "Civil rights should not be taken from one race and given to another. That is intrusion of privacy and freedom."

A week later, on August 5, 1966, Hart's column included five letters that either opposed integrating neighborhoods or criticized Idealist. Two letter writers noted that Idealist should move into an all-black neighborhood if she believed in integration. Others wrote that it was natural for races to live separately. Bill from Miami wrote: "Our freedoms have been tragically breached. I believe zoning should be legal in building a neighborhood of a specific race if a majority so desires."[73]

The topic was again addressed two weeks later on August 19, 1966, with the publication of three letters. The first simply noted that an integrated Girl Scout troop felt comfortable throughout Miami as times were changing. The second letter addressed Idealist as well as other letters who had responded. She encouraged integration and wrote about the complexity of the process. The third writer was critical of integration and suggested that the black community did not want to end segregation.[74]

On September 11, 1966, Hart's column included two pro-integration letters from black writers. The first letter was from a retired Miami Air Force lieutenant colonel who had gone through problems buying a home when he lived in Syracuse, New York. He said the housing policies in Miami were too restrictive for black homebuyers. He wrote, "As long as the attitude exists that one Negro family in a white community is too many, so will the problems and potential problems." A second letter writer responded to the question over whether a "model colony" for the different races should exist, an issue raised earlier. He wrote, "When we learn to live together as Christians and friends, when we realize God made us all regardless of color, when we resolve to throw off the yoke of prejudice, ungodliness and selfishness, then we will be living in a 'model colony.'"[75]

The final column ran on September 25, 1966, and included six letters. Hart began by indicating that this would be the final column on the issue. The first letter noted that social class was also a form of segregation. A second went back to the original letter writer who felt swayed by friends. She noted, "To follow the crowd instead of one's conscience is what the masses of Germans did while Hitler exterminated millions of Jews." A third letter writer noted the difficulty of doing what is correct, in general terms. A fourth writer from Fort Lauderdale wrote that he or she believed in segregation. The final two letter writers were also against integration for no particular reason. The issue was clearly complex for the letter writers.[76]

Adding S for Sexism

While there were several men in journalism who supported the women's cause—some education was still needed in terms of equality. Take, for example, John S. Knight, editorial chairman of Knight Newspapers, headquartered in Miami. He had supported Jurney and then Anderson's work updating the women's page. Yet, he was not necessarily encouraging women's liberation. On April 15, 1970, Knight sent a letter to Vera Glaser. He thanked her for sending a copy of the President's task force on women's rights and responsibilities report. He promised to read the report "at the first opportunity."[77] Four days later, he penned an editorial. He wrote: "I have nothing against women's rights so long as its advocates stay out of the men's bar and don't clutter up the golf course on weekends."[78] In other words, as long as it did not impact his social life, liberation was fine.

The reason for the column was Betty Friedan's protest of the men-only Tiger Bay Club. He criticized her aggressive style, writing, "You girls should know that a man doesn't want to be driven, compelled or commanded to accept something he doesn't want to buy."[79] The column also noted that he promised to read *The Feminine Mystique*, which he described as "a highly touted discourse on why women must have their rights NOW."[80] It's worth noting that the book had been published seven years earlier and had been reviewed by the women's section of the *Miami Herald*.

Creating Quilted News

A review of the women's pages in the 1950s and 1960s revealed a mix of hard and soft news. They created a new kind of news within the social fabric of their communities—a kind of quilted news.[81] Quilts have become recognized as art—largely women's art—in recent decades. Some credit the counterculture's arts-and-crafts movement in the 1960s for the renewed attention to the craft. Others view the country's bicentennial celebration in 1976 as the spark for a renewed interest in quilts. From an artistic standpoint, the real status came when New York's Whitney Museum featured a quilt show in 1971.[82] The following explains the art of quilting: "In the production of cloth, the sense of personal creation and connection to one's production is so direct that the exploitation of this kind of work arouses one's personal core and powers of resistance all the more strongly."[83]

Jurney explained her approach to news in an article in the January 1956 American Society of Newspaper Editors' publication. She suggested that editors cover home and health stories from more of a hard news than a soft news perspective. She wrote that the home beat should be "no different fundamentally than the police beat."[84] She echoed her approach in a 1988 speech at the Penney-Missouri Winners' Banquet: "What is generally regarded as 'soft' news should be elevated in the editor's mind. What the community is talking about, thinking about is vital to readers. The story might not be an event that happened yesterday. It may be a lot more nebulous."[85]

Notes

1. Mei-ling Yang, "Women's Pages of the Washington Post and Gender Ideology in the Late 1940s and the 1950s" (master's thesis, University of Maryland, 1992), 51.
2. Zena Beth McGlashan, "Club 'Ladies' and Working 'Girls': Rheta Childe Dorr and the New York Evening Post," *Journalism History* 8, no. 1 (Spring 1981): 7.
3. Yang, "Women's Pages," 371.
4. Yang, "Women's Pages," 372.
5. Yang, "Women's Pages," 367.
6. Sam N. Lehman-Wilzig and Michal Seletzky, "Hard News, Soft News, 'General' News: The Necessity and the Utility of an Intermediate Classification," *Journalism* 11, no. 1 (2010): 38.
7. Gaye Tuchman, "Making News By Doing Works," *American Journal of Sociology* 79 no. 1: 110–131.
8. Carsten Reinemann, James Stanyer, Sebastian Scherr, and Guido Legnante, "Hard and Soft News: A Review of Concepts, Operationalization and Key Findings," *Journalism* 13, no. 2 (2012): 221–239.

9. Lehman-Wilzig and Seletzky, "Hard News, Soft News," 39. Dhyana Ziegler and Alisa White, "Women and Minorities on Network Television News: An Examination of Correspondents and Newsmakers," *Journal of Broadcasting & Electronic Media* 34, no. 2 (1990): 215–223. Catharine Lumby, "Feminism and the Media: The Biggest Fantasy of All," *Media Information Australia* 72 (1994): 49–54.
10. Cokie Roberts, *We Are Our Mothers' Daughters* (New York: Perennial, 2000), 114.
11. Letter from Harry Tyson, manager of the Florida State Employment Service, to Roberta Applegate, June 10, 1953, Papers of Roberta Applegate, National Women and Media Collection, State Historical Society of Missouri.
12. Letter from *Miami Herald's* Editor George Beebe to Laura Ross, undated, Papers of Roberta Applegate, National Women and Media Collection, State Historical Society of Missouri. In the letter, Beebe wrote how great these stories were.
13. Gaye Tuchman, *Making News* (New York: Free Press, 1978), 147; Susan Douglas, *Where the Girls Are: Growing Up Female With the Mass Media* (New York: Random House, 1995), 157.
14. Anderson's files include letters to and from Dorothy Jurney, as well as correspondence with other women's page editors.
15. Letter from Jurney to Anderson, 1970, Box 1, Papers of Marie Anderson, National Women and Media Collection, State Historical Society of Missouri.
16. Betsy Israel, "The Sexes: Pages of Their Own?" *New York Times*, October 3, 1993.
17. Janet Senderowitz Leongard, letter to the editor, "Embracing the Four Fs," *New York Times*, November 7, 1993.
18. Colleen Dishon, "The Tea Party Was Over a Long Time Ago; Please Take the Tea Cups Away," *What's Wrong With Women's Pages*, The University of Chicago Center for Policy Study, 1971, 17.
19. Dishon, "The Tea Party," 19.
20. Koky Dishon, "We've Come a Long Way – Maybe," *Media Studies Journal* 11 (1995): 95.
21. Edee Greene, "How to Hurdle Your Girdle Or: Sex and the City Room," Theta Sigma Phi Seminar, Cleveland, Ohio, August 24, 1963, 2.
22. Dick Sherry, "Women's Page Revolt: To the Classifieds!" *Editor & Publisher*, December 26, 1964.

23. "Penney-Missouri Workshop is Another Classic Event," *Southern Advertising and Publishing*, April 1967, 15–16.
24. Pam Hanlon, "Women's Rising Status Will Affect News Coverage," *Columbia Missourian*, March 17, 1967.
25. Vivian Castleberry, "Women in Journalism Oral History Project," Washington Press Club Foundation, Session 1, 60.
26. Castleberry, "Women in Journalism," 160.
27. Ibid.
28. Castleberry, "Women in Journalism," 162–163.
29. Jeannette Walls, *Dish* (New York: Perennial, 2000), 76.
30. "Pages for Women," *Time*, May 19, 1967.
31. *Household Hints* (Chicago: Chicago Daily News, 1933).
32. Jan Jarboe, "Heloise: Armed and Ingenious," *Chicago Tribune*, May 14, 1989.
33. Heloise Cruz, *Heloise's Housekeeping Hints* (New Jersey: Prentice-Hall, 1962), 7.
34. Dorothy Jurney, "Talk at Carolina Symposium," 4, Papers of Dorothy Jurney, National Women and Media Collection, State Historical Society of Missouri.
35. Kathryn Robinette, "Foster Mothers Fill Gap," *Palm Beach Post-Times*, May 12, 1968.
36. Marie Anderson, "Commencement Speech," 5, Papers of Marie Anderson, National Women and Media Collection, State Historical Society of Missouri.
37. Anderson, "Commencement Speech," 5.
38. Marie Anderson, "Women in Journalism Oral History Project," Washington Press Club Foundation, Session 1, 42.
39. Anderson, "Women in Journalism," 66.
40. Jurney wrote several letters to friends while staying at Anderson's home. Letter from Dorothy Jurney to Virginia Allen, February 25, 1980, Folder 5, New Direction for News, National Women and Media Collection, State Historical Society of Missouri; Letter from Dorothy Jurney to Virginia Allen, January 3, 1984, Folder 22, New Direction for News, National Women and Media Collection, State Historical Society of Missouri.
41. Letter from Dorothy Jurney to J. Edward Murray, August 20, 1979, Folder 2, Papers of Dorothy Jurney, National Women and Media Collection, State Historical Society of Missouri.

42. Judy Lunn, "Dressing by Codes," *Houston Post*, May 1, 1974.
43. Judy Lunn, "Even Though School Years Are Coming to an End, Dress Code Controversies Continue," *Houston Post*, May 8, 1974.
44. The "Hunger in Kentucky" series included: Irene Nolan, "First of the month means prosperity"; John Filiatreau, "Large Families Struggle to Feed the Children"; Irene Nolan, "$9 a week in food stamps is elderly woman's lifeline"; John Filiatreau, "Debts take a slice of mountain's food resources," *Courier-Journal*, November 23, 1297.
45. Martha Ingle, "Take Care When House Becomes a Tent," *Miami Herald*, July 28, 1965.
46. Grace Whipple, "Tell-Tale Symptoms Signal Poor Vision," *Fort Lauderdale News*, October 2, 1961.
47. Louise Dameron, "First Aid To Speech," *Fort Lauderdale News*, May 23, 1963.
48. Jo Werne, "Music Camp … as Home," *Miami Herald*, July 28, 1965.
49. Janet Chusmir, "Menopause: Confidence, Understanding a Must," *Miami Herald*, September 23, 1968.
50. Vera Glaser, "White House Doctor Packs Her Black Bag," *St. Petersburg Times*, May 2, 1965.
51. Roberta Applegate, "'Women Keep Peace at Home; They Can Do It in Industry," *Miami Herald*, October 31, 1958.
52. Roberta Applegate, "Dimples Don't Sway a Woman's Vote," *Miami Herald*, August 29, 1959.
53. Beverley Morales, "Candidate Use of Sex Appeal Woos Women," *Sun-Sentinel*, October 7, 1966.
54. Associated Press, "GOP? It Means Gals' Own Party," *Miami Herald*, June 18, 1964.
55. No byline, "What Katie Did – Use Imagination," *Miami Herald*, June 18, 1964.
56. Vera Glaser, "What America and American Can Expect in National Politics in the Coming Decade, 1960–1970," *Miami Herald*, 1959, Papers of Vera Glaser, Heritage Center, University of Wyoming.
57. Vera Glaser, "12 Who Skirt Laws," *Miami Herald*, January 31, 1965.
58. Amy Clark, "Another Note From President," (Cocoa, Florida) *Today*, June 7, 1970.
59. Doris Eastman interview with Janet Gallagher, April 10, 1985, Heritage Commission.
60. Ibid.

61. Robert N. Pierce, *A Sacred Trust: Nelson Poynter and the St. Petersburg Times* (Gainesville, FL: University Press of Florida, 1993), 244.
62. Ibid.
63. Dorothy Jurney, "Women in Journalism Oral History Project," Washington Press Club Foundation, Session 4, 127.
64. Jurney, "Women in Journalism," Session 1, 49.
65. Jurney, "Women in Journalism," Session 1, 49.
66. Roberta Applegate letter to George Beebe, February 16, 1962, Papers of Roberta Applegate, National Women and Media Collection, State Historical Society of Missouri.
67. Ibid.
68. Reva Berger Tooley, "untitled," in *Anyone Who Enters Here Must Celebrate Maggie*, ed. Jim Bellows (Los Angeles: Ward Ritchie Press, 1972), 19.
69. Ponchitta Pierce, "Negro News – Why Isn't More On Women's Pages," *Matrix*, June 1968, 4.
70. Chris Porterfield, "Practicality, Significance Prevail Over Less Urgent, Familiar Ideas," *Penney Press*, March 1973, 6.
71. Column with a Heart, "Homeowner's On the Spot: Should He Sell to Negro," *Miami Herald*, July 22, 1966.
72. Column with a Heart, "Negro Family Helped Improve Neighborhood," *Miami Herald*, July 31, 1966.
73. Column with a Heart, "Integration Ideal Must Be Lived," *Miami Herald*, August 5, 1966.
74. Column with a Heart, "Integrated Scout Troop 'is Welcome Anyplace,'" *Miami Herald*, August 19, 1966.
75. Column with a Heart, "Whites Can End Block Busting," *Miami Herald*, September 11, 1966.
76. Column with a Heart, "Varied Faces of Segregation," *Miami Herald*, September 25, 1966.
77. John S. Knight letter to Vera Glaser, April 15, 1970, Papers of Vera Glaser, Heritage Center, University of Wyoming.
78. John S. Knight, "The Tigress of Tiger Bay Wasn't Shy," *Miami Herald*, April 19, 1970.
79. Ibid.
80. Ibid.
81. Kimberly Wilmot Voss and Lance Speere, "Quilted News: Mixing Hard and Soft News to Create a New Definition for Women's News," Florida Communication Association Conference, Orlando, October 18, 2013.

82. Dorothy Clifford, "Kaleidoscope Effect: Quilters Are as Diverse as the Patterns They Create," *Tallahassee Democrat*, August 1, 1999.
83. Radka Donnell, *Quilts as Women's Art: A Quilt Poetics* (Canada: Gallerie Publications, 1990), 20.
84. Jurney, "Women in Journalism," Session 1, 5.
85. Dorothy Jurney, "Penney-Missouri Winners' Banquet speech," March 30, 1988, folder 106, 3, Papers of Dorothy Jurney, National Women and Media Collection, State Historical Society of Missouri.

7

The Demise of the Women's Pages

In *Perspectives on Mass Communication History*, historian Wm David Sloan addressed the lack of attention historians have paid to women's page journalism. He reviewed several areas of research and suggested research questions for further study, including one particularly germane to this research: Why did most "women's pages" die?[1]

The answer is complex, but one thing is clear: many women's page editors did not want their sections to be eliminated. Many identified themselves as feminists and were a part of the women's movement in their own ways, including covering movement news and being active in local women's organizations. According to journalist Zena Beth Guenin in 1973: "First-rate women's sections do exist and some were doing a top reporting job long before the theme of women's liberation was heard. And there have been women who strived for excellence despite the indifference from management."[2]

The evidence list of a changing women's page is lengthy. For example, speakers at the 1970 Penney-Missouri Awards Workshop were full of ideas for the content of the women's pages. Betty Ann Raymond of the *Montana Standard* recommended stories about women sky divers, women who make candy, and women who were circus clowns. Kathy Hoersten of the *Dayton Journal Herald* recommended a feature on black female

K. W. Voss, *Re-Evaluating Women's Page Journalism in the Post-World War II Era*,
https://doi.org/10.1007/978-3-319-96214-6_7

DJs, recovery for mastectomy patients, and treatment for premature babies. Jean Henniger of the *Oregonian* suggested stories about single fathers, women in state legislatures, and married couples who worked together in the workplace. Katherine Stokes of the *Fort Lauderdale News* suggested a series about rape, a story about birth control pills, and an article about men having a vasectomy versus women undergoing sterilization. Doris Eastman of the *Fargo Forum* suggested a story about the barriers preventing women from working the night shift, the efforts to help the mentally challenged to get jobs, and the impact of children's fashion choices based on television.[3]

While changes were clearly on the way for the women's pages, it is usually Ben Bradlee who is given credit for transforming women's pages into lifestyle sections.[4] In the late 1960s, Bradlee said he thought the *Washington Post's* section, "For and About Women," was dated in relation to women's developing roles in society. He wanted a new section with a new focus. He said that the mission of the new Style section was "first, to treat women as people and not as appendages to men, and second, to make the paper better organized."[5] The intent of the new section was to broaden the definition of women's news beyond that of interests only to wives and mothers. In her memoir, *Washington Post* publisher Katherine Graham described her concern and then pride over the changed women's section:

> What was right was that we had broken an old mold and were inventing an important and entirely new one—one for the new times that were dawning, in which women's and men's interests were coming together, in which neither one nor the other wanted to hear about women holding teacups around a table, or as Ben [Bradlee] put it: 'We had become convinced that traditional women's news bored the ass off of all of us.'[6]

The *Washington Post* was not the only newspaper looking to transform its women's pages. It was happening at newspapers across the country. One of the most visible transformations occurred during the spring of 1964 in St. Petersburg, Florida. At the time, five journalists from the newspaper (known as the "Filthy Five") gathered in a hotel room with different afternoon newspapers from across the country and compared old copies of their own newspaper—the daily *Evening Independent*—a newspaper owned by the *St. Petersburg Times*. The meeting was the result of women's page editor Anne Rowe speaking with Executive Editor Don Baldwin about how to improve the afternoon newspaper. She wrote to a friend about the project: "The intent was to make it a strictly local newspaper. We never quite made it. And we found it wasn't selling because readers were saying there was too much duplication in the *Times* and the *Independent*."[7]

The Filthy Five—which included Rowe—spent three days at the hotel. They began on a Monday morning talking about what the newspaper's mission should be. They felt that as the *Times* had become more of a statewide newspaper; there was less city coverage. They felt the *Independent* could excel in truly local coverage—an area where the women's pages also excelled. They brainstormed everything from news approach to layout to reporting beats. Rowe wrote of the experience: "For those three days we lived and breathed that new *Independent*. It really was a marvelous experience."[8] They returned from the hotel and little changed initially. After a few weeks, staffing reorganization began. She wrote in a letter: "Now all we can do is wait and see. It could flop. It's so different. Whether the *Independent* is successful or not, it was great fun to do something different and it's been a real challenge."[9] For Rowe, it was a lesson in creativity and management.

By April 1969, she put that knowledge and experience to work in what was really a revolution in newspapers: replacing women's pages with a lifestyle section. At some newspapers, there was a change in name only and the traditional content continued. But at the *St. Petersburg Times*, there was real change, and they became leaders in a new form of journalism: the introduction of the DAY section. It was a way of updating the women's pages without abandoning the heart of the section. Various other newspapers were in the process of changing names, although not always content. For example, the *Democrat & Chronicle* in Rochester, New York, changed the section's name to "Feminique" in September of 1968.

The result of the arguments against women's pages led to the end of these sections—at the expense of women's editors' positions. Marjorie Paxson recalled a friend telling her that she was a casualty of the women's movement because she lost her job as a women's editor. Paxson responded, "Well, of course, that's true and lots of other women were casualties, too, but I'm sure they had just as rough a time as I did."[10] She said:

> When you've got Gloria Steinem and people like her writing in her magazine and making speeches about (eliminating the sections)—and the National Organization for Women and other women's groups hammering at this in everything they say, every time they speak to an editors' group. They began to hammer and pound and hammer and pound.[11]

Many of the original women's movement leaders, such as Susan Brownmiller, Betty Freidan, and Gloria Steinem, had been journalists and were aware that men controlled the media. They hoped by criticizing women's pages and arguing for more women in the media, the movement's message would be portrayed with a positive tone. At the time, the few women who held jobs in journalism outside of the women's pages were not in a position to make a difference. According to historian Winifred Wandersee, "That women played almost no role in this process was certainly a factor contributing to the trivialization of their issues and the general negative treatment of the politics of the movement."[12] Although the movement did lead to more women in newsrooms, it also led to the elimination of many women's page editors' jobs.[13]

The negative impact of the sections' elimination was noted by some women journalists who covered general news. Journalist Peggy Simpson wrote that in the late 1960s, news about the women's liberation movement "gradually crowded out the more traditional coverage of society balls and debutantes."[14] She did not think this was totally a good move in terms of keeping women readers. In fact, after the elimination of the sections, some women's section editors questioned the decision. Women's page editor Marie Saulsbury, who went on to become a city editor, said:

> The trend away from women's sections toward modern living was a lot like the French revolution. It was destined by history to take place, it eliminated much that was bad, it cleared the way for a new day, BUT … too many heads were lopped off as the movement went too far. No one denies that the blood bath was worth it. (Of course, it was our blood that was

> shed.) So long overdue that who can blame us when, in retrospect, we see that perhaps we became a little carried away with the swish, swish of the guillotine.[15]

Women's liberation leaders wanted newspapers to eliminate the women's pages and put news about women on the front pages. It was an interesting theory, but it did not work in practice. Instead, much of the news about women was eliminated. Some women's page editors wanted to save their sections and raise the standards of the sections. Among those were Marie Anderson, Vivian Castleberry, and Dorothy Jurney. Koky Dishon also did not support abolishing the sections. Years later she would lead the revival of a modern women's section at the *Chicago Tribune*. She wanted to see more issue-oriented sections instead, commenting:

> I see an unmistakable opportunity for women's pages to report in depth the changes in women's world and the problems women face. We can use our space to report on discrimination, women in poverty, infant deaths, politics—all of the things that are vital to women and to everyone in society.[16]

Journalist Cokie Roberts wrote, "Jurney and her contemporaries used the women's pages to underline women's problems."[17] These women saw stories where their male peers did not. According to historian Kay Mills, some women reporters said they remembered "the glazed looks that came over editors' eyes when they suggested stories on child care or women in politics" in the early 1970s.[18] It was women's page editors who pursued these topics. Some of these editors encouraged their reporters to cover news differently from male reporters. "Many female editors ask questions that their male counterparts do not ask, and thus their editing may seem different even though both have the same training in the elements that make up a news story," Mills contended.[19] These editors created a new framework for what constituted news. "Sometimes having a woman strategically placed in the news hierarchy determines whether an entire set of stories is done, and once completed, prominently displayed," she wrote.[20]

These editors saw great potential in women's pages but were caught in the controversy over the elimination of the sections to their detriment.

The journalists worked to empower women in their communities and to include women's voices in newspapers. Their efforts helped to define feminist concepts as they endeavored to add to women's knowledge about their lives. Each made a substantial contribution to the content of news for women and to the role of women journalists.

Women's page journalists who wanted to report on the movement had to battle both their management for better gender coverage and the leaders of the women's movement for credibility. In 1970, Janet Sanford, then women's editor of the *Phoenix Gazette*, went to cover a speech by Steinem. After learning of Sanford's job title, Steinem responded, "That shows what your paper thinks about women's issues."[21] In other words, she saw being covered in the women's pages as an insult, a slight. She and other movement figures believed that real news was found only in other sections of the newspaper. While Steinem initially called for the end of the women's pages, a few years later she found the significance of the sections.[22] Although, at that point, most sections were already eliminated.

Handful of Promotions

As society began to question the lack of women in management, it was natural for newspapers to look at women's page editors for promotions. For example, Gloria Biggs became the head of women's sections for the Gannett chain in Florida in 1966. Seven years later, she was promoted to publisher of the *Melbourne (Florida) Times*—the first woman to be named a publisher among the Gannett Company's many newspapers. The promotion garnered national media attention—just as the women as "firsts" stories were running across the country.

Yet, in reality, Biggs's new position was only a title. Although her title was "publisher," she could not make final decisions. Instead, she had to report to the nearby *Cocoa Beach Today* publisher. The fact was revealed in a 1974 *Editor & Publisher* article about Christy Bulkeley being promoted to publisher of the Gannett newspaper *Times-Union* in Rochester, New York. The article revealed, "Technically, Bulkeley is the first woman to be put in full control of a Gannett Group newspaper."[23] In retrospect, it makes sense that Biggs would not be given full control as women's page editors rarely had budgetary nor personnel control. Biggs did not have the experiences that would have prepared her to be a publisher.

Ultimately, Biggs was named a Gannet special projects coordinator. Later, she edited the *Handbook for Caribbean Journalists* publication with the World Press Freedom Committee.[24] She also taught news and reporting classes at the University of the West Indies branch in Trinidad.[25] Her legacy may have been the kind of feature writing that she promoted. She also left a lasting impact on the media's coverage of gender roles. In an article about women in journalism, Gannet executive Philip Currie wrote that he learned the importance of not making assumptions about gender roles from Biggs.

Women's page editor Carol Sutton's experiences were similar to Biggs's limited-term promotion. Sutton was named managing editor of the *Louisville Courier-Journal* in 1974. It was a "first" nationwide for a major metropolitan newspaper, and her accomplishment was lauded as a breakthrough for women. It led to national recognitions, including being one of twelve "women of the year" on the cover of *Time* magazine in 1976. Sutton said she never thought of herself for the position: "I came from a generation when women didn't think of long-term career plans. No woman had ever held that job at a major newspaper. It just didn't occur to me."[26] It was not surprising. A 1978 national study of 1,700 daily newspapers revealed women held 2.7 percent of management positions at daily newspapers with circulations above 25,000.[27]

By May 1976, after less than two years in her position, Sutton was removed as managing editor and reassigned as an assistant to the editor and publisher. The demotion was poorly handled. Although she had been promised the reason for her demotion would be handled privately, the media column in the *Louisville Times* soon ran a story that an unnamed source said Sutton was removed for incompetence. Her boss, Barry Bingham, Jr., confirmed the demotion and was quoted as saying, "Nobody wanted to look like he was knifing Carol."[28] Sutton responded to Bingham, "the newspaper game is still played by boys' rules."[29] The rest of her response, which she put in a memo to Bingham, was even more forceful:

> I waited a week to write this, until the blood stopped flowing from the large wound in my back, but I do think you should know that I consider Bob Schulman's column of last Monday the ultimate betrayal. To treat a 21-year career and reputation—built, in my view, with a helluva lot of blood and brains and devotion and personal sacrifice—as grist for a public gossip mill is reprehensible.[30]

These "firsts" from women's page journalists to management paved the way for others. In 1976, Paxson heard from the senior vice president for news at Gannett. He said there was an opening for an assistant managing editor in Boise, Idaho. She took the position at the 60,000-circulation newspaper, earning the same salary as the man in the previous position. At Boise, Paxson received management training: "I regarded this as a kind of a training ground. And this was the first time that I learned about working with budgets, for the whole editorial department."[31] After more than a year in Boise, Paxson was offered the position of publisher of the *Public Opinion*, a Gannett newspaper in Chambersburg, Pennsylvania.

At the newspaper, Paxson's management skills were tested. She had to fire a circulation manager, and the lack of authority given to her in her past women's section positions left her unprepared to take this action. She said, "It was a totally new experience for me because I had never had the authority to fire anybody up to this point."[32] The regional president recognized that she lacked experience and joined in on a conference call with the employee. After two years and eight months, Gannet named her publisher of the *Muskogee Phoenix*, in Muskogee—a town of about 40,000 in Oklahoma. She remained there until retirement.

Sutton's experience at Louisville had a happy ending for reporter Irene Nolan, who as a rookie reporter was surprisingly chosen by Sutton to cover an important story that would get big play in the Sunday section. Years later, Nolan asked why Sutton had assigned such a green reporter to such an important story. "Because I knew you could do it and you needed to know you could do it," Sutton responded.[33] She went on to become a full-time reporter in the women's section. Sutton believed that Nolan was being "groomed" to be the second woman in the management positions. According to Nolan, "We talked about what had happened to her and how I could make sure it didn't happen to me when and if I became managing editor."[34] Sutton died in 1985 at age 51. Nolan would be named managing editor about 18 months after Sutton's death.

At the *Chicago Tribune*, Koky Dishon created more than seventeen new sections. As soon as one was created, other newspapers across the country quickly copied it. For example, Dishon created a new feature section called "Tempo." It included a novel kind of feature writing by focusing on trends. The day before its debut, the *Tribune*'s women's page ran a banner headline announcing: "Closed for Remodeling." In the process, she created a new type of women's news.

In 1982, Dishon became the first woman to be listed in the *Tribune's* masthead. She later was promoted to associate editor, then senior editor. "Hard news," Dishon commented, "can hide behind late, breaking events and churn out pyramid-style stories. They shine spotlights on things. Feature writers light up stories from the inside, for the benefit and pleasure of readers." According to James Squires, *Chicago Tribune* editor for most of the 1980s: "For someone just five feet tall, Koky Dishon was as close as you can come to being a giant in journalism. At one point, she could have been the most influential woman in journalism."[35]

Another women's page editor to have a successful promotion to newspaper management was Janet Chusmir at the *Miami Herald*. She joined the paper in 1968 as a general assignment reporter for the women's pages and also covered the Republican Convention and the Florida Legislature. In the early 1970s, she was named the editor of the News For and About Women section. In 1972, when she won a Penney-Missouri Award, she described herself this way:

> I'm typical of the woman we often write about who launches a career after she had launched the kids. A native of Boston, Mass., I earned a degree in journalism from Boston University in June 1949, got married a week later then took a 12-year hiatus to rear the children who give me some of my best story ideas.

She stayed at the *Miami Herald* until 1982 during which the women's section became the Living Today section and she was named assistant managing editor for features. She left in 1982 to take a position as the first female executive with Knight Ridder—president and publisher of the *Daily Camera*, the chain's paper in Boulder, Colorado. She returned to the *Herald* in February 1987 becoming at age 57 the paper's executive editor.[36] She died of a brain aneurysm in 1990 at the age of 60. Under her leadership, the newspaper won two Pulitzer Prizes. Just prior to her death, Chusmir, a feminist, told a group of Hispanic women: "Pick your battles. It's not good to be fighting over each little thing and male chauvinistic action. Instead, fight for the important things: equal pay and equal respect. Fight smart."[37]

Other women's page editors slowly rose through the ranks. Ruthe Deskin became the longtime assistant to legendary *Las Vegas Sun* Publisher Hank Greenspun. Her position included authoring a regularly appearing column. Jean Sharley Taylor was promoted to associate editor at the *Los Angeles Times* and helped to establish the *Los Angeles Times* Magazine and the Book Review. In 1973, Dorothy Jurney was named the assistant managing editor of the *Detroit Free Press* and became a member of the American Society of Newspaper Editors. She also was the first woman board member of the Associated Press Managing Editors. Later that same year she moved to the *Philadelphia Inquirer* as an assistant managing editor.

While there were a few success stories of women being promoted out of the women's section to the news section or loftier editor positions, the stigma of the section hurt other women's page reporters. By 1977, the *Milwaukee Journal* had its first female Pulitzer Prize winner in Margo Huston, who won for general reporting. She was honored for a series of stories about the elderly who were struggling to live independently. She had written the stories for Spectrum—the renamed women's pages. She learned that the top prize in journalism did not trump her gender. She started applying for jobs in other departments at the newspaper only to be asked if she had ever written a news story. Another editor asked for her resume despite her being at the newspaper for a decade. Two years after the Pulitzer Prize win, she was finally transferred to the business desk and then the editorial page.[38]

Taking Other Paths: Higher Education

In 1964, Roberta Applegate was hired as an assistant professor of technical journalism at Kansas State University. Upon hearing that Applegate was leaving, women's editor Billie O'Day remarked "what a loss for Miami."[39] Applegate was one of the few women in this position in the country. She taught classes on reporting, magazine writing, and media law. Rather than being limited by the more traditional women's page content described in textbooks, Applegate subscribed to the newspapers that won the Penney-Missouri Awards, which recognized progressive content, to be used in its place.[40]

Marie Anderson left the *Miami Herald* in 1972 to become a dean of University Relations and Development at Florida International University, which was established in 1965. In a response to a survey request, she wrote she "was offered a new and challenging job at a time I felt I was in a rut in the newspaper business."[41] Anderson remained at the university for five years but was not happy in the position.[42] It may have been that she did not have the kind of control that she had at the newspaper. "The mere fact that I'm sitting at this typewriter the day after Christmas has everybody on this floor thinking I'm either a genius or a nut and either way you're not a follower,"[43] she wrote in that questionnaire sent to female administrators.

Contributions to the Women's Liberation Movement

The end of the women's pages did not mean that the impact of the women helming them also disappeared. The women themselves were actively involved in advocacy work on behalf of the women's liberation movement. Many were members of or officers in groups such as NOW. Others, using their journalism training and expertise, helped compile government reports on women's issues or edited newsletters and news reports from women's conferences.

Anderson was a member of the Florida Commission on the Status of Women from 1967 to 1973. In 1973, the governor named Anderson as co-chair of the Commission.[44] She worked to make sure that women were able to make the transition from homemaker to career woman with the establishment of the Council for the Continuing Education of Women. There was often a connection between the women's pages and the Commissions. For example, there was a NOW meeting in Washington, DC, that officer Kathryn Clarenbach did not want to attend. She suggested Milwaukee women's page journalist Dorothy Austin go to the meeting instead where the reporter "could keep her eyes and ears open and report back to me."[45] She went and Clarenbach got several phone calls, including one from Betty Friedan: "Who is this Dorothy Austin? This meeting is closed to journalists. We're not allowing any journalist to be here, even women journalists." Clarenbach explained, "I wasn't suspicious of Dorothy Austin because she has been an ally, and a very important ally to us here in the state, but apparently others there had had negative experiences with journalists making fun of it in their stories."[46] In May 1971, Austin wrote about a Wisconsin NOW meeting where Clarenbach was the speaker: "We haven't begun to use our political clout in this or any other state and this is one of the tasks to which NOW must address itself."[47]

In 1975, while an editor at the *Philadelphia Bulletin*, Paxson received a phone call asking if she would be interested in editing the daily newspaper to be published in Mexico City for the United Nations World Conference for International Women's Year. With the approval of the managing editor, she was given five weeks of unpaid leave to edit the newspaper for the conference that included 1,300 delegates from various countries. The name of the paper was *Xilonen*, in honor of the Aztec goddess of tender corn. Although Paxson's title was editor, she was more of a publisher.

Paxson worked in a difficult environment with few resources. One of her biggest problems was the heavy pressure from special interest groups. In an article about her experience published in the *Matrix*, Paxson wrote that one woman shoved her against a wall and shook her fist in Paxson's face because she refused to run the writer's "three-page, hand-written opus."[48] On the other hand, many influential writers eagerly contributed to the publication, including Germaine Greer.[49]

After becoming an assistant managing editor at the *Detroit Free Press* and then the *Philadelphia Inquirer*, Dorothy Jurney retired from newspapers in 1975. In the first few years of her retirement, Jurney worked for the National Commission on International Women's Year in Washington, DC. She was the writer and editor of the commission's 1976 report to President Gerald R. Ford, "To Form a More Perfect Union." It was a difficult assignment as she dealt with fifteen committees to produce the report.[50] She also continued to speak about the role of women and journalism. In a 1978 speech, Jurney said the roles of wife and mother in the lives of women added to their journalistic abilities—allowing them to place more of an emphasis on human concerns. "These experiences do not rob an able woman journalist of traditional news concepts," she said. "Rather they add dimension. She sees news value in many areas that seldom occur to a man to be important."[51]

New Directions for News

Several former women's page editors were involved in studying how the media covered women in the 1970s. It began as an attempt to better understand the role newspapers played in the defeat of the ERA. Jurney said one of the most significant projects during her retirement was a study of how newspapers covered particular issues related to women. In 1979, Virginia Allan, then chair of the Women's Studies Program and Policy Center at George Washington University, created the New Directions for News project to analyze American newspaper coverage. Jurney co-authored the 1983 report from the research.

Reviewing more than a thousand clippings from ten newspapers, the project examined the newspaper coverage of five other women's issues and events from 1972 to 1980 (essentially the period during which the women's sections were beginning to be phased out or replaced with feature sections) in addition to the ERA to increase objectivity and provide a context. The events included the 1977 Women's Conference at Houston, Texas, and the 1980 United Nations World Conference for Women at

Copenhagen, Denmark. The study was later expanded to include coverage of Title IX, education, housing, family law issues, and equal pay for comparable work.

The report's recommendations were published in 1983. The front page included an image that symbolized the approach many managing editors took to the women's sections. It included a drawing of men in shirts and ties sitting in front of computers in various newspaper departments—government news, sports, and entertainment. The last department was the women's section and behind the desk sat a Neanderthal character using a manual typewriter. (The *Miami Herald* ran the cartoon in its newspaper.[52])

The report's overall conclusion was that newspaper coverage of the gendered topics was inadequate. According to the report, many editors either lacked knowledge of the topics or had no understanding of the topics' impact on the readers.[53] The study found that all of the newspapers examined during this post-women's page era, with the exception of the *St. Louis Post-Dispatch*, had failed to cover the ERA in a way that allowed readers to understand the legislation. Instead, the media treated the assertions of each side equally and did not analyze the claims. In a 1976 talk to newspaper executives, Jurney addressed the false myths the poor reporting was perpetuating such as the ERA leading to unisex bathrooms. She cited an article that did not question a John Birch Society speaker about statements against the ERA. For example, Jurney said, the speaker "fails to point out that there is a discriminatory practice applied against women who want to join the military. A woman has to be a high school graduate; a man does not; a woman has to score 40 points higher than a man in qualifying exams."[54] The lack of analysis allowed for a simplistic representation of the fight for and against the ERA.

The introduction to the study began with a quote from the American Society of Newspaper Editors' statement of principles: "The primary purpose of gathering and distributing news and opinion is to serve the general welfare by informing the people and enabling them to make judgments in the issues of the time."[55] Jurney wrote that the hook of a newspaper story did not have to be confrontational. Instead, the hook could be issue-oriented—from economic or financial to family-oriented.

She wrote that too often reporting focused on the confrontations and obscured the focus on social change.[56]

The study pointed out the areas where the remaining women's page editors or the editors of the new sections were neglecting their responsibilities as gatekeepers. One of the main conclusions was that newspapers needed to expand their definition of what was newsworthy, particularly putting a stronger emphasis on human interest or soft news. According to the research findings: "Reporting soft news is more difficult than covering hard news because there is little action and guidelines are few. But when it is done with expertise, the rewards for the public and for the newspaper are large."[57]

Conclusion

Women's page journalists navigated career paths in uncharted waters. They created career paths within the parameters of what was acceptable for women at the time. They stretched the definition of women's news in the 1950s and 1960s—being sure to be inclusive of homemakers and women in the workforce. Women's page content was changing and, in doing so, they helped create a foundation for women's liberation movement leaders. This was done at newspapers across the country—from Phoenix to Milwaukee to Miami. Most women's sections changed as society's expectations for women changed.

While the reporters and editors of these sections were marginalized, they made the most of their positions. The women's pages were an important place for women to gain journalism experience for decades and a significant place for women's page readers to find information in their communities. Unfortunately, too many newspapers ignored the women's pages in their own histories. Newspapers need to acknowledge their mistakes and reward the value of the women's pages. The stories of numerous women's page editors are included at the end of this book. These women played major roles at their newspapers and in their communities. Yet, there are still more stories to be told.

A few years ago, it was women's page editor Maggie Savoy who was discovered by another *Arizona Republic* journalist, Karina Bland. The newspaper was preparing to celebrate its 125-year anniversary, and in doing some historical research to commemorate the occasion, Bland discovered Savoy and noticed that the content of her section went beyond the preconceived ideas of what was generally covered in the women's section. "Among the recipes and women's club calendar listings, she slipped in news of another kind: the social, economic and political issues of the growing women's movement," Bland wrote in a story titled "Ariz. woman journalist led way for next generation—including me." "She wrote about society events but also about the environment and preservation. Rather than just covering the benefit luncheon, she looked a little more deeply at what would benefit."[58]

Bland wrote that when she started at the *Republic* in 1986, she was able to cover any beat she wanted to cover—a far cry from the limitations of the women's pages. She wrote: "Funny, by then, nobody told me the cop beat was too dangerous for a woman. They just told me I'd have to work nights, and to get moving." Yet, she appreciated the role that women like Savoy played for future women journalists:

> Under women like Savoy, the women's pages were about what was wrong in the world and how it could be right. The women's pages stopped running long ago, but they didn't vanish. They became every page. What's wrong and how it can be right. What's being lost and how it can be saved.[59]

Women like Savoy and her fellow women's page editors were in many ways selfless. They knew they were not valued by many in newspaper management but often adored by their readers. They championed women who were in the spotlight for the first time and validated the few women leaders who were often devalued by the news side. They did the best they could with what they were given. They were very much aware what they were doing would benefit the next generation. Let's hope that journalism history can do a better job of preserving their legacy.

Notes

1. Wm David Sloan, *Perspectives on Mass Communication History* (Hillsdale, New Jersey: Lawrence Erlbaum Associates, 1991), 102.
2. Zena Beth Guenin, "Women's Pages in the 1970s," *Montana Journalism Review* 16: 27.
3. "Ten Best Story Ideas," Penney-Missouri Awards Workshop, 1970, Papers of the Penney-Missouri Awards, National Women and Media Collection, State Historical Society of Missouri.
4. Kay Mills, *A Place in the News: From the Women's Pages to the Front Pages* (New York: Columbia University Press, 1990), 118.
5. Mills, *A Place in the News*, 119.
6. Katharine Graham, *Personal History* (New York: Random House, 1997), 414.
7. Anne Rowe letter to Paul Myhre, August 31, 1964, Papers of the Penney-Missouri Awards, National Women and Media Collection, State Historical Society of Missouri.
8. Ibid.
9. Ibid.
10. Marjorie Paxson, "Women in Journalism Oral History Project," Washington Press Club Foundation, transcript, Session 3, 87.
11. Paxson, "Women in Journalism," Session 3, 73.
12. Winifred Wandersee, *On the Move: American Women in the 1970s* (Boston: Twayne, 1988), 169.
13. Mills, *A Place in the News*, 124.
14. Peggy Simpson, "1979: Covering the Women's Movement," *Neiman Reports*, Summer 1979, accessed May 5, 2018, http://niemanreports.org/articles/1979-covering-the-womens-movement/.
15. Marie Saulsbury, *Associated Press Managing Editors, 1975*, 26, Box 2, Papers of Marie Anderson, National Women and Media Collection, State Historical Society of Missouri.
16. Colleen 'Koky' Dishon, "We've Come a Long Way – Maybe," *Media Studies Journal* (1997): 93–102.
17. Cokie Roberts, *We Are Our Mothers' Daughters* (New York: Perennial, 2000) 123.
18. Kay Mills, "What Difference Do Women Journalists Make?" in *Women, Media and Politics*, ed. Pippa Norris (Oxford: Oxford University Press, 1997), 44.

19. Mills, "What Difference," 42.
20. Mills, "What Difference,"47.
21. Mills, *A Place in the News*, 118.
22. Dustin Harp, *Desperately Seeking Women Readers: U.S. Newspapers and the Construction of a Female Readership* (Lanham, Maryland: Lexington Books, 2007), 43.
23. Jane Levere, "Woman Publisher-Editor Appointed by Gannett," *Editor & Publisher*, April 20, 1974, 72.
24. Gloria Biggs, ed., *Handbook for Caribbean Journalists* (St. Michael, Barbados: Caribbean Publishing and Broadcast Association, 1983).
25. Gloria Biggs letter to Marie Anderson, January 31, 1978, Papers of Marie Anderson, National Women and Media Collection, State Historical Society of Missouri.
26. Interview with Carol Sutton, University of Louisville Oral History Project, July 21, 1982, CD 2, Part 1.
27. Jean Gaddy Wilson, "Future Directions for Females in the Media," in *Communications at the Crossroads: The Gender Gap Connections*, ed. Ramona Rush and Donna Allen (Norwood, NJ: Ablex, 1989), 161.
28. Bob Schulman, "An Untouched Story Behind the Story," *Louisville Times*, May 24, 1976.
29. Susan E. Tifft and Alex S. Jones, *The Patriarch: The Rise and Fall of the Bingham Dynasty* (New York: Summit Books, 1991), 309. Nolan confirmed the memo in a telephone interview, June 14, 2010.
30. Ibid.
31. Paxson, "Women in Journalism," Session 4, 105.
32. Paxson, "Women in Journalism," Session 4, 112.
33. Author interview with Irene Nolan, July 10, 2006.
34. Irene Nolan email to the author, June 14, 2010.
35. Kimberly Wilmot Voss, "Koky Dishon: Journalism Legend," *Timeline*, July/September 2010: 2–17.
36. Associated Press, "*Miami Herald* Names Editor from Colorado," *New York Times*, February 12, 1987.
37. Dennis Hevesi, "Janet Chumir, Executive Editor of the *Miami Herald*, Dies at 60," *New York Times*, December 23, 1990.
38. Robert Wells, *The Milwaukee Journal: An Informal Chronicle of Its First 100 Years* (Milwaukee, Wisconsin: Milwaukee Journal, 1981), 452.

39. Roberta Applegate letter to parents, June 15, 1964, folder 75, Papers of Roberta Applegate, National Women and Media Collection, State Historical Society of Missouri.
40. In a January 26, 1965 letter, Kansas State University Professor Roberta Applegate wrote to Nevada women's page editor Florence Burge and explained the students in the "Home Page" class read the winning sections of the Penney-Missouri Awards competition rather than a textbook. University of Nevada, Special Collections, Florence Burge Papers.
41. Marie Anderson, "Questionnaire for the Woman Administrator," Box 4, Papers of Marie Anderson, National Women and Media Collection, State Historical Society of Missouri.
42. Marie Anderson, "Women in Journalism Oral History Project," Washington Press Club Foundation, Session 1, 61.
43. Anderson, "Questionnaire for the Woman Administrator."
44. Margaria Fichtner, "Florida Status Commission Reactivated by Askew," *Miami Herald*, February 13, 1973.
45. "Oral History Interview: Kathryn Clarenbach," UW-Madison Oral History Program, 1989, 130–131.
46. Ibid.
47. Dorothy Austin, "New NOW Network," *Milwaukee Sentinel*, May 24, 1971.
48. Paxson, "Mexico," *The Matrix*, Women in Communications Inc., 1975.
49. Paxson, "Women in Journalism," Session 4, 96.
50. Catherine East letter, January 29, 1984, folder 104–105, Papers of Dorothy Jurney, National Women and Media Collection, State Historical Society of Missouri.
51. Jurney, "Talk at Carolina Symposium," 4, Papers of Dorothy Jurney, National Women and Media Collection, State Historical Society of Missouri.
52. Jurney, "Women in Journalism," Session 2, 99.
53. Papers of New Direction for News, description, National Women and Media Collection, State Historical Society of Missouri.
54. Dorothy Jurney, untitled talk to Knight Ridder newspaper executives, Point Clear, Alabama, 1976, Papers of Dorothy Jurney, National Women and Media Collection, State Historical Society of Missouri.
55. Virginia Allan, Catherine East, and Dorothy Jurney, "New Directions for News," Women Studies Program and Policy Center of George Washington University, 1983, 2.

56. Allan, East, and Jurney, "New Directions for News," 2.
57. Allan, East, and Jurney, "New Directions for News," 10.
58. Karina Bland, "Ariz. Woman Journalist Led Way for Next Generation – Including Me," *Arizona Republic*, May 15, 2015.
59. Ibid.

8

Women's Page Journalists Across the Country

The women who became women's page journalists came from a variety of backgrounds. Most had journalism degrees and plans to become reporters. They came together during the American Press Institute seminars, the Penney-Missouri Awards workshops, and state press club meetings. They were largely forgotten by the late 1970s. As gender roles were changing, the women's pages seemed to represent a backward time for women. The sections were assumed to reinforce traditional roles. Yet, in examining these sections, the content was more complex. This fact was often revealed in the obituaries of the women where their progressive approaches were mentioned. Below are summaries of numerous women's page journalists with details drawn from those obituaries, along with oral histories, newspaper clippings, and archival papers.[1] This is not an exhaustive list. There are many more women's page journalists whose stories remain to be told.

K. W. Voss, *Re-Evaluating Women's Page Journalism in the Post-World War II Era*,
https://doi.org/10.1007/978-3-319-96214-6_8

Arizona

Maggie Savoy

Margaret Case Savoy was a graduate of the University of California, Los Angeles. She worked at the women's pages of newspapers in Arizona and Southern California, including at the *Arizona Republic* and the *Los Angeles Times*. She won several Penney-Missouri Awards and spoke at the award workshops about updating women's page content. In an article for the American Society of Newspaper Editors, she took editors to task for not fully explaining the issues central to the women's movement. She challenged male editors to catch on to the issues. She asked them, "Do you duck the responsibility of helping your women's editor achieve excellence for her 51 percent of your readership? Or do you just listen to one, two or a dozen irate society women and sign, 'Don't rock the boat.'" When the feminist organization KNOW, Inc. issued a list of "Reporters You Can Trust," Savoy's name was on the list. In her final newspaper column before her death in 1970, Savoy wrote about the need for real equality and for the end to negative liberation stereotypes. She married three times and had one child.

Betty Milburn

Betty Milburn Schumacher was the women's page editor at the *Tucson Citizen* from 1950 to 1970. She earned a journalism degree from the University of Missouri before joining the newspaper. Her first husband, the late William Milburn, worked in the newspaper's editorial department. In 1964, she took a leave of absence to become press secretary for Peggy Goldwater when her husband ran for president. While some women's page editors were limited by what they could cover, she lobbied the newspaper publisher William Small until he agreed women's page reporters could write "about anything of interest to women." She made sure it included a broad range of topics for her reporters. By the mid-1960s, she and a women's page colleague decided to write about the stock market by buying stocks and tracking the progress. They went to a brokerage office and learned they could only invest if their husbands signed off on the forms. After it was explained that the women had earned their own money, they ripped up the forms. She served as a Tucson Baseball Commissioner, a Tucson Family Service Agency board member, and a member of the Junior League of Tucson. She was married and had a daughter.

California

Thelma Barrios

Thelma Barrios was the longtime women's page editor at the *San Fernando Valley Sun*. She started working at the paper in the 1960s, working in the collections department. She soon moved on working in the society section, covering women's clubs and weddings. For her section called "People in the Sun," she wrote a weekly column, "Chit-Chat." She also covered the "Food and Fashion" section. She also edited an annual publication about the women's clubs. She won a Penney-Missouri Award for her work. She and her family later bought the paper, and she worked as the publisher. She was married and had two children, as well as a parakeet named "Deadline."

Frances Moffat

Frances Moffat was the longtime society columnist for the San *Francisco Examiner* and later the *San Francisco Chronicle*. She earned a journalism degree from Stanford University. She had wanted to be a hard news reporter, but when she began her career in the 1930s, women were relegated to the lifestyle and society pages. As a result, she took a hard news approach to writing her columns. Her career began at the *Call-Bulletin*. In 1939, she went to work at the *Examiner* as assistant to society editor Peggy Tomson. She went to the *Palp Alto Times* in 1943 as women's editor, and then rejoined *The Examiner* in 1952 as society editor after Tomson's death. In 1963, *The Chronicle* hired her to become its society editor, a position she held until the mid-1970s when she retired. During her career, she covered the opening of the San Francisco Opera, the coronation of Queen Elizabeth, and the signing of the United Nations Charter in San Francisco. She also covered the Eisenhower and Kennedy inaugurations, the Kentucky Derby, and the Royal Dublin Horse Show, as well as following the jet set from Pebble Beach to Lake Tahoe, Puerto Vallarta, Southampton, and London. She founded and was first president of the San Francisco Women's Press Club. She also wrote a book, *Dancing on the Brink of the World: The Decline and Fall of San Francisco Society*, in 1977. She married twice.

Betty Preston Oiler

Betty Preston was a women's page editor at the *Glendale News-Press* in California. She went from an award-winning women's page editor to a top editor during her career in Glendale, California. A Michigan native, she graduated from Petoskey High School and attended Michigan State College (now Michigan State University). She graduated in 1941 with a degree in journalism. She was taught by the chair of the journalism program, Albert A. Applegate, who had a daughter, Roberta, near Preston's age. Roberta would also go on to be a significant women's page journalist. She said: "My dad was extremely supportive of women who were highly ambitious."

After moving to California to be with her parents and escape the snowy winters, Preston made an impression on *Glendale News-Press* Publisher Carroll Parcher. He later noted, "We didn't exactly have a job open at the time but something told me this girl was too good to let get away." She quickly became editor of the women's page and made her mark on it. Former *News-Press* reporter Avery Keener Econome noted, "The woman was really a pioneer in progressing those old-fashioned society sections into real feature sections that appealed to both sexes and all age groups. Times were changing and she wanted to be on top of that." She won four Penney-Missouri Awards in the 1960s and also attended the American Press Institute sessions for women's page editors. After the elimination of her section, she went on to be a city editor, managing editor, and executive editor before her retirement. She was married and had a step-daughter.

Ethel Taylor

Ethel Taylor was the longtime women's page editor of the *Van Nuys News*, which she helped establish at the newspaper. After high school graduation in 1927, she passed up a journalism scholarship to the University of Southern California to work at the newspaper. She became a writing protégé for the newspaper's editor. During her career, she won three Penney-Missouri Awards.

Colorado

Lois Cress

Lois Cress was the longtime women's editor at the *Denver Post*. She also served as the section's club editor. A scholarship is given out in her name at New Mexico State University, which was funded by her brother.

Florida

Marie Anderson

Marie Anderson was a groundbreaking women's page editor at the *Miami Herald*. She graduated from Duke University with a degree in English. After working in New York and then the Servicemen's Pier in Miami, she started working at the *Miami News*. Later, she began working at the Herald in the 1950s, while being mentored by Dorothy Jurney. When Jurney moved on to Detroit, Anderson became the women's page editor. She won so many Penney-Missouri Awards during the 1960s that she was retired from the competition. She was considered a national expert about the women's pages. She was interviewed for the Washington Press Club Foundation's Women in Journalism oral history project. Her papers are part of the National Women & Media Collection.

Roberta Applegate

Roberta Applegate earned a languages degree from Michigan State University—where she took two classes from her journalism professor father, Albert A. Applegate. She grew up regularly visiting the *Idaho Statesmen* newspaper where her father was a journalist. After graduation, she became a women's page journalist in Michigan and then earned a master's degree in journalism from Northwestern University. During World War II, she worked on the hard news side of newspapers. After the war, she served as press secretary to Michigan's governor—one of the first woman to work in this role in the country. In the 1950s and early 1960s, she worked as the club editor in the women's pages of the *Miami Herald*. She left the newspaper in 1964 to become a journalism professor at Kansas State University where she taught classes about women's pages.

Janet Chusmir

Janet Chusmir earned a journalism degree from Boston University and got married the next day. She stayed at home and raised two children. Later, she became a women's page journalist at the *Miami Herald* in the late 1960s and rose to the position of Executive Editor at the *Herald*. She died suddenly in 1990. According to her obituary, "During her tenure she pushed the *Herald* to be more sensitive to ethnic and racial concerns, to think about how the events of the day affected real human beings, to publish a newspaper that, in her words, 'connects with the community.' As the newspaper's first executive editor, she also brought diversity to the newsroom by creating new opportunities for women and minorities."

Dorothy Clifford

Dorothy Clifford was the women's page editor at the *Tallahassee Democrat* in Florida. Dorothy Ring Clifford was a native of Kingsport, Tenn., where she was the youngest of eight children of a steel foundry owner and his homemaker wife. Clifford earned a bachelor's degree from Agnes Scott College (Ga.) and later attended the University of Tennessee. She started her journalism career at her hometown *Kingsport Times-News*, covering police and courts as well as serving as women's editor for morning and evening editions. She moved on to work at the morning and afternoon newspapers in Savannah, covering city government schools and editing the women's sections. She spent more than four decades at the Florida newspaper—winning a Penney-Missouri Award in 1960. According to her obituary: "For decades, Clifford was the newspaper's social historian." Most famously, she wrote the *Democrat's* weekly "Capital Scene." After a 10-year hiatus to raise her three children, Clifford returned in 1971 as assistant city editor, before moving back to editor of the women's section. In 1974, after she had returned as its editor, the women's section name was retired in favor of the name, "People," and Clifford approved of the rebranding. She was married and had three children.

Dorothy-Anne Flor

Dorothy-Anne Flor, a New York City native, joined the newly created *Sun-Sentinel* in Florida in 1961. Within a few months, she became the women's page editor. After a few years at the *Lakeland Ledger*, she became assistant women's page editor at the *Miami Herald* in 1968 and later the editor of the newspaper's renamed Living Today section in 1971. She twice won Penney-Missouri Awards. She returned to the *Fort Lauderdale News* and *Sun-Sentinel* in 1979 as a feature writer and was later a writing coach. She was divorced and had one child.

Edee Greene

Edith "Edee" Greene was the longtime women's page editor of the *Fort Lauderdale News*. She won several Penney-Missouri Awards for her work. She was a Florida resident since the age of 12. Her career in the media began with a show on radio station WSUN in St. Petersburg, Florida, in 1932. She wrote soap opera scripts and had her own show about movies.

A year later she left her job when she married. She helped her first husband with his business. After 17 years of marriage, she found herself a single mother looking for work. She found work in the women's pages of the *Orlando Sentinel*; she worked there from 1950 to 1957. She later married a fellow journalist at the newspaper. The newspaper's policy, like many, did not allow for married couples. They were then hired at the *Fort Lauderdale News*. She penned a witty column, "AhMen," which ran for 17 years. She left the *News* in 1976. She married twice and raised three children.

Dorothy Jurney

Dorothy Jurney was known as the godmother of the women's pages. She was a groundbreaking women's page editor who encouraged other editors to improve the content of their sections. Her father was a newspaper publisher and her mother was a suffragette. They informed her career as a journalist and a feminist. After earning a journalism degree from Northwestern University, she initially worked at her father's newspaper before becoming women's editor of the *Gary* (Indiana) *Post-Tribune*. She worked on the news side during World War II and was forced back to the women's pages in peacetime. In the 1950s, she revolutionized the women's pages of the *Miami Herald* while an editor there before moving on the larger circulation *Detroit Free Press* as women's page editor in 1960. In 1973, Jurney was made assistant managing editor of the *Free Press* and became a member of the American Society of Newspaper Editors. She also was the first woman board member of the Associated Press Managing Editors organization. Later that same year she was asked to move to the *Philadelphia Inquirer* as assistant managing editor during a period of transition for the paper. She was one of four women's page editors included in the Washington Press Club Foundation's Women in Journalism oral history project, and her papers are at the National Women and Media Collection. She was married for several years.

Beverley Morales

Beverley Brink Morales grew up on a Montana ranch where she punched cattle, dehorned calves, and herded sheep. She graduated from Montana State University and was then hired by a newspaper to cover snow ski competitions and boxing prizefights. She spent some time in public relations and then became the society editor at a newspaper in Mexico City. She married Hector Morales, the newspaper's sports editor. They moved to the United States in 1956 and ran a newspaper in North Dakota. By 1959, she became an assistant editor of the *Miami Herald* women's pages. When the Pompano Beach *Sun-Sentinel* was started in April 1960, she was heading up the women's section. In September 1960, she won three Florida Women's Press Association awards. After an argument with her editor, brought on by her Penney-Missouri Award-winning ways, she was fired in 1961. She worked on several projects before the *Sun-Sentinel* management rehired her in 1966. She divorced her husband and became a women's page editor in Ohio for a few years. In the 1970s, she moved back to Montana and became a grant writer, while continuing to be a freelance journalist. She helped Native Americans gain millions of dollars in grants. While there, she married and became Beverley Badhorse. She eventually moved to Alaska and continued to work as a grant writer. She married three times and was the mother of three children.

Helen Muir

Helen Muir made a significant contribution to her beloved Miami. She raised funds and awareness for the city's libraries. She reported for the women's pages of the *Miami Herald* in the 1950s and 1960s and wrote significant books including the classic books *Miami USA* and a memoir about her friendship with poet Robert Frost. She was the center of a significant group of women who included Dorothy Jurney, Jeanne Voltz, Marie Anderson, and Marjory Stoneman Douglas. Muir gathered those women, and others, together at her annual tea parties, which created a lifelong connection.

Kay Murphy

Kay Murphy was a longtime women's page journalist at the *Miami Herald* where she largely covered furnishings. She earned the top award in that field—the Dorothy Dawe Awards from the American Furniture Mart—five times. She graduated from Ohio University where her classmate was future journalist Eleanor Hazlett Ratelle. This was in the 1930s. Murphy's newspaper career began at the *Columbus Dispatch*. She left after six years after learning about an opening at the *Miami Herald* from Ratelle. Murphy established a scholarship for students at her alma mater with an interest in newspaper or magazine journalism; it was given as recently as 2017. She was also an artist, a poet, and a gourmet cook. She was married and retired from the Herald after 33 years in the industry.

Billie O'Day

She was born Billie Corinne Womack (O'Day was her radio name that she began using as her own name) in Pine Bluff, Arkansas, in 1919. Her dad, William Womack, was a piano tuner and a music store owner. An only child, she both played football and music instruments. Her journalism career started early. She was the first sports editor in Pine Bluff history. She earned an undergraduate degree in music at Hendrix College. After graduation, she moved to Miami with her mother and began taking graduate classes at the University of Miami. She also played violin for the University of Miami Symphony for several years. In 1944, she became the music librarian at Radio WIOD. She then teamed up with Jack Berry for the weekday program "Billie and Jack." O'Day was hired as the club editor in the women's pages at the *Miami News* in 1958. O'Day soon became the women's page editor at the *Miami News* where she won her Penney-Missouri Awards. The women's section of the *Miami News* ended in the 1970s and became a lifestyle section—as was common at most newspapers. O'Day went on to be the music and television editor at the *Miami News* before retiring from the newspaper in 1984. She did not marry.

Eleanor Ratelle

Eleanor Ratelle majored in journalism at Ohio University in 1936. With a journalism degree in hand, she went to work at the *Akron* (Ohio) *Times-Press*. She arrived in Miami, Florida, on January 14, 1940, at age 24. She rented a room at the local YMCA for $3.75 a week and started working in the women's section at the *Miami Herald*. She wrote a local advice column "A Column With A Heart" under the penname "Eleanor Hart" for the *Miami Herald*. It ran in the newspaper during the 1950s and 1960s. It addressed social issues including race and gender—including integrating neighborhoods and whether married women should work outside the home. She also had a popular column about make overs and losing weight. She was married with two children.

Anne Rowe

Anne Rowe moved to St. Petersburg, Florida, from New Jersey at a young age. She began working in the library of the *St. Petersburg Times* a few days after high school graduation in the 1950s. During the next 12 years, she worked as a copy editor and a women's page editor at the *Times*. Later, she became the women's page editor of the *St. Petersburg Evening Independent*. She won several Penney-Missouri Awards for her work. In 1966, she was promoted to the *Times* as newsfeatures editor, becoming the first woman in the newspaper's history to lead a department that included as many men as women. Three years later, the features section was redesigned. At this point, she oversaw a staff of 22 editors and writers, plus specialists in religion, fashion, food, and arts. The section was called DAY. *Times* Editor and President Donald Baldwin said: "Anne was a very special person. Of all the journalists I've worked with over the years, she was among the very best." She was married with three children.

Jo Werne

Jo Werne often covered furnishing. Yet, in 1972, she won a Penney-Missouri Award for fashion. For the award-winning story, Werne combined her hobby with her work, and it led to the 1972 Penney-Missouri Award for fashion writing. A reporter on numerous beats, she had been sewing for years. Raised on an Ohio farm, she joined the 4-H when she was nine years old and given the choice of a project. Her options were to learn to sew or raise a hog. She chose the former. Her handmade bean bag won a blue ribbon and her interest was sparked. She described her hobby as "therapy, after pounding a typewriter all day long." Her award came after her search for inexpensive fabrics.

Helen Wells

Miami women's page journalist Helen Wells served as a Gray Lady for the Red Cross during World War II. In the 1950s, she was the society editor at the *Miami News*. She went on to be a women's page journalist at the *Miami Herald*. She retired in 1969 with a party at editor Marie Anderson's home.

Hawaii

Drue Lytle

A native of Pittsburgh, Pennsylvania, Druzella Goodwin earned a bachelor's degree from the University of California, Los Angeles in 1926. She worked for more than two years for the State Department in Washington, DC. She then earned her master's degree in English from Occidental College, known as Oxy, a small liberal arts college in Los Angeles, in 1937. Lytle was visiting her second husband at the Hawaii newspaper where he worked when she had a conversation with the society editor and was quickly hired at the *Honolulu Advertiser*. By the early 1960s,

Lytle oversaw 15 reporters. Her section placed at the Penney-Missouri Awards in 1962 and 1963; she oversaw investigative articles that earned numerous accolades. She also wrote a recurring standard column called "Talk About Women," which was a collection of news and opinions. For example, in one column, she declared her enjoyment of books, petting zoos, and a dry martini. She also wrote about cooking and travel.

Pat Millard Hunter

One of Drue Lytle's reporters was Pat Millard (later Hunter). *Honolulu Advertiser* columnist Bob Krauss called the women's page reporter, "Hawaii's most prolific winner of newspaper writing awards." She was born Patricia Wing Williams in Hilo, the daughter of a Big Island sugar-plantation manager. She earned a degree in architecture from Stanford University. Later, she joined the promotion and advertising department of the *Advertiser* as a copywriter. She became a reporter at the newspaper in 1957, covering homemaking and cooking. (In 1974, she wrote *The Hawaiian Cookbook* full of local recipes.) She later covered health issues and took on investigative assignments.

Idaho

Betty Penson

Betty Penson was a third-generation Idahoan who grew up in Boise. Her journalism career began at the *Boise Capital News* as a proofreader. She later worked as a church editor, weather editor, and society editor. She moved on to the *Idaho Statesman* in 1937 as the police and court reporter. Two years later, she started in the women's pages where she stayed for 25 years. She also wrote the book *Idaho Women in History*, where she documented the stories of 500 women from the state. She married three times and had two children. Her papers are available at the Northwest Digital Archives.

Illinois

Lorraine Bannon

Lorraine Bannon was the women's page editor at the *Evanston Review* in Illinois. She started college at Northwestern University before leaving for a job at the *Chicago Sun*. She became a clubs editor and then the society editor. She moved on to the Evanston newspaper where she had a feature column and a cooking feature. She won several Penney-Missouri Awards. She was married and had two children.

Colleen "Koky" Dishon

Colleen "Koky" Dishon started her newspaper career when she was in high school—covering baby news. She went to college for journalism but left to cover hard news for the Associated Press during World War II. After the war, she was a progressive women's page editor in Columbus, Ohio, and Milwaukee, Wisconsin, before moving on to Chicago. In 1975, she was hired by the *Chicago Tribune* and, in 1982, Dishon was named associate editor, becoming the first woman listed in the *Chicago Tribune's* masthead. At the *Tribune*, Dishon created 17 special sections that were often quickly copied at newspapers across the country. In the words of *Tribune* Managing Editor Ann Marie Lipinski: "Whether you have ever worked for Koky, or ever heard her name before today, if you are a newspaper reader, you are the beneficiary of her genius. She defined modern features coverage with her work in Chicago, creating the so-called 'sectional revolution' in American newspapers." According to former *Chicago Tribune* newspaper executive Jim Squires, "For someone just 5 feet tall, Koky Dishon was as close as you can come to being a giant in journalism. At one point, she could have been the most influential woman in journalism."

Mattie Smith Colin

Mattie Smith Colin is best known for her civil rights coverage of Emmett Till's body as it arrived in Chicago and later at the child's funeral when his mother insisted on an open casket. She was raised in Chicago and studied journalism at Roosevelt and Northwestern universities. She was hired by the black newspaper, the *Chicago Defender*, in 1950. After covering Till, she went on to cover food and fashion for the newspaper. She was an invited guest at the presidential inauguration of Lyndon B. Johnson and served as grand marshal of the largest African-American parade in the country—the Bud Billiken Parade.

Eleanor Page

Eleanor Page was well-traveled with time spent in Italy and France, but did not go to college. She began covering society for the *Chicago Tribune* in 1933. She covered charity events and rewarded those who helped the community. A former colleague said: "In the years that society coverage counted for something, she pretty much set the standard for coverage in Chicago." She was known for saying that in other US cities, society positioning was based on money or a family history. Yet, in Chicago, society status was based on "only charity work," which "had the power to allow someone to know everyone and go everywhere." She covered society for more than four decades.

Kansas

Nell Snead

Nell Snead earned a college degree and taught English in Nebraska. While in vacation in the 1930s, she applied for a job at the *Kansas City Star*. After a brief stint on the city desk, she became the women's page editor after being promised she would be able to go to New York City to cover fashion. She also covered food, and her recipes were included in the

1952 *Coast to Coast* cookbook. Her initial staff included four women, and she encouraged hiring more women. She trained 16 female reporters who became known as "Nell's chicks." She survived a 1957 plane crash in France; she said she regretted not being able to complete the French meal that was being served on the flight. According to the executive editor of the newspaper: "No label fits Nell Snead. She is a free spirit, and you will never know another like her." She worked for the women's pages for more than 40 years.

Kentucky

Carol Sutton

Carol Sutton graduated from the University of Missouri's journalism school and was initially hired by the *Louisville Courier-Journal* as a secretary. She eventually became a reporter before taking over the women's pages and transforming the section in the 1960s. Later, she was promoted to managing editor of the newspaper. She was the first woman in such a management position at a newspaper that her family did not own. During her tenure, the newspaper won Sigma Delta Chi and Roy Howard awards for public service for coverage of school desegregation in Louisville. She was a winner of a Penney-Missouri Award. She was one of several women named *Time* magazine's people of the year in 1975. She remained at the newspaper after she was demoted. In 1985, she died of cancer.

Irene Nolan

Irene Nolan was a native of Brooklyn, New York, and a graduate of the Indiana University School of Journalism. After college, Nolan's first job was a brief stint as a news writer at WAKY radio in Louisville. She joined the *Louisville Courier-Journal* as a clerk in the women's department in 1969. She soon became a features writer for what was then called Women's World and later with the Today's Living and Accent sections. Her positions included assistant editor and then editor of the features section and later editor of the arts and leisure section. From 1979 to 1984, she was the *Courier-Journal* assistant managing editor for features. She became managing editor of the *Courier-Journal* in 1987.

Massachusetts

Marian Christy

Marian Christy was a significant fashion reporter in the 1960s before she became a celebrity columnist. She started as a fashion reporter at the *Boston Globe* in April 1965, and her work was later picked up by the syndicate UPI. Her work then ran in 104 different newspapers. For example, she described the see-through blouse from a late-1960s Saint Laurent fashion show: "Haute couture is a laboratory for new ideas. Saint Laurent was not advocating public near-nudity. It was poetic exaggeration to shock the eyes. Once you see the extreme overstatements, watered-down versions seem reasonable and palatable. This was the late sixties and Saint Laurent seemed to be suggesting that women's bodies should be unharnessed." She won Penney-Missouri Awards in 1966, 1968, and 1970. Christy took a progressive, sociological approach to fashion, rather than writing for advertisers, which eventually cost her the position of fashion reporter. Her less than flattering report on the Paris fashion show led to a brief revocation of her French press card in 1972.

Michigan

Marjorie Goldsmith

Marjorie G. Goldsmith was a longtime women's page editor at the *Kalamazoo Gazette* in Michigan. She earned a degree from Ohio State University. She had been working in Washington, DC, for the Truman administration and lost her job with the election of Eisenhower. In 1953, she became the women's page editor at the *Gazette*, where she remained for four decades. She was credited for modernizing her section and was known for running a tight ship. A colleague said of Goldsmith: "She was dedicated to her job and was dedicated to the community, too."

Minnesota

Mary Ann Grossmann

Mary Ann Grossmann graduated from Macalester College in 1960 with a degree in journalism. After graduation, she worked at the United Press International's Minneapolis bureau. She then was hired by the *St. Paul Pioneer Press* where she spent decades. When she arrived in 1961, she recalled there was still a spittoon in the newsroom. After some time in the newsroom, she moved over to the women's pages. It was what she described as the end of the "society days" with an emphasis on brides and women's club coverage. While in the women's pages, she was the fashion editor and got to cover the New York City fashion shows. When she became women's page editor, she fought for maternity leave for employees. She described the changing time: "I have to compliment the men running the paper at the time; this was a confusing time. They wanted to get the paper into contemporary times, but they didn't want to lose readers, and we had a lot of very conservative readers. Covering things like abortion—which we did, from both sides—was a big departure from what we used to write about."

Montana

Betty Ann Raymond

Betty Ann Raymond may be most well known for her column, "The Livin' End," which made its debut in the *Montana Standard* on March 10, 1968. A year later her column was selected as the best column in Montana by the Montana Press Women. She went on to become the

Women's Editor and later the Feature Editor at the Standard. She was also the recipient of many awards including a Penny Missouri Award in 1971. She was president of the Montana Press Women and a member of the Symphony Guild, a book club and bridge club. She married Dick Raymond in 1941, and they had several children before divorcing.

Nevada

Flo Burge

Reno journalist Florence Sanford Burge was born in 1912 in Rochester, New York, and lived in Ypsilanti, Michigan, before graduating from high school in Los Angeles. Burge attended the University of California at Los Angeles and studied journalism before leaving school to attempt a professional dancing career. In 1956, Burge attended the University of Nevada, Reno, and again studied journalism, while also freelance writing for the *Reno Evening Gazette*. In 1959, she became women's editor of the newspaper. She remained in that position until 1966. While there, Burge was the 1964 recipient of the Penney-Missouri Award for best women's pages for a newspaper with circulation of up to 25,000. It was Burge who explained the transformation to her readers and sources. She wrote in an industry publication, "while it is difficult, the transition from 'club calendar' pages to international, national and local news of interest to women can be made." She suggested that this approach could be used to cover topics such as birth control, medical research, and abortion legislation.

Ruthe Deskin

Ruthe Deskin majored in journalism at the University of Nevada and was a staff member of the *Sagebrush*, the student newspaper. Deskin worked for the government during World War II. After the war was over, Deskin moved back to Reno and became the women's page editor of the *Reno Evening Gazette*. She described the newspaper as "very business-like." This prevented her from getting truly involved in the community as she later would in Las Vegas. The *Reno Gazette* used a more objectivity-driven approach to journalism which lacked the advocacy approach that Hank Greenspun favored at the *Las Vegas Sun*—where she became a columnist and executive. She married twice and had two daughters.

New York

Charlotte Curtis

Charlotte Curtis was the first woman to head the Op-Ed section of the *New York Times*, beginning in 1974. She had taken a traditional path for women journalists at the time—starting in the women's pages. She earned her undergraduate degree from Vassar College and then spent 11 years as a reporter and a society editor at the *Columbus Citizen* in Ohio. Curtis began at the *Times* as the fashion reporter in 1961 and, four years later, she became the women's page editor of the newspaper. She was known for her witty and sometimes biting columns—a combination of reporting and observation at the *Times.* She served as a social critic at her newspaper—especially about issues of social class, race, and gender. A collection of her columns was published in the 1976 book, *The Rich and Other Atrocities.* She died in 1987 at age 58.

Dorothy Roe

Dorothy Roe Lewis was a graduate of the University of Missouri's Journalism School. After graduation, she started work at the *Eldorado Daily News* as the shopping news columnist. A few years later, she landed both a part-time position with International News Service (INS) and a freelance feature writing job with the *New York World.* Lewis later quit her job with INS and took a full-time writing position at the *Brooklyn Times.* Later, she moved back near her family in Arkansas, where she gave birth to a daughter during her first marriage. Upon her return to New York, Dorothy was hired by Universal News Service as a feature writer. She remained there until 1937, when she married reporter John Lewis. In 1940, she began working for King Features as the assistant women's editor. A year later, and after the birth of a second daughter, she became the women's editor for the Associated Press. By 1960, she was writing a column for the *Chicago Tribune-New York News* Syndicate. She continued writing the column even after she began teaching journalism at the University of Missouri. She retired from the faculty in 1974, but remained active, editing the *Missouri Republican* for the next six years.

Eugenia Sheppard

New York-based fashion reporter Eugenia Sheppard helped to define a new kind of American fashion society in the post-World War II years. Her reporting ran in the women's pages of the *New York Herald Tribune*. Artist Andy Warhol wrote of Sheppard, "She invented fashion and gossip together." Her writing had a distinctly gossipy tone which was different from previous fashion journalism coverage that was more straight forward. She was known for her discovery that the rich "no longer craved privacy, and loved nothing better than to have their taste validated by attention in the public prints." Sheppard also worked with fashion publicist Eleanor Lambert to create the ultimate prize in fashion and gossip—the official best-dressed list. In 1987, the Council of Fashion Designers of America began giving out the Eugenia Sheppard Award for best fashion journalism; it continues to this day.

North Carolina

Bette Elliott

Bette Elliott was the women's page editor of the *Raleigh Times*. When she became a single mother in 1949, she relocated to Raleigh with her two-year-old son and infant daughter. A dogged journalist, she was a Penney-Missouri award winner in 1962. She also had a local television show.

For years, she rang the Salvation Army bell in front of a downtown department store. Shoppers were reportedly afraid not to give a donation because their names might appear in Elliott's column.

Zoe Kincaid

Zoe Kincaid Brockman was the longtime women's page editor of the *Gazette* in North Carolina. For more than 60 years, she worked at the newspaper. During that time, she wrote the column, "Unguarded Moments." She was the author of two books and a drama. In 1946, she authored *A Century of Growth* about Gaston County's centennial celebration. Her book of poetry, *Heart on My Sleeve*, was published in 1951, and a collection of essays, *Unguarded Moments*, was published in 1959. In 1934, Brockman was nominated for Poet Laureate of North Carolina. A charter member and past president of North Carolina Press Women, Brockman received many awards from that organization for her newspaper writing. An organizer and first president of the North Carolina Poetry Society, she won top awards from that organization. *Unguarded Moments* was long considered required reading in the journalism department of the University of North Carolina at Chapel Hill. More recently, Mrs. Brockman was spotlighted with other outstanding authors on a literary map of North Carolina. She was married and had one child.

North Dakota

Doris Eastman

Doris Eastman wrote and edited for the women's pages of *The Fargo Forum*—a section that later changed to the family section and then lifestyles. After an initial stint at the newspaper, she returned to the newspaper in 1950 and, eight years later, she became the women's editor. She covered society and local events. She retired in 1978. At the time, she said: "Through the years, we hope, it has reflected the changing world of women and family and, in some cases, helped to stimulate changes for the better."

She was married and had three children. In 1973, she printed an appeal from an Irish woman asking Americans to open their homes to children of war-torn Northern Ireland. Reportedly, Eastman was the only American reporter to reprint the request, which led to an exchange program, the Children's Program of Northern Ireland. During the next four decades, more than 6500 children came to the United States.

Syblann "Syb" Gullickson

Syblann "Syb" Gullickson worked with Doris Eastman in the women's pages of *The Fargo Forum*. She graduated from St. Cloud University with an education degree, expecting to become a teacher. In the 1960s, the North Dakota newspaper needed someone to cover weddings and social events so she was hired. Later, she helped transform the women's pages into a lifestyle section. Her reporters recalled the significant journalism she championed including writing about social issues such as sexual abuse and addiction. "It wasn't fluff. She had us do some really important reporting." She spent more than three decades at the newspaper. She married and had three children.

Ohio

Marj Heyduck

Marj Heyduck was a Dayton native who graduated from Ohio State University and began working as a columnist at the *Dayton Journal Herald* in 1944. She also had a radio show on WING. Five years later she became the women's page editor. She also covered food including contributing to the 1952 *Coast to Coast* cookbook. She had a popular column, "Third and Main," that was published in several books. She was a discussion-leader about women's pages at the American Press Institute. She was editor of the women's department for 16 years until becoming the assistant to the editor of the newspaper in 1966. Her columns were collected into three books. She was married and had no children.

Betty Jaycox

Betty Jaycox was the longtime women's editor at the *Akron Beacon Journal*, beginning in the 1950s. She wrote a witty Sunday column known as "Nancy Dear" (written as if it was a note to her sister). It took readers inside her upper-middle-class life. For example, she once recommended fixing a flat tire by wearing white gloves and looking helpless until someone came along to change it. She came from a prominent Akron family. She covered society events after graduating from college—although she had never used a typewriter. She quit her job when she married and started a family, but returned in the 1940s when her children were older.

She could be a champion for causes, including local preservation. Some have noted that despite her sometimes gender stereotypical advice, she was an early champion for women. She wrote a significant column charging her male colleagues for barring her from the press tent when she covered the local 1960 PGA Championship at Firestone Country Club. As she wrote: "Here I am, assigned to write PGA stories to tell about the crowd, about the wives of players, about the color of the scene, about the interested women have in the game that probably has as many women devotees as men, and I have no place to write, no spot for a typewriter, no hook for messages. Why? Because men sports writers decided in the historic past that golf is a man's game, and that no woman journalist will ever clutter up the confines of their cluttered sanctuary."

Tina Satterthwaith

Tina Satterthwaith was the home furnishings editor at the *Toledo Blade* from the 1950s through the 1970s. She attended several schools including Northwestern University, Wellesley College, and the Chicago Art Institute before graduating from the University of Toledo. She was hired by the *Blade* in 1950. Colleague Mary Alice Powell said: "I remember her as a writer with a vision, ahead of her time in furniture design." Satterthwaith was a five-time winner of the Dorothy Dawe Award for top furniture coverage: 1958, 1963, 1966, 1972, and 1973.

Pennsylvania

Barbara Cloud

Barbara Cloud reported about fashion in Pittsburgh for 33 years. Her writing was truly for a local market—her sources were often based on who visited her city and the department stores that dominated the local market. While her job did include traveling to fashion shows across the country and abroad, it was not as glamorous as some may have thought. "Fashion writers do not spend leisure hours on the Riviera or in fashion salons," she wrote in a 1991 column. "I've never been to the Riviera. And it's a myth that fashion writers get their clothes for free. Newspaper's ethics policy forbids it."

Cloud's reporting was done at an important time—as fashion went from having well-defined rules to a time of a casual anything-goes attitude. She recalled her mother's generation—one of corsets and hosiery. And, women of a certain age would never bare their arms. As Cloud wrote of her mother, "She was following the rules of her day." Ultimately, her reporting was about the heart of journalism: people. For all the talk of trends, hemlines, and fabrics, she quoted Halston: "Fashion is made by fashionable people—not designers."

Texas

Vivian Castleberry

Vivian Castleberry was the longtime women's pages editor at the *Dallas Times Herald.* She graduated with a degree in journalism from Southern Methodist University. While in college during World War II, she was able to head the newspaper—something unheard of during peacetime. After graduation, she worked in public relations before beginning a job in the women's pages of the *Dallas Times Herald.* She worked there from 1956 to 1984 and won several Penney-Missouri Awards. She was the first woman named to the newspaper's editorial board. After retirement, she was a leader in the peace movement, and the Peace Institute at the University of North Texas is named in her honor. She was married and had five daughters. She was one of four women's page editors included in the Washington Press Club Foundation's Women in Journalism oral history project. She wrote several books about Texas women.

Val Imm

Dallas women's page journalist Val Imm was born as the daughter of a newspaperman, editor of the *Mankato News*, a small daily paper in Minnesota. She worked in various parts of the newspaper. She graduated from Mankato Teachers College and traveled throughout Europe. After some writing experience, she went to visit her sister in Fort Worth, Texas—and she never left the state. After writing for a fashion publication, she became the society editor of the *Dallas Times Herald*. She won awards for her stories about abused children. Her coverage caused the Dallas city government to investigate the issue and make changes in its social welfare system.

Graydon Heartsill

Graydon Heartsill was a longtime fashion editor at the *Dallas Times Herald*, beginning in 1943. Dallas was a significant fashion city because of the high-end Neiman Marcus department store, which hosted the country's first boutique fashion show. Five years later, she went to Europe to cover the first fashion shows after World War II. By July 1955, she was honored for attending the fashion shows in New York City 25 times. Heartsill noted the clothes shown at the major fashion shows would later be shown at Neiman Marcus. She won numerous prizes for her work, including a Penney-Missouri Award for fashion writing in the 1960s.

Judy Lunn

Judy Lunn took a different path to her position as a fashion editor. While she had a knack for writing, it was fashion that caught her interest so she attended the Rhode Island School of Design to study fashion design. (She liked to draw and design but hated to sew.) She and her family relocated to Houston in 1968, and she took time off to be a stay-at-home mother for her two daughters, Linda and Susan. It was her daughter, Linda, who led Lunn to the eventual post of fashion writer. In hopes of earning some change, Linda knocked on a neighbor's door with an offer to recite the Pledge of Allegiance for a quarter. That neighbor was the fashion editor of the *Houston Post*, Lynn Van Deusen. She asked to meet the mother of the precocious child, and her fashion journalism began in 1971. Lunn developed the Fashion Today section for the *Post* and won many national fashion prizes with that section, including a Penney-Missouri Award. She traveled to the major fashion markets twice a year, every year. She visited the home of Coco Chanel. She visited with Bob Mackie when he visited Houston and Galveston. She had strong opinions about fashion. She believed that Tommy Hilfiger was a non-designer and instead just a smart marketer. She believed that when Versace died, the magic died with him.

Marjorie Paxson

Marjorie Paxson graduated from the journalism program at the University of Missouri. She was able to cover hard news for a wire service during World War II and signed a waiver to quit when peacetime returned. She spent years as a women's page journalist in Texas, Florida, and Pennsylvania. She went on to become the fourth women to be a publisher in the Gannet newspaper chain. In her position, she allowed women to wear pants (rejecting the previous publisher's policy) and encouraged support for the ERA. In retirement, she created the National Women and Media Collection archive in Missouri. She was one of four women's page editors included in the Washington Press Club Foundation's Women in Journalism oral history project.

Washington, DC

Marie McNair

Marie McNair began her career at the *Washington Post* in 1921 as a social reporter. Later in the 1920s, she lived in New York, then returned here in 1929 and joined the society department of the *Washington Herald*. She was the *Herald's* society editor before rejoining the *Post*, also as society editor, in 1942. During her last years at the paper, she wrote the popular Town Topics column for a section of the *Post* then called "For and About Women." McNair covered not only Washington society but also the White House social life of every president from Herbert Hoover through Lyndon B. Johnson. She retired from the *Post* in 1965. She was married and had a daughter.

Marie Sauer

Marie Sauer earned a master's degree in journalism from Columbia University. She joined the *Washington Post* in 1935 as an assistant Sunday editor. In 1942, she joined the US Navy as a lieutenant. She was the first woman staff member of the *Post* to join the armed forces in World War II. After her return in 1946, she became woman's editor where she remained until her retirement in 1969 (and the launch of Style). Her women's section was a progressive mix of hard and soft news in a city where political decisions were often crafted at social events. It was she who wanted to change the name of the section in the 1950s to "For and About People," but her request was denied. Sauer's women's section offered readers much news that was not available elsewhere. It won recognition as required reading for anyone hoping to understand how Washington worked. She earned several recognitions for her section, including the top prize for the women's pages, the Penney-Missouri Award in 1963 and 1965. She was honored for her distinguished journalistic achievement by Columbia University in 1963. She also served as president of the Women's National Press Club in 1952, at a time when women were not allowed to be members of the National Press Club.

Malvina Stephenson

Malvina Stephenson spent most of her life in Oklahoma while not in Washington, DC. She applied for her first newspaper job at the *Tulsa World* in the 1930s. She recalled being nervous because there were so few women in journalism. She earned a master's degree in journalism from the University of Oklahoma in 1936. Four years later, Stephenson moved to Washington, DC, to create a one-woman news bureau and quickly became a political correspondent for several newspapers. She also wrote freelance stories for King Features Syndicate and the North American Newspaper Alliance news service. In addition, she reported for the West Virginia Network's weekly radio program. From 1951 to 1963, Stephenson worked as press secretary for Senator Robert S. Kerr of Oklahoma. After the senator's death in 1963, she returned to journalism and contributed stories to the *Tulsa World*. In 1969, Stephenson and Vera Glaser formed what was likely the initial female political columnist team, writing the syndicated column, "Washington Offbeat."

Vera Glaser

Vera Glaser was a Washington, DC-based wire service reporter whose stories and columns typically ran in the women's pages. She was born and raised in St. Louis, Missouri. She was interested in journalism since high school and visited the newsroom of the local newspapers. She graduated from high school first in her class. That position typically meant a scholarship to Washington University. Instead, the honor went to a male who had only been at the school for a year. Decades later, she recalled the snub turned her into a "fighting feminist."

After a variety of writing and public relations work in 1950s, she became a reporter for the North American Newspaper Alliance in the 1960s. She was one of the first women to be a Washington bureau chief. She had regular interaction with many of the women at the *Miami Herald*, the newspaper that eventually syndicated her column. Together, Vera Glaser and Malvina Stephenson wrote the syndicated "Offbeat Washington" column in the late 1960s. She was a member of President

Nixon's Task Force on Women's Rights and Responsibilities from 1969 to 1970. In 1971, she was elected the president of the Washington Press Club. She was the first president to oversee the Club as men were allowed to become members. The two clubs merged in 1985.

Washington

Dorothy Brant Brazier

Dorothy Brant Brazier was hired by the *Seattle Times* in 1931—when one of the only options for a woman at a newspaper was in the society section. Born in Seattle in 1907, Brazier attended Ballard High School and the University of Washington. Initially, she covered society and women's clubs, but she preferred to cover hard news. During World War II, she had new opportunities covering federal courts and offices. Brazier reported on visits of royalty from several countries, covered the coronation of England's Queen Elizabeth, and interviewed celebrities including Beverly Sills and Clark Gable. Brazier pioneered changes in the way the newspaper covered women's issues as the section evolved through various name changes. The women's section reflected her philosophy that there was more to women's interests than just high society. She was named by *Time* magazine in 1967 as a leader in broadening women's news coverage. Brazier had started a column in 1958, which earned four Washington State Press Awards, and she earned a 1964 Penney-Missouri Award for her series about alcoholic women. She was married to a fellow journalist at the newspaper.

Lettie Gavin

Lettie Gavin was a women's page journalist at the *Seattle Post-Intelligencer* who was a trailblazer for women both as a role model in the newsroom and as someone who changed content for readers. She wrote for her high school and hometown newspapers. She graduated with a degree in English from the University of Michigan in 1944 and later joined the *Seattle Post-Intelligencer*. After she retired in 1982, she wrote the book

American Women in World War I—They Also Served. Gavin, along with reporter Susan Paynter, wrote about abortion rights and the ERA.

Bobbi McCallum

Bobbi McCallum, a Cornell University graduate, was a women's page journalist at the *Seattle Post-Intelligencer*. In 1968, at age 25, McCallum won the top national reporting award from the Penney-Missouri Award competition. Her five-part series about young pregnant women, "Unwed Mothers—The Price They Pay," examined the lives of women facing significant social stigma. She interviewed teens, hippies, career women, and African-American women. She told warm yet probing stories of young women whose voices often went unheard. Her work demonstrated what was happening at newspapers across the country in the 1960s when women's pages were changing. Later, the *P-I* assigned McCallum her own column "Eye-to-Eye." In one column, she wrote about an interview she conducted with a Mississippi women's page editor about racial strife in the south. McCallum wrote, "She was a Southern editor talking Southern problems with a Southern accent. And trying to make a Western writer understand." McCallum received other accolades. She was cited by the National Federation of Press Women for her article, "Teen-Agers Dig Young Life's Bible Beat."

Susan Paynter

Seattle women's page journalist Susan Paynter dropped out of college when she got a job at the *Bremerton Sun*. Her exposure to women's reproductive issues began early. Because she was newly married, the editor requited her to bring in proof that she was on birth control. In order to get that birth control, she had to show proof to her doctor that she was married. She soon became the women's page editor at the newspaper. She later moved on to the *Seattle Post-Intelligencer* where she wrote significant stories about abortion, women in the workforce, and the ERA. She later became a columnist at the newspaper.

Sally Raleigh

Sally Raleigh was the women's page editor at the *Seattle Post-Intelligencer* in the 1960s and 1970s. While some people did not describe her as a feminist, her actions demonstrated her role as women's rights leader. She oversaw a significant series about the ERA and encouraged her reporters to cover progressive social issues, including lesbian mothers and women's reproductive health.

Wisconsin

Aileen Ryan

Aileen Ryan was the longtime women's page editor at the *Milwaukee Journal*. She studied journalism at Marquette University but left before graduation to work at the newspaper. During her first summer of work in 1921, Ryan attended a meeting to hear the newspaper's editor say he was happy to have females on the staff because "women have cleaned up newspaper offices." Ryan later recalled the statement made her feel she had been hired to use a mop. Ryan started under the editorship of women's page journalist Elizabeth B. Moffet. Moffett had been recruited from the *Kansas City Star*, where she had pioneered a new method of covering fashion that went beyond simply promoting the clothing of the advertisers. Moffett would visit the local fashion houses and bring along an artist to sketch the clothing. She would then give a critical analysis of the styles.

During her first trip to New York in 1931, Ryan made fashion journalism history. At the time, only magazine reporters and buyers were allowed into the fashion shows. Ryan would not accept that policy. She knocked on numerous showroom doors and got access to about a third of them. Ryan continued to fight for more access each year, and she slowly was able to get access for her photographer, too. This meant other newspapers had to buy their fashion photographs from the *Milwaukee Journal*. In 1937, images from Ryan's trips to the fashion shows in Europe became the first color photos in the Wisconsin newspaper.

Lois Hagen

Lois Hagen graduated from the University of Wisconsin and later became the furnishings reporter at the *Milwaukee Journal.* She spent the bulk of her career in the women's pages of the newspaper. She set new standards for women at the newspaper, being the first mother to return to the Journal after having a child. She traveled extensively covering furnishings, and she won a Penney-Missouri Award for her reporting.

Dorothy Kincaid

Dorothy Kincaid was the longtime women's page journalist at the *Milwaukee Sentinel.* She came to the *Sentinel* in 1962 after earning a journalism degree from the University of Minnesota. She was the *Sentinel* women's page editor from 1966 to 1974. She then became a reporter in the Trend section. In 1982, she became the food editor. When she retired, she shared this memory of being banned from the press box during the 1963 Rose Bowl when she traveled to California with the University of Wisconsin Badgers football team. Her assignment was to write a feature article about the parade and game. She had tried to make advance plans to cover the game knowing she would likely not be allowed in the press box due to her gender. The plans fell through and she asked to have space to file her story. Instead, she had to file her story from a public phone booth located under the stadium as the University of Southern California marching band was practicing, making a difficult assignment.

Jean Otto

Jean Otto was a stay-at-home mother of three children before she began writing a column for the Appleton, Wisconsin, newspaper. By 1968, she was hired by the women's pages of the *Milwaukee Journal.* Four years later, she became the first woman to serve as an editorial writer with the *Journal*—and one of the first women in that position. And one of the few women in that position in the country. She was later named editor of the newspaper's Op-Ed page. In 1979, she became the first female president of the Society for Professional Journalists. It was an organization that had only allowed women to be members a decade before. She wrote a book about her life, *First Love: Memoirs of a First Amendment Freedom Fighter*.

Note

1. For information about the food journalists who worked in the women's pages, see Kimberly Wilmot Voss, *The Food Section: Newspaper Women and the Culinary Community* (Lanham, Maryland: Rowman and Littlefield, 2014).

Index[1]

[1] Note: Page numbers followed by 'n' refer to notes.

K. W. Voss, *Re-Evaluating Women's Page Journalism in the Post-World War II Era*, https://doi.org/10.1007/978-3-319-96214-6

Printed by Printforce, the Netherlands